Anonymous

The Home Cook Book

Anonymous

The Home Cook Book

ISBN/EAN: 9783744781145

Printed in Europe, USA, Canada, Australia, Japan

Cover: Foto ©Lupo / pixelio.de

More available books at **www.hansebooks.com**

THE HOME COOK BOOK

TRIED, TESTED, PROVED.

THE
HOME COOK BOOK.

COMPILED BY
LADIES OF TORONTO AND OTHER CITIES AND TOWNS
IN CANADA.

Toronto:
ROSE-BELFORD PUBLISHING COMPANY,
1881.

Entered according to Act of the Parliament of Canada, in the year one thousand eight hundred and seventy-seven, by BELFORD BROTHERS, in the Office of the Minister of Agriculture.

PRINTED AND BOUND
BY
HUNTER, ROSE & CO.
TORONTO.

A LETTER TO THE PUBLISHERS.

My Dear Sirs,

I have read your Cook-Book, and now I know how it is done. The mystery is solved. The question which puzzled King George the Third is no longer an enigma. I know now how the apples get into the dumplings, how to baste a chicken, make a pork pie, and fry dough-nuts. I have read your book carefully, and can say it is full of good things. I can only compare it to old Dr. Kitchiner's recipe-book, Dr. Sir Theodore Mayerne's *Archimagirus Anglo-Gallicus*, which you may remember on account of the title. A badly cooked dinner, the records of crime will shew, has caused nearly half the suicides of the nation, and matrimonial infelicities may be traced to the same direct cause. We have no Schools of Cookery, as you know, in our Dominion, where our young ladies may learn that art which the ancients deemed second only to medicine. The Home Cook-Book is intended, as far as I can learn from a perusal of its contents, to supply the place of the Academy. A man is not necessarily a *gourmand* or an alderman because he enjoys a good dinner. Many persons are blessed with a taste for gastronomics, and can descant as fluently and as pleasantly on this science as others can of the theories of Huxley or the " Social Studies " of Herbert Spencer. Poets have sung of the stomach and of good eating. Novelists have lingered lovingly over the matutinal meal, and even the historian has not neglected to chronicle events intimately associated with generous living. The subject of cookery is of national importance. The Scotsman discusses his haggis, the Englishman his chop, the Frenchman his pâté, and the American would be uncomfortable all day Sunday, if his plate of beans and brown bread were forgotten. In Canada proper, we have no national dish yet, but in Quebec, in the old French parishes, our friends enjoy a mysterious black pudding, which savoury compound is fearfully and wonderfully made. I say it is mysterious to me, because the Home Cook-Book does not tell me how it is made. I sometimes wonder if it really is made at all. I think it must grow somewhere in Vaudreuil or Longueuil or St. Hyacinthe. That pudding and French Canadian cheese are triumphs of the culinary art. How lonely the world would be without them—and Scotch haggis! Do you know I sometimes feel glad that St. Andrew's day only comes once a year—a little haggis goes a long way!

The volume you have sent me is not only, in my opinion, an admirable receipt-book, but it is a perfect companion of the housewife. The hints, suggestions, and

THE HOME COOK BOOK.

HOUSEKEEPING.

Word of grace to women; word that makes her the earthly providence of her family, that wins gratitude and attachment from those at home, and a good report of those that are without. Success in housekeeping adds credit to the woman of intellect, and lustre to a woman's accomplishments. It is a knowledge which it is as discreditable for any woman to be without as for a man not to know how to make a living, or how to defend himself when attacked. He may be ever so good an artist, ever so polished a gentleman; if deficient in these points of self-preservation you set him down for a weakling, and his real weight in society goes for very little. So, no matter how talented a woman may be, or how useful in the church or society, if she is an indifferent housekeeper it is fatal to her influence, a foil to her brilliancy and a blemish in her garments.

Housekeeping ought not to be taught in classes and by professors; though when early training is lacking they may be of use. It is one of those things to be imbibed without effort in girlhood, instead of being taken up at marriage and experimented on with varying certainty for the rest of one's natural life. There is no earthly reason why girls, from eight to eighteen, should not learn and practice the whole round of housekeeping, from the first beating of eggs to laying carpets and presiding at a dinner party, at the same time that they go on with music, languages, and philosophy. The lessons would be all the better learned if, instead of sitting down at once out of school hours, the girl was taught to take pride in keeping her room nice, or in helping about such work as canning fruit for the season, hanging clean curtains, or dusting every day. The wealthiest women of the oldest families in society are not above seeing to these things themselves, and they know how it should be done. They were bred to it as part of a lady's duty. But if a woman finds herself ignorant or half taught how to keep house, there is nothing so difficult to learn that she may not be proficient in a year or two at most. An intelligent woman will succeed in most duties at first trying. Housekeeping is an exact science, and works like the multiplication table if one only has learned it. But if one is shaky in figures how is he ever to keep accounts? There is no chance about housekeeping. If Mrs. Smith's sitting room is always neat and fresh, it is because she sweeps it with tea leaves, and sponges the carpet with ox gall, and dusts it with a damp cloth, and keeps a door mat on the porch, and sends the boys back every time to use till they get the habit of keeping clean. While you hang a newspaper before the what-not and throw one over the work table, sweep with a soft broom, butting the broad side of it at every stroke against the moulding; instead of carrying all the dust clean from the crevice next the wall by one lengthwise sweep with the corner of the broom, you blow the dust off some places and give a hasty rub at others; pass the stove with a touch from the hearth brush instead of blacking it, and let the boys track in mud and dust enough to deface a new carpet its first season, while you take it out in scolding—which was never known to brighten rooms yet. So, when your feather cake fails, though you made it precisely by the rule which the other day came out like bleached sponge, there is a very good reason for it, you did not stir it as much as the first time, or you beat it a little too long and lost the best effervescence of your soda, or your baking powder had been left open a few minutes at a time on baking days and lost strength. By practicing the same recipe carefully all these and other points fix themselves in your mind, so that success is certain. Those clever cooks, whose success is so much a matter of instinct, observe all these points unconsciously each time, and lay it to luck! There's no such word in housekeeping.

This labour does not only mean keeping things clean, and having plenty to eat. It goes from the outside of the house to the inside of the travelling-bags of those who leave it. The mistress must observe the outside of her house regularly; on Saturday is the most convenient time to see if window-blinds need washing, if the catches are in repair, if the shades inside hang straight, and the curtains drape well, if the walks, steps, and piazzas are neat, and the door knobs and paint in order, making a note of every want, and having it attended to *at once*. Dexterity with tools is very convenient to any one, and I have known accomplished women who would set a pane of glass, put on a door knob, and hang a gate in the best style. One of the valued contributors to the New York press is a woman who reads Horace in Latin, and Bastiat's political economy, makes point-lace and embroiders beautifully, who at the gold mines with her husband built the chimney to her house, and finished most of the interior with her own hands. A little care, weekly, keeps a place in that bright order that so attracts and welcomes one at sight. It looks as if whole people lived in it, with live sensibilities and intelligence. Indoors the same spirit is reflected. The bell-pull never is left for weeks after it gets loose, the gas burners are never suffered to leak, or grow dim; the kerosene lamps are large enough to give good light, and of the best pattern for safety, and for the eye. The stoves are the open "Fireside" kind, the modern version of the old Franklin stoves—giving the ventilation and delight of an open fire, burning either coal or wood, with bars and fender like a grate; yet, capable of being shut up as tightly as any base-burning heater by two tight fitting covers that may be removed and put away at pleasure. The health, the comfort, the luxury of such an addition makes up for many a deficiency beside. The carpet was well-chosen at first in small figure and warm colours of good quality, whether Brussels or three-ply, and it looks well as long as it lasts, and kept clean by shaking twice a year.

laid straight and stretched smooth over a soft lining, which saves the carpet and saves noise; darned at the first break with wool, matching the pattern, it will not be shabby in ten years. It is pleasant to have things last with the family, and grow to seem a part of it. The true sentiment of the sharp, genteel woman, was expressed by the housekeeper who "liked to have her carpets wear out so she could have new ones." She let lodgings to have company, and money to dress by, against her husband's wish, and her only dread was that of "settling down and having a lot of children with no theatres, no opera, nobody to see." The home feeling, the attachment that grows for the pleasant enduring objects of daily use is one of the rare plants of sentiment that the housekeeper does well to cherish. There should be care at first to have things agreeable and handsome as possible, that they need not be a daily eyesore, and there need be no reason for wishing them to wear out. Manufactures constantly add service to trade by placing better patterns in reach of moderate purses. Thus, the mottled carpets in oak and brown, ash and crimson, maroon and elm-leaf yellow, with borders to match, so admired in velvet and Brussels, are found in fine three-plys and ingrain, and in the newer Venetians of hemp and wool, like the old-fashioned stair carpet that lasts so long. A word for these new Venetians, which is on account of their artistic quality, likely to be overlooked, because they are so cheap. All the best colours and patterns of Brussels, in two shades, in mottled, moss or leaf designs, are afforded in this carpet, which is durable as the conscience of a housekeeper could exact. Two rules are enough for the looks of a carpet; choose small figures and avoid contrasts of colour. Small figures, however, have different meanings to different people. As a rule, a small figure is not more than three inches at most, any way across. Very, very few rooms there are, but look better with carpets of small design. Then the oil-cloth under the stove must match, if possible, and be bound with leather strips to keep the edge from getting unsightly. The woodbox or basket is covered with wool work on canvas, or applique of bright cloth on Turkish toweling, making a handsome bit of furniture. A scrap basket, with applique border, and a bright lining, goes far toward keeping a room tidy. The mistress will try to have her rooms in keeping with the style by a few pieces of furniture in the fashion of the day, a Turkish chair embroidered in wools, a straight-backed one in unbleached toweling and applique of crimson, blue, black and gold, a stand covered with velvet, or a home-made easel with the single good picture the house affords on it, a jardiniere of titles or wickerwork in the window, or a bamboo lounge, things not expensive in themselves, yet lending a graceful air to quiet surroundings. As for chairs, sofas and lambrequins, artists have been insisting on chintz for the last ten years, and women have as steadily bought woollen reps, which the doctors tell us harbours dust, absorbs vitiated matter from the air, and is absolutely dangerous in disease from the contagion it holds. But women of the best taste, who like to have their rooms pretty, will choose chintz, when they cannot afford silk and satin, and often when they can, for its intrinsic beauty.

It is of more account to have broad seats and deep cushions to chairs and sofas, than to have them covered with rich material. See that there are plenty of low seats in your sitting-room, for much of the furniture seen is of very little use for rest and ease, points essential to the health and comfort of women and children. If a woman will only start with the intention of making her house comfortable, she will gain all the admiration she wants. There are many elegant rooms in private houses, where there are only one or two that come up to the idea of comfort. Now that is a very important word one that cannot be infringed on without losing health. The mistress of a house must see that it is ventilated from top to bottom, by having every window and the skylight, if there is one, open at least once a day—if possible when the sun is shining. She is responsible for the health of the household, and must allow no scent of decay, whether from vegetables or meat, barrels or refuse in the cellar, no slops anywhere about the premises, no mouldering food in closets, no confined bedrooms or closets with old clothes or soiled linen to taint the air, no dead, musty smell in any room, however seldom used, no sickly smell escaping from rooms where there is illness. She must see that fires are started as early in the fall and kept as late in the spring as the weakest, chilliest of her family desires, for these slow chilly days take more life, and play more mischief with nerves and blood than she could bear to think of, could she see their effects. She must look after the clothing from a hygienic view, to see that her children and family are warm enough and cool enough, so warding off many an attack of cramps, coughs and neuralgia. The food must be of the best quality, and she must *know* that it is. It pays to give an extra shilling on the half barrel for selected potatoes and apples, as they go farther and make more muscle than poor ones, and don't poison anybody. Sharp scrutiny of eggs, meat, butter, and milk, is a benefit to others as well as her own family, by raising the standard of provisions, besides more direct gain. More disease comes into the world in the shape of tainted butter and milk, than any one dreams of but the doctors. If she gets the hygienic craze about food, don't let her carry it to the verge of confounding things "healthful" with things uneatable, for badly cooked oatmeal and graham "gems" are as distressing to delicate organisms as the richest mince pie and old cheese together. That slight sour tinge, which nobody noticed, in the home-made bread, that solid pudding, which yet was not quite rejected at dessert, are responsible for the bad breath of the children and the beginning of a sick headache in their elders. Never be satisfied with any but the nicest cooking, with variety enough to make your table a delight as well as a necessity. And don't let anybody lay it to you that you are pampering your family, and devoting yourself to a low sphere of action. You are doing no such thing, but are giving them strong, active bodies, steady nerves and tempers, and clear brains to meet their work with. By just so much as you neglect your part of the work, they will fail in theirs. You are the engineer to feed the fires, and keep the wheels oiled, and the whole family system depends on you. Don't dare to call such work low.

There is a great work to be done in American kitchens. You may and ought to delegate as much to hired helpers as you can, but you must see that all is done as it should be. And one receipt for training service is given, that is the whole secret in a nut-shell. If child or servant leaves anything undone, or ill-done, don't scold, but insist on having it done immediately as it ought to be. Put the badly ironed shirts in the basket to be done over, have the house-girl who left the china badly washed, take it out of the closet and do it right, time after time, and let her get tired of doing her work over before you get tired of telling her. It is no harder to do work nicely than to half do it, indeed the careless way is the hardest. Finally, let your housekeeping be as liberal as you can. Whether well-to-do, or in narrow circumstances, you will hold that waste is a sin, against yourself and the world. By keeping strict account of every cent received and paid out, you can gauge your means, laying by what is proper, but within that limit be good to yourself and yours. Make the most of your money. It was no less a divine than the orthodox Doctor John Hall, who said that, of the two faults, he had far rather see people extravagant than penurious. Stint nowhere in cleanliness, light, and warmth, and let what you have be the best and prettiest for the cost. By these things men live, in body at least, and the soul is very dependent on its surroundings, or at any rate greatly assisted by favourable ones. It is an every-day wonder to see how little rich people get for their money; the common-place houses, with so little that is light or striking or original in them, the dull service, the narrow round of enjoyments. In some sense housekeeping is making the most of life, bringing taste and variety into it, compassing difficult ends with invention. Those who disdain it lower themselves. Never think that anything is too good for you or yours that you can obtain. Everywhere there are people living in small common ways, because they are absolutely afraid of the expense or the notice which a pleasanter life would bring. Half the niceties of life involve only care to secure them, without a dollar of expense. Good manners cost nothing, good taste is saving, and good housekeeping actually makes money. Though this book is an aid to the ambitious housekeeper in one direction only, that is on the way to all the rest. People grow refined first in their eating. How is it that the most brilliant and cleverest nation in the world has also the best cooking? Put these things together, and do your best according to their result.

TABLE TALK.

In all attempts at refinement, one cardinal point should be kept in view—that manners were made for men, not men for manners. Nice customs courtsey to great kings, and the greatest of these is convenience. Most rules will be found to serve convenience, and there is no good breeding where etiquette is not observed for this end, the order and comfort of all concerned, *not* for the sake of definining one's social position. When any one begins to study manners as a set of arbitrary rules, followed because every other desirable acquaintance does the same, politeness breeds a sort of pharisaism that the best bred persons look down on as supremely vulgar. If any mistress of a house looks here for rules that will aid her to affect a trifle more of style than her neighbours she will only be disappointed. If any woman wishes hints how to reduce her household to regularity and make her children neat and gentle in habits, it may be that she will not find this chapter in vain.

Martinet regularity as to hours and minutes is no longer held the saving virtue in a household. The rule in many families keeps all the rest waiting for a meal if one is tardy. Modern custom both for the family and for dinner parties takes the sensible course of sitting down to table when the hour comes, and the principal part of those expected. No guest should feel affronted, if he is late, and finds the party at dinner, provided the indispensible care has been shown to keep his portion warm over dishes of hot water, by which they neither grow cold or are dried up in the oven. Order the table daily with the same care as for a dinner party. This is the only way to insure success for hostess and servants when one does come off, and gives mistress and waiter the luxury of getting used to nice style, so that it is just as easy as common ways, and no sudden visitor can put them out. Home tables do not always compare to advantage with those at the restaurant or club, and the housemother should see that a man finds as careful service at home as he does anywhere else. Unlimited laundry work should be one of the indulgence's of one's own house, and it should be of the utmost nicety. Why should it be too much to provide clean napkins and table-cloth daily at home as well as at a hotel? They would cost half an hour's extra work a day, and this is not too much for the refinement it gives. We should then expect to see the table spread with a snowy cloth, less starched than many housekeepers think necessary, finish and pliancy given by plenty of wax in the starch, which will keep it clean the longer. It should fall below the table half a yard all round, and be pinned up at the corners to keep it from the floor if necessary. For ceremonious occasions a common white cloth is laid under the table-cloth to protect a handsome table, keep the upper cloth from wearing, and because dishes make less noise when set down on it.

For breakfast the coffee is set before the mistress, the cups and spoons ranged in their saucers in front of it, in two rows if there are many of them; the meat and plates, which should be warm, before the master; salt, butter and castor at the corner to the right of both, head and foot, if the table is a large one, when two sets of these things will be convenient. Otherwise put them in the centre with the dishes in regular order around them, and relishes at the corners. To meet this order, it is a trifle to have dishes in pairs of the same size, and use them always together for different things. Fruit, whether berries, baked apples, or pears, is served first at breakfast, then oatmeal or wheaten grits, now found on every good table in cities at least, then meats and vegetables, with toast, hot cakes and coffee following. Hot rolls come wrapped in a napkin to keep them warm, griddle-cakes between two hot plates, and all meats covered. Baked potatoes are scrubbed with a manilla brush, the ends cut off, rinsed twice, and eaten without paring, as the best flavour goes with the skin. This is the custom with the best society in this country and abroad. Eggs are washed with a cloth in cold water before boiling, and eaten in egg cups from the shell, chipping the small end off, or broken into larger glasses, or held in the napkin and eaten from the shell with entire good form, in either method. Where individual salt-cellars are used they should be emptied after each meal, and the salt thrown away, that one person may not use it after another, and they should be very small, that there be less wasted. Butter should be piled round a lump of ice in little pats. To be very nice, as many have learned to like it from living abroad, it should be churned daily from perfectly sweet cream, worked without being touched by the hands or with water, and without a particle of salt. Thus it has the delicate flavour of cream at its best. Honey is especially a breakfast delicacy, and so is maple syrup, which should be served in small saucers to be eaten with hot biscuit. A basket of crisp cakes, toasted rusk and crackers, will accompany coffee.

For lunch the coloured table cloths may be used if ever, though their use is gradually dropped because the colours do not wash well. White cloths with striped border in colours, or fine gray or unbleached damask, with napkins to match, assist the easy half-dress style of this repast. Cups of broth and thick chocolate, with light meats, hashes, croquettes, and stews. Salad and fruit are the staple variety, and rather more attractive than the cold meat, tea and cracker fare too often set apart for this hurried meal. Nowhere is negligence more annoying than at luncheon, and the cloth, glasses, and arrangements should be fastidiously neat to do away with the disagreeable feeling that everybody is too busy with drudgery to look after comfort. Insist that the girl who waits on the table has her hair neat, her hands washed, and a clean apron and collar on. An unkempt servant will spoil the best dinner appetite was ever sharp-set for. Ceremonious lunches mean an hour's visit with a meal, at which salads, shell-fish, chops, in paper frills, and broiled chicken play a part, with ices, tarts, and fancy cakes for dessert. **Mixed** drinks, like Regent's punch, or claret sup, with ale and beer, are more in keeping at lunch than wines. These drinks are served from the side-board, the malt liquors in common goblets, the claret cup in tumblers, the punch in small cups. Beef tea is taken from cups held in small saucers, or in small Chinese bowls, with little saucers. The absence of all ceremony with the presence of light charming detail makes the luncheon attractive.

For dinner, the family table wants to have less the air of hotel arrangements. More delicate napery and ware, whether the latter is only "seconds," or the finest egg-shell china; lighter, more convenient, knives and forks, and heavier teaspoons, nice thin glass for drinking, thick cut crystal for sweets, with above all things a well kept cruet stand, make the difference in favour of home taste and home comfort. Keep all cracked and nicked ware from the table. Buy nothing that cannot be replaced without regret, but let each article be the best of its material. There is choice in the quality of stone ware and blown glass as well as in the shapes of each. The plainest is always most satisfactory of inexpensive things. The old fashion of furnishing dining-rooms in dark and heavy styles is reversed. The room is light, cheerful, warm in colour, the chairs broad and substantial, the table lower than it used to be, two points which add sensibly to the comfort of those who use them. Have the chair feet shod with rubber tips which come for the purpose, or if on castors, cover the wheel with rubber so that they can move without noise. See that the room is light and especially warm, for people want comfort at meals of all times, and they feel the cold more in sitting.

DINNER ETIQUETTE.

Directions for a ceremonious dinner naturally include those for the family table, as much form in serving being kept as may be convenient. The number of guests for a state dinner rarely exceeds twelve.

Written invitations are always complimentary and in finer style than any other for small parties, but persons who entertain often, have engraved cards with blanks left for the name of guest, and date, for convenience. The following is a form adopted for dinner cards, a large, nearly square form being used:

Mr. and Mrs ———————————————————

    Request the pleasure of

——————————————Company (name.)

————————————————————date and No.

——————————o'clock.

The favour of an answer is requested.

(or) R. s. v. p,

For a gentleman's party the host's name alone appears on the invitation. An early answer must be sent in all cases, either to accept **or decline. Not to do so is the grossest rudeness.**

Invitations are always sent to persons in the same town by private messenger. Outside envelopes are necessary only when sent by mail to another city. No particular excuse need be sent. It is enough to say "Mr. and Mrs. ——— regret that they are unable to accept Mr. and Mrs. ——— kind invitation for the date named." When the dinner is to meet any particular guest or distinguished person, it is made known by the words, "To meet So-and-So," at the head of the invitation, or after the name of the invited person before the date.

Written invitations are on note sheets of mill-finished paper with side fold, the fancy rough and the highly glazed papers of eccentric shapes and fold being out of use. The large envelope, nearly square, allows the sheet to be doubled once to fit. Cards have the same finish, neither dull nor highly polished. The cipher of initials entwined is preferred to the monogram, and occupies the corner of the note sheet.

Guests arrive at any time during the half hour before dinner, and after leaving wraps in the dressing room, are met by the host and hostess at the door of the drawing room. Introductions follow if the guest is a stranger. If the party is given in honour of any distinguished person, or favourite visitor, the other guests are brought up to him or her and presented. It is an omen of success for her evening if the hostess can make conversation general before dinner. To this end, have some novelty at hand, either in the shape of a personage whom everybody wants to meet, or a new picture, a grotesque group, a rare plant in the drawing-room, the latest spice of news to tell, or a pretty girl to bring forward. Whatever the attraction, bring it on at once, to prevent that very stupid half hour. At the hour, the servant comes in and tells the hostess dinner is served. The arranging of the guests has all been considered beforehand. If she wishes people to think her dinner a pleasant one, the hostess will see that the likings of her guests are consulted in pairing off for the table. Host and hostess intimate to the gentlemen whom they are to escort. "Mr. Lance, will you be kind enough to take Miss Dart in to dinner. Mr. Curtis, be so good as to see Mrs. Vane. Jermingham, I know you'd prefer Miss Olney, she's such a good listener. Mr. King, if you want to finish telling that story to Mrs. Capron, suppose you give her your arm," and so on. If the guest to be honoured is a lady, the host offers her his arm and goes out first, the hostess last. If a gentleman, he escorts the hostess, and the host follows the company. Before dinner is announced, after the guests have arrived, the host has the names of each person written on a card and laid on the plates at the place where he or she is to sit. This does away with that awkward moment when the guests are in the dining room waiting to be told their places. The method long used at public dinners is now adopted for private ones in the best circles.

The standard size for dinner tables is four and-a-half feet wide, by any length desired. Round tables for gentlemen's dinners, where all are wanted in the conversation are made seven feet across. Dining chairs should have cushioned seats covered with fine leather, but no arms, or very low ones, that will not impede the flow of ladies' dresses. People who make a study of entertaining are particular on such points. Each gentleman offers his right arm to the lady he takes to dinner and seats her on his left, which gives occasion for a pretty piece of attention on his part. On reaching their places, he draws out her chair for her, and as her hand leaves his arm he takes the tips of her fingers and hands her to her seat, relinquishing his touch with a slight bow or glance of acknowledgment. Of course, the honoured guest, if a lady, takes the right hand of the host; if a gentleman, he is at the right of the hostess.

Small can-shaped pitchers of engraved crystal, holding about a quart, are placed with ice water between each pair of guests. The napkins are folded flat, with a thick piece of bread on each, a cruet-stand and silver salt celler is at each corner, and a silver butter dish at each end. The small individual salt cellars and butter plates, have an air of hotel arrangements which it is desirable to avoid at home dinners, though entirely admissable and convenient at breakfast. If wax lights are used, there should be as many candles as guests, according to the old rule. These are in branches held by Sevres and Dresden figures, above the heads of the guests. Nor are wax lights by any means the extravagance they seem. Dinner napkins are from three-quarters to seven-eighths of a yard square, and should match the cloth, for which Greek, Moresque, and Celtic filigrees and diaper patterns are preferred to large arabesques and fruit pieces. French napkins of fine fringed damask, with crimson figures of lobster and crawfish woven in the centre, are sometimes used at first and removed with the fish. Decorations must be choice and used with discretion. Flowers should be fine but few, for cultivated senses find their odor does not mingle pleasantly with that of food. All artificial contrivances, like epergnes and show-pieces, tin gutters lined with moss and filled with flowers for the edges of a table, or mirror plates to reflect baskets of blossoms, are banished by the latest and best taste. The finest fruit grouped in the centre of the table, set off with leaves, the garnished dishes, the lustre of glass and silver, and the colours of delicately painted china, need no improvement as a picture. A low silver basket of flowers at the sides, and a crystal bouquet holder with a delicate blossom and leaf, sparingly introduced, are all that is allowed for ornament's sake. Large dinner services of one pattern are no longer chosen. The meats and large dishes are in silver or electrotype ware, the sweets come in heavy English cut crystal, and each course brings with it plates of a different ware.

The order of wines is sometimes perplexing, and the novice should remember that Chablis or Sauterne comes with the small oysters before soup, and that Sherry is drank after soup. Claret may be taken by those who prefer it during a whole dinner with entire propriety. Champagne comes with the roast, and Burgundy with game. The French and Germans reserve champagne for a dessert wine, but we drink it with both roast and dessert. After dessert comes coffee, which should be served, however, in the drawing-room. Fingerbowls with warm water are placed on the napkin on the dessert plate, and removed by the guest to the left, to be used by dipping the fingers in lightly and drying them on the d'oylay. When the ladies are quite through with dessert the hostess catches the eye of each or raises her gloved hand slightly, as a signal, and they leave the table, the oldest lady going first, the youngest last, followed by the hostess—the youngest gentleman, or the one nearest the door, taking it on himself to hold the door open. After half an hour a guest is at liberty to withdraw, but a dinner party rarely breaks up till half past ten or later, if cards and dancing follow.

As to the individual etiquette of the table, on seating himself a guest draws off his gloves, and lays them in his lap under the napkin, which should be spread lightly not tucked in the dress. The raw oysters are eaten with a fork; the soup, only a ladleful to each plate, is sipped from the side of the spoon, without noise, or tilting the plate. The head should never stoop toward the plate or cup, but the shoulders kept straight and the food lifted to the mouth, the head bent naturally a little. A quiet celerity in eating is preferable to the majestic deliberation which many people consider genteel. Bread should be broken, never cut at table, and should be eaten morsel by morsel, not crumbed into soup or gravy. Food should not be mixed on the plate. Sweet corn is brought on, tied in its husk by a strip of leaf, and should be eaten from the cob, breaking the ear in two, and holding the piece in the left hand. Asparagus should *not* be touched with the fingers, but the tender part cut up, and eaten with the fork. Fish is eaten with the fork, assisted by a piece of bread in the left hand. Maccaroni is cut and taken with the fork, unless served with the tomatoes, when a teaspoon is allowed, as with green peas, and stewed tomatoes alone. Cheese is crumbled with the fork and eaten with it, never touched by the fingers. Pastry should be broken by the fork without the aid of a knife. Game and chicken are cut up, never picked with the fingers, unless in the indulgence of a family dinner, when the bone may be held in one hand and eaten. Pears are held by the stem to be paired, and then cut and eaten like apples, beginning to remove the skin at the blossom end. Oranges are held on a fork while peeled and divided without breaking the skin. Cherries in pie, or natural, should have the stones passed to the napkin held at the lips and returned to the plate, and grape seeds and skins are disposed of in the same way. Salt is left on the edge of the plate, not on the table. Ladies take but a single glass of any wine at most, having their glasses half-filled with champagne a second time. It is beginning to be the custom to take soft bread as well as ice-cream with cake. Cocoanut pudding looks pie, but is helped and eaten with a spoon. Small meringues are best eaten with a spoon, though the practice is to take them in the fingers.

SOCIAL OBSERVANCES.

The simplest society duty is, that of making calls. A new comer should return each call within two weeks after it is made. After this, a call once in six months, or a year, serves to keep up acquaintance. Calls are due to a hostess two days after a dinner party, and two days after a ball, and a week after a small party, though these are amply fulfilled by leaving one's card in the case of a gentleman, a personal call being polite from a lady who has more time.

In town, leaving a card with the corner bent signifies that it was left by its owner in person, not sent by a servant. Bending the edges of a card, means that the visit was designed for the young ladies of the house, as well as the mistress of it. If there is a visitor with the family whom you wished to see, a separate card should be left for that person, naming him or her to the servant. A card should also be left for the host, if the call was designed as a family matter, but more than three are not left at one house.

Visits of condolence are paid within a week after the funeral, and are as well expressed by leaving a card and kind inquiries of the servant. This is the only proper thing to do in case of sickness, beside asking if one can be of use. Visits of congratulation are paid in person. After the birth of a child, cards and inquiries are left at the door, when the lady is able to receive her friends, she sends her card in return " with thanks for kind inquiries," after which calls are made on her in person.

Bending the corners of the cards to signify "condolence," "felicitation," "to take leave," etc., is not used so much as a penciled word or two, to express one's "kind inquiries," if there is trouble in the house, or "best wishes," if there is a wedding, or engagement.

The P. P. C. card when one is going away, is a convenient way of letting friends know of your absence, the initials of "*pour porendre conge*" being often relinquished for the plain English "to take leave." On returning, cards are sent to all the friends one wishes to see, with one's address, and receiving day, when one day of the week is set apart for company.

From three to six are proper calling hours, and a visit may be from five minutes to half an hour, never longer, unless with a very intimate friend. A gentleman leaves his umbrella in the hall, but carries hat and cane with him, keeping the former in his left hand, never venturing to lay it on table, or rack, unless invited to do so by the lady of the house. Her not doing so is a sign that it is not convenient for her to prolong his call.

A soft hat is tolerated, but the dress hat is usually carried.

The lady of the house rises to receive any guest, unless it be a very young one, and gives her hand. After the visit, she receives a gentleman's bow, and if disposed to be very polite, walks with him to the door of the room. She sees a lady visitor to the street door, if the parlour is on the same floor. If not, going to the head of the stairs is sufficient courtesy except to elderly guests. A gentleman must escort a lady who makes him a business call to the outer door, and to her carriage, if she has one. A caller should take leave as soon as possible on the arrival of another visitor, unless asked to stay.

Where a lady has a large acquaintance, it is most convenient for her to set apart a day for receiving their calls, of which she admonishes them by her visiting card on which the day of the week is pencilled.

Unless specially invited otherwise, her friends will confine their visits to that day of the week.

To these afternoons the hostess appears in usual afternoon dress; her rooms are attractive with flowers and pictures, but no refreshments are served. Her guests find her, not sitting at the receipt of customs, but busy with some elegant trifle of lace or wool-work, writing letters, or touching a sketch, to be laid aside on the entrance of visitors.

The set afternoon reception is announced by this form of card, the hostess usually preferring to have some young lady with her to add to the attractions of her house.

Mrs. L. Persifer,
Miss Arnold,
At Home,
Saturday, January thirteenth,
from three until six.
(Name and No. of street.)

If there be a card receiver in the hall, the visitor's card is left in it, that the hostess may have the pleasure afterward of recalling all the friends who favour her with their presence.

Coffee, chocolate, cake and ices, are to be found in a side room at such receptions.

The form of card for afternoon tea, which means ladies in visiting or carriage dress, a harlequin tea service, each cup different, or a set of choice East India China, rooms coosy with warm curtains, and signs of womanly occupation, everything in short to have the daintiest home-look possible, are issued in this fashion :

Mrs. Bradley Cowles,
Friday, January 18th,
Tea at 4 o'clock.

(Name and No. of street.)

Guests arrive in the five minutes before the hour, or the five minutes after. The tea is brought in punctually and placed on the hostess' table in the corner, where are the urns of black, green and Russian tea for those who like each, a basket of wafers, delicate sandwiches of chicken or thin sliced meats, and a basket of fancy cake. If the English style is followed, the cups of tea are carried to the guests on a tray, and a tiny table to rest the cups on placed in reach of each group.

Cards are issued for dinner parties and afternoon receptions in distinction from evening parties and weddings, invitations to which are engraved on notepaper. Written invitations are more complimentary than printed ones, but the idea of cards and engraved requests is to save the labour of writing notes for a large party, or where one entertains continually. Written invitations for the honour and style of the thing, cards and engraving for convenience, though this is perhaps contrary to the popular notion. Written invitations should be as fastidiously correct as printed ones, on mill-finished side-fold note sheets with cipher in the corner, and written in the same form as cards, unless to a familiar friend, when such precision would be absurd. Outside envelopes are only used when invitations are sent by mail. And whether so requested in the note or not, answer to accept or decline should be sent as soon as possible, no matter how slight the invitation may be, even to dine with a gentleman, or go to a picture gallery. It will not do to present oneself without a word to announce one's coming, or to stay away and apologize the first time of meeting. Good breeding is hardly shown in nicer points than this.

The person entering a room is the one to salute the company by a good morning, or how do you do, and to make his adieus, to which the rest respond. Where a stranger enters a small company, each one should be separately presented. The guest salutes hostess and host before speaking to anyone else, and if the party is large, is introduced to two or three convenient persons that he may have somebody to talk to, though in a private house guests may accost each other without formal presentation. Near the close of a party, the host and hostess usually are to be found near the door of the parlour, and guests take leave of them with a bow and compliment for a pleasant evening, then pass to the dressing rooms after wraps and vanish without further—

ceremony. In small circles a bow should be given to each person about one, and leave taken of any special friend whose conversation has been particularly pleasant.

A gentleman does not shake hands with a lady not of his kindred, unless she offers to do so. Unmarried ladies do not give their hands in salute to any but gentlemen relations. Ladies in any case give the hand, the gentleman respectfully presses it without shaking. It is a piece of stupid bad breeding, however, not to take the hand of anyone offered in ignorance of the rule. The best breeding always adapts itself to the customs of those about one.

When a gentleman escorts a lady to a party, he waits for her near the door of the ladies' dressing-room till she shows herself, gives her his right arm, or gives it to the elder lady if he takes two, and goes up to the hostess with her to make salutations, then after a sentence or two, turning away to join the company. After a dance with any lady it is proper to take half a turn round the room in promenade with her, and take her to the refreshment room if she wishes, always leaving her with her chaperone. An unmarried lady does not ask gentlemen to call, but the gentleman asks permission for the favour of her, or waits to be invited by her father or mother.

THE LITTLE HOUSEKEEPERS.

It often happens that a good deal of knowledge which we are not conscious of possessing—but which finds its way somehow into the brains of big and little people as well—comes very readily to hand when it is needed. It so happened with Annie and Jennie, whose first practical lessons in housekeeping began after breakfast, one morning when Bridget was absent, at her sister's funeral, and in consequence of an accident by which mamma sprained her ankle.

And the doctor had said, with a very wise shake of his head, and any amount of wisdom in his eye, that "Little Mother" must not step on that foot for three days, she grew still whiter with dismay, for Bridget would not be back until quite late in the day, and how was all the house work to be done and nobody to do it?

It was thus that Annie's and Jennie's first practical experiences in housekeeping began, and as our object in telling you how and what they did is to give you some ideas how you should manage in similar circumstances. I must not pass over their mother's first caution: *Before commencing your work prepare yourselves for it.* This they did by putting long sleeved aprons over their dresses, rolling back their sleeves when it was evident the right place to begin with was

THE DINING ROOM.

The first thing here to do, was the clearing of the table. In this, all the clean silver, china, and dishes that had not been used, were first put away in the silver drawer, the china closet and on the side-board. Next, the dishes to be cleaned were collected together; the silver and the knives were first put into a pitcher of hot water, with the bowls and blades downwards. Next, the water was emptied from the glasses, and the coffee from the cups into a basin, and while Annie took these into the kitchen and placed them there on the table, Jennie gathered the plates in a pile, the cups and the saucers, each by themselves, in which way they were quickly and easily carried to the kitchen.

They were careful not to take too many at once, as they would be liable to break them. Then the table-cloth was folded and laid in the side-board; the napkins were put in the napkin basket; the dining room floor was nicely swept and the furniture dusted; the coal stove was attended to, that the fire was not too lively and not too low; and then, after kissing and petting mamma a few minutes, the little housekeepers set about

THE WASHING OF THE DISHES.

This, of course, with "Little Mother" at the head of affairs, was no disagreeable work, you may be sure. The large tin dish-pan, as bright as silver, was placed in the sink; the hot and cold water faucets turned on until the temperature of the water was hot enough for cleansing the dishes, and not too hot for the hands; then the suds was made by stirring about in the water the soap-shaker (a little tin box with soap in it, and perforated with holes having a long handle like a dipper). Then the glasses were first washed and quickly wiped on clean dry towels; then the silver; then the pretty china cups, saucers, plates and other dishes, which were then rinsed by pouring clear hot water over them in another pan, from which they were wiped with the coarser towels. This finished, Jennie removed the dishes from the kitchen table, putting the silver, glass and china away, while Annie washed the sauce-pans and the tins, putting them in their places in the kitchen; then brushed the range and swept the kitchen floor; after which they washed their hands well and dried them on the roller-towel; and then our little housekeepers set themselves about preparations for

THE CHAMBER WORK.

First, the two little girls went into mamma's room, and put on over their bright glossy curls two little Martha Washington dusting-caps of pink and blue cambric, trimmed around the edges with scolloped ruffles, and ornamented with pretty little fanciful bows of pink and blue cambric, with scalloped edges. Then Annie took the pails and cloths, and Jennie the brushes, and brooms, and went up stairs.

The first rule of chamber work is to open the windows and turn down the bed clothes to air them well; beating up the pillows and the mattress. As Annie and Jennie always did this the first thing after dressing in the morning, and before going down to breakfast, the first thing now to do was to make up the bed. While Annie went to the further side, Jennie remained on the other, and thus, each sheet and blankett was brought up and laid over straight and smooth, with not a wrinkle in sheet or blanket, or a single article out of line. When all was done, the spread and blankets were turned neatly back, with the pretty ruffled sheet lying back on the nice white counterpane; the clothes were all neatly tucked and folded at the sides and the corners, and the pillows put up against the headboard. Then, while Annie washed the bed-room service, first emptying the waste water, and then washing out the cleanest dishes in warm suds, Jennie brushed the room, dusted the furniture and put the hair and clothes-brushes in order, and arranged the bureau and toilet table. They followed the same order in their brother John's room, which was all of the chamber work to be done that day, and then went down stairs.

By this time the little housekeepers began to feel tired, and so they rested a while in their two little easy chairs in mamma's room, talking to mamma and each other until it came the time for getting ready for the

LUNCHEON.

As John took his dinner with him to school, and papa ate his luncheon down town, and would not be home until the five o'clock dinner, there was only mamma and the two little girls to partake of this repast together; and as mamma's luncheons were such cosy, tasteful though simple meals, we may gain some suggestions from the way our little housekeepers prepared them. The first thing to do in getting any meal, is to decide upon the various dishes to be served. A look at the supply of prepared food was quite disheartening to the ambitious desires of the little housekeepers, as there was bread and cake and cold meat in plenty, and it seemed as though there would be no opportunity for practicing their skill in cooking. But mamma, who saw the troubled look on the little faces, made out the following

BILL OF FARE:

Tea.

White Bread.   Brown Bread.   Crackers.

Ham.

Cheese Sandwiches.

Jumbles.   Preserved Strawberries.

Whipped Cream.

Now, it must be remembered, that in this arrangement, the bread was at hand ready to slice; the ham was boiled, ready to cut; and the strawberries ready in the little glass can to be opened. There remained, therefore, jumbles and tea to make, and the cheese sandwiches to prepare. Following mamma's advice, they first undertook the jumbles, of which they were to make but half the recipe. They selected for this "Excellent Jumbles," in the Home Cook Book, and while Jennie held the book and read the ingredients, Annie collected them together. Thus: one-half a cup of butter, one cup of sugar, and one-half cup of cream, and one-half teaspoon of soda. When Jennie came to the one egg of the recipe, they had some trouble how they should manage to make it half an egg; but after consultation with mamma, they concluded to vary from the given rule, and put the whole egg in. Then Jennie read on: "A little nutmeg; flour enough to stiffen it, so as to bake in rings; bake quickly."

The flour was sifted; the butter and sugar first creamed together by Annie, while Jennie beat the yolk of the egg, and added it to the creamed sugar and butter; then they put in the nutmeg, the cream and the soda; then the beaten white of the egg, and the sifted flour; then they put the jumbles into the buttered rings and baked them. As the oven was quick and hot, I am happy to say these jumbles were a success. In taking them out of the tins when done, they did not pile them on one another, but placed them carefully about on a large plate to cool. Then the little housekeepers made the tea, according to the directions in the Cook Book, and also the cheese sandwiches, which were a complete success. The cutting of the bread was a difficult task, since to be nice the slices should be even and thin, but it was managed nevertheless with patience and care. When all was ready, the cream nicely whipped, the strawberries put in the preserve dish, the little round table in mamma's room drawn out, and the luncheon arranged, they were just ready to sit down to enjoy the fruits of their labour, what should they hear but Bridget's voice at the door. So it came to pass, that with the luncheon ended for this time the practical experiments of our little housekeepers. But it all goes to prove that, if we live with our eyes open, we shall all of us find that, with such help as our Home Cook Book, we shall be ready for those emergencies which come to big as well as the little housekeepers, when Bridget is not at hand.

OUR SUSAN'S OPINION OF A KITCHEN.

"My opinion of a kitchen?" said Susan, in a tone, with a glance, and a wave of her fork that spoke unwritten volumes, as she translated the perfection of fried cakes from the frying kettle to a tin colander to drain; "my opinion of a kitchen? Well, that would vary somewhat with the mansion that contained it. In any case, however, it would be the pleasantest room in the house, if I had the ordering of things."

The queen of our kitchen said this with a half smile and a half apology, as she continued: "It makes a good deal of difference, you know, to one who is to spend the best part of her time there. I often think that many people with whom money is no object, have very limited ideas of their responsibilities when it comes to the servant's quarter in the houses they build, with all they may have of modern improvements and conveniences.

"I have no conceit of those fine houses," said she, with considerable asperity of manner, "with not a room in it but where a regiment might meander comfortably about among the furniture but the kitchen, which is only large enough for the range, the sink, the ironing table, and the —— cook. Neither for my part, could I ever see what those people are thinking about who do not keep servants, and where the mistress expects to do her own work, who allows, of all rooms in the house, her kitchen to be built a dark little box of a place, pervaded with the sole idea of *work*. Of work, too, without one gleam of cheerfulness about it, and from which every one who enters escapes with a glad feeling of relief. For my part," she continued, "I don't see why making fried cakes, and baking biscuit, and washing dishes, might not be made as bright and attractive as, —— well, as any thing else one has to do in the way of house work.

"My opinion of a kitchen, 'as is a kitchen,' is one with room enough about for the many little things and comforts that give it a home-like look; a 'living room,' as we used to call our kitchen in the old home. For instance *this* comes the nearest my idea of it; always excepting *that*," she said, with a gratified glance around at the pretty clock on its pretty bracket, and the newspaper rack, (for Susan enjoyed the papers,) at the various nicknacks, and the landscapes, and home views, which Susan prized far above the costly conventional fruit and game pieces on the dining room walls. And then Susan's glance wandered, with a pleased softened look to the sunny window, with its geranium pots and hanging basket, near which the most cheerful of canaries in his cage made all the air melodious with song. Here, also, stood an easy chair inviting rest for those moments of waiting upon work which so often occur, and near it a stand with drawers for all sorts of little treasures which contained all of fancy work in which Susan ever indulged, "That easy chair, and that window, are great comforts to me," she resumed. "Now, if there was but one window to my kitchen, and the sink before *that*, as I see in so many kitchens, if I had to take refuge in a stiff-backed chair in a dark corner or the middle of the room where I could reach out and touch the walls all around while I was waiting for the biscuit to rise, or the cake was baking, as I sat there glaring at some dark melancholy paper, instead of this bright cheerful tint of gray, with its hints of rose and violet, and then with the wood-work about, of an ugly, dingy blue, or mud coloured brown, instead of this bright-grained wood, with gleams of sunshine in it on the darkest days, and that is so easy to keep clean and is as pretty as a picture. I think if *this* was *that* kind of a kitchen, I would run away with the milkman some bright morning—I actually think I would." This is a standing joke of our Susan's, but one nevertheless that brings fear and consternation in our household whenever it is revived. "I suppose I was spoiled for that sort of thing in my early days," said she, meditatively, with a look in her eyes that went out for the moment, "over the hills and far away," to the kitchen, where we first found our Susan.

It was a wide, long room—so wide and long that the dresser and clock and tables and large old-fashioned furniture that stood here and there, never intruded themselves, but in large, comely, decorous, but uncompromising dignity, formed each a part of the harmonious whole. There was an indescribable charm about it, always orderly, always bright and the centre of a home-life where its duties went on in that easy cheerful way, a pleasure both to sight and sense. About its many windows, all the summer time, the roses clambered in sweet confusion, and through which the scent of the fragrant sweet-briar came floating in, with the song of the woodland birds and the pleasant farm sounds, and a vision of the far away hills, in their ever varying beauty of light and shadow; while within, in conscious enjoyment of it all, was Susan, stepping merrily about, making custard pies, or folding the fragrant linen, fresh from the line, for the morrow's ironing. But the prettiest picture of that old kitchen was of a winter evening, when the winds blew furiously without, of the grand old fire-place, with its heaping wood fire, over which on the crane the kettle hung, humming and singing, and sending up the chimney white clouds of steam, while before it stood the tin baker, which held the rich juicy roast, or the light snowy biscuit, the like of which never came out of any range that ever was, or will be invented; while the fire lighted up the fine old room with a rich warm glow, as Susan set the table with its snowy linen and polished ware, and golden butter, and luscious honey in the comb, and all those charming fancies she knew so well how to prepare. And to complete the picture, the comfortable easy chairs by the fire where the grandmother sat in placid enjoyment with her knitting, and not very far away, the father, tired with the work of the day, giving himself to the rest and comforts of the evening hour. This is the picture that rose so vividly before me, but which had faded all too suddenly from our Susan's past.

Ah, well! said she, after a time coming out of her reverie with a little sigh and back again, to her opinion of a kitchen.

"It is not all of life to live"—making a hap-hazard

selection from her small stock of poetical fancies, but checking herself before reaching the concluding lines of this stanza.

"My opinion," she said, with a sudden change of tone and manner as she sniffed the air—is—that until some contrivance is invented to carry out all the steam, smoke, and smell of frying, that with all my care, and in spite of windows, and doors, and ventilators, will hang about my kitchen, the millenium won't come; and if it does, *I* shan't be in it."

As she said this, we looked around, and there stood the Pater. And we knew by the look in his eyes that he had heard these words of Susan's. And thus it will happen, that the Pater who is a born inventor, but who in the hurry and worry of business life has limited opportunities for the indulgence of this natural bent of his genius, will seize upon this idea with the pretext of a duty, and with which he will retire to the depths of his inner consciousness, there to evolve some stange contrivance hereafter to assume form and shape for the perfecting of "Our Susan's" kitchen.

UTENSILS

NECESSARY IN THE KITCHEN OF A SMALL FAMILY.

WOODEN WARE.

Kitchen Table; Wash Bench; Wash Tubs, (three sizes); Wash Board; Skirt Board; Bosom Board; Bread Board; Towel Roll; Potatoe Masher; Wooden Spoons; Clothes Stick; Flour Barrel Cover; Flour Sieve. Chopping Bowl; Soap Bowl; Pails; Lemon Squeezer; Clothes Wringer; Clothes Bars; Clothes Pins; Clothes Baskets; Mop; Wood Boxes, (nests).

TIN WARE.

One Boiler for Clothes; one Boiler for Ham; one Bread Pan; two Dish Pans; one Preserving Pan; four Milk Pans; two Quart Basins; two Pint Basins; two quart covered Tin Pails; one four-quart covered Tin Pail; Sauce Pans with covers, two sizes; two Tin Cups with handles; four Jelly Moulds, (half-pint); two Pint Moulds for rice, blanc-mange, etc.; one Skimmer; two Dippers, different sizes; two Funnels, (one for jug and one for cruets); one quart measure, also, pint, half-pint and gill measures, (they should be broad and low as they are more easily kept clean); three Scoops; Bread Pans; two round

Jelly Cake Pans, and two long Pie Pans; One Coffee Pot; one Tea Steeper; one Colander; one Steamer; one Horse Radish Grater; one Nutmeg Grater; one small Salt Sieve; one Hair Sieve for straining jelly; one Dover's Egg Beater; one Cake Turner; one Cake Cutter; one Apple Corer; one Potato Cutter; one dozen Muffin Rings; one Soap Shaker; Ice Filter; Flour Dredge; Tea Canister; Coffee Canister; Cake, Bread, Cracker, and Cheese Boxes; Crumb Tray; Dust Pans.

IRON WARE.

Range; one Pot with steamer to fit; one Soup Kettle; Preserving Kettle (porcelain); Tea Kettle; large and small Frying Pans; Dripping Pans; Gem Pans; Iron Spoons of different sizes; one Gridiron; one Griddle; one Waffle Iron; Toasting Rack; Meat Fork; Jagging Iron; Can Opener; Coffee Mill; Flat Irons; Hammer; Tack Hammer; Screw Driver; Ice Pick.

STONE WARE.

Crocks of various sizes; Bowls holding six quarts, four quarts, two quarts, and pint bowls; six Earthen Baking Dishes different sizes.

BRUSHES.

Table Brush; two Dust Brushes; two Scrub Brushes; one Blacking Brush for stove; Shoe Brush; Hearth Brush; Brooms.

SOUPS.

> "No useless dish our table crowds;
> Harmoniously ranged and consonantly just,
> As in a concert instruments resound,
> Our ordered dishes in their courses chime."

The basis of all good soups, is the broth of meat This may be made by boiling the cracked joints of beef, veal or mutton, and is best when cooked the day before it is to be eaten. After putting the meat into the pot, cover it well with cold water and let it come to a boil, when it should be well skimmed. Set the pot where it will simmer slowly until it is thoroughly done, keeping the pot closely covered the while. The next day, when the soup is cold, remove the fat, which will harden on the top of the soup. After this, add the vegetables and the herbs you use for seasoning, cooking all well together. Before sending to the table, the soup should be strained. A good stock for soups may be made from shreds and bits of uncooked meat and bones, poultry and the remains of game. When these are all put together and stewed down in the pot, the French term it *consomme*, and use it chiefly in the preparation of brown soups.

Soups may be varied in many ways, chiefly in the kinds of vegetables and different seasonings used,—as in herbs, burned caramel, eggs or slices of bread fried to a crisp in butter, which impart a savoury relish.

EGG BALLS FOR SOUP.
Mrs. Frisbie.

Rub the yolks of three or four hard boiled eggs to a smooth paste, with a little melted butter, pepper and salt, to these add two raw ones, beat in light, add enough flour to hold the paste together, make into balls, with floured hands, and set in a cool place until just before your soup comes off, when you put them in carefully and boil one minute.

ANOTHER SOUP FOR SUET.
Mrs. G. B. Wyllie.

One tea-cup pearl barley in about one pint *cold* water, bring to the boil till it swells, boil in a tin pail, in hot water, four quarts milk, put in your barley and keep simmering for three or four hours, add, *then serving*, one teaspoonful of salt.

POTATO SOUP.

Boil a shank of beef two days before you want your soup, strain into a crock and let stand till you need it, the fat will rise to the top, this you must take off before beginning to make your soup, now take your soup pot, and in about two tablespoonfuls of this same fat, fry brown four large onions sliced, put in half your stock, have ready a pot of nicely mashed potatoes, stir the potatoes into the soup till about the thickness of thick cream, and season with pepper and salt. The remaining stock is valuable for gravies, &c., or Scotch broth instead of mutton.

SCOTCH BROTH.

Mrs. G. B. Wyllie.

Take one-half teacup barley, four quarts cold water bring this to the boil and skim now put in a neck of mutton and boil again for half an hour, skim well the sides of the pot also; have ready two carrots, one large onion, a small head of cabbage, one bunch parsley, one sprig of celery top: chop all these fine, add your chopped vegetables, pepper and salt to taste. This soup takes two hours to cook.

SUET SOUP.

MADE WITHOUT MEAT.

In your soup pot put about a quarter of a pound of butter, set on the stove, slice into it four large onions; fry them a nice brown, stirring all the time. Now put in four quarts of cold water, one large coffee cupful of split peas previously washed; boil four hours. Before serving stir smartly with your potato-masher, strain through a colander into your tureen. Many like tomato catsup in this, but it is better to serve that separate.

TO KEEP STOCK FOR SOUP.

Mrs. G. B. Wyllie.

Cover your crock with a cloth, and tie down, as a lid causes it to ferment.

POTATOE SOUP FOR LENT.

Mr. G. B. Wyllie.

Slice and fry to a nice brown four large onions in quarter pound of butter in your soup pot, add four quarts of skim milk, have pealed and boiled a good three pints of potatoes, mash them fine and reduce smooth with the milk from your soup pot; repeat this till all the potatoes are in your soup pot; just bring to a boil and add pepper and salt to taste.

OX TAIL SOUP.

Miss Brokovski.

Take two ox tails and two whole onions, two carrots a small turnip, two tablespoonfuls of flour, and a little white pepper, add a gallon of water, let all boil for two hours; then take out the tails and cut the meat into small pieces, return the bones to the pot, for a short time, boil for another hour, then strain the soup, and rinse two spoonfulls of arrowroot to add to it with the meat cut from the bones, and let all boil for a quarter of an hour.

BEEF SOUP.

Mrs. Wm. H. Low.

Cut all the lean of the shank, and with a little beef suet in the bottom of the kettle, fry it to a nice brown; put in the bones and cover with water; cover the kettle closely; let it cook slowly until the meat drops from the bones; strain through a colander and leave it in the dish during the night, which is the only way to get off all the fat.

The day it is wanted for the table, fry as brown as possible a carrot, an onion and a very small turnip sliced thin. Just before taking up, put in half a teaspoonful of sugar, a blade of mace, six cloves, a dozen kernels of allspice, a small tablespoonful of celery seed. With the vegetables this must cook slowly in the soup an hour; then strain again for the table. If you use vermicelli or pearl barley, soak in water.

JULIENNE SOUP.

M. A. T.

Shred two onions and fry brown in a half spoon of butter; add a little mace, salt and pepper; then a spoonful or so of stock; rub a tablespoonful of flour smooth with a little butter and let fry with the onions; strain through a colander, then add more stock if desired; cut turnip, carrot and celery in fillets; add a few green peas; boil tender in a little water and add both water and vegetables to the soup. If wished, the flour can be left out, and it will make a clear light-coloured soup. In that case the onions should be cut in fillets and boiled with the vegetables.

MUTTON SOUP.

Mrs. Whitehead.

Boil a leg of mutton three hours; season to your taste with salt and pepper, and add one teaspoon of summer savory; make a batter of one egg, two tablespoons of milk, two tablespoons of flour, all well beaten together; drop this batter into the soup with a spoon, and boil for three minutes.

VEAL SOUP.

To about three pounds of a joint of veal, which must be well broken up, put four quarts of water and set it over to boil. Prepare one-fourth pound of macaroni by boiling it by itself, with sufficient water to cover it; add a little butter to the macaroni when it is tender; strain the soup and season to taste with salt and pepper; then add the macaroni in the water in which it is boiled. The addition of a pint of rich milk or cream and celery flavour is relished by many.

TURKEY SOUP.

Anonymous.

Take the turkey bones and cook for one hour in water enough to cover them; then stir in a little dressing and a beaten egg. Take from the fire, and when the water has ceased boiling add a little butter with pepper and salt.

OYSTER SOUP.

M. A. T.

Take one quart of water, one teacup of butter; one pint of milk, two teaspoons of salt, four crackers rolled fine, and one teaspoon of pepper; bring to full boiling heat as soon as possible, then add one quart of oysters: let the whole come to boiling heat quickly and remove from the fire.

OYSTER SOUP.

Mrs. T. V. Wadskier.

Pour one quart of boiling water into a skillet; then one quart of good rich milk; stir in one teacup of rolled cracker crumbs; season with pepper and salt to taste. When all come to a boil, add one quart of good fresh oysters; stir well, so as to keep from scorching; then add a piece of good sweet butter about the size of an egg; let it boil up once, then remove from the fire immediately; dish up and send to table.

CLAM SOUP.

Mrs. A. A. Carpenter.

Cut salt pork in very small squares and fry light brown; add one large or two small onions cut very fine, and cook about ten minutes; add two quarts of water and one quart of raw potatoes sliced; let it boil; then add one quart of clams. Mix one tablespoonful of flour with water, put it with one pint of milk and pour into the soup and let it boil about five minutes. Butter, pepper, salt, Worcestershire sauce to taste.

LOBSTER SOUP.

Mrs. Robert Harris.

One large lobster or two small ones; pick all the meat from the shell and chop fine; scald one quart of milk and one pint of water; then add the lobster, one pound of butter, a tablespoonful of flour, and salt and red pepper to taste. Boil ten minutes and serve hot.

PLAIN CALF'S HEAD SOUP.

Mrs. F. D. J.

Take a calf's head well cleaned, a knuckle of veal, and put them both into a large kettle; put one onion and a large tablespoon of sweet herbs, into a cloth and into the kettle, with the meat over which you have poured about four quarts of water. If you wish the soup for a one o'clock dinner, put the meat over to boil as early as eight o'clock in the morning; let it boil steadily and slowly and season well with salt and pepper. About one hour before serving, take off the soup and pour it through a colander, pick out all the meat carefully, chop very fine and return to the soup, putting it again over the fire. Boil four eggs very hard, chop them fine, and slice one lemon very thin, adding at the very last.

VERMICELLI SOUP.

Anonymous.

A knuckle of lamb, a small piece of veal, and water to cover well; when well cooked, season with salt, pepper, herbs to your taste, and a small onion, to which you may add Halford or Worcestershire sauce, about a tablespoonful. Have ready one-quarter of a pound of vermicelli, which has been boiled tender; strain your soup from the meat, add the vermicelli, let it boil well and serve.

GUMBO SOUP.

Anonymous.

Put on half a peck of tomatoes in a porcelain kettle and let them stew; have half a peck of ochra cut in fine shreds; put them with thyme, parsley and an onion cut fine, into the tomatoes and let them cook until quite tender. Fricassee one chicken in ham gravy; then take the yolk of four eggs, a little vinegar, the juice of one lemon, and season to taste, beating the eggs into the vinegar; pour this over the chicken, and put all then into the tomatoes, letting the kettle be nearly filled with water. Boil all together four or five hours.

MOCK TURTLE SOUP.
Mrs. C. H. Wheeler.

One soup-bone, one quart of turtle beans, one large spoonful of powdered cloves, salt and pepper. Soak the beans over night, put them on with the soup-bone in nearly six quarts of water and cook five or six hours. When half done, add the cloves, salt and pepper; when done, strain through a colander, pressing the pulp of the beans through to make the soup the desired thickness, and serve with a few slices of hard-boiled egg and lemon sliced very thin. The turtle beans are black and can only be obtained from large grocers.

TOMATO SOUP.
Mrs. Whitehead.

Boil chicken or beef four hours; then strain; add to the soup one can of tomatoes and boil one hour. This will make four quarts of soup.

TOMATO SOUP WITHOUT MEAT.
C. O. Van Cline.

One quart of tomatoes, one quart of water, one quart of milk. Butter, salt and pepper to taste. Cook the tomatoes thoroughly in the water, have the milk scalding, (over water to prevent scorching.) When the tomatoes are done add a large teaspoonful of saleratus, which will cause a violent effervescence. It is best to set the vessel in a pan before adding it to prevent waste. When the commotion has ceased add the milk and seasoning. When it is possible it is best to use more milk than water, and cream instead of butter. The soup is eaten with crackers and is by some preferred to oyster syrup. This recipe is very valuable for those who keep abstinence days.

ASPARAGUS SOUP.
Mrs. D.

Three or four pounds of veal cut fine, a little salt pork, two or three bunches of aparagus and three quarts of water. Boil one-half of the asparagus with the meat, leaving the rest in water until about twenty minutes before serving; then add the rest of the asparagus and boil just before serving; add one pint of milk; thicken with a little flour and season. The soup should boil about three hours before adding the last half of the asparagus.

GREEN PEA SOUP.
Anonymous.

Four pounds of lean beef cut in small pieces, one-half peck of green peas, one gallon of water; boil the empty pods of the peas in the water one hour; strain them out; add the beef and boil slowly one and a half hours. Half an hour before serving strain out the meat and add the peas; twenty minutes later add one-half cup of rice flour; salt and pepper to taste; and if you choose, one teaspoon of sugar. After adding the rice, stir frequently to prevent burning.

CORN SOUP.

Mrs. W. P. Nixon.

One small beef bone, two quarts of water; four tomatoes, eight ears of corn; let the meat boil a short time in the water; cut the corn from the cob and put in the cobs with the cut corn and tomatoes; let it boil about half an hour; remove the cobs; just before serving add milk, which allow to boil for a few moments only; season with salt and pepper.

CORN SOUP.

Anonymous.

One quart of corn cut from the cob in three pints of water: when the grain is quite tender, mix with them two ounces of sweet butter rolled in a tablespoon of flour; let it boil fifteen minutes longer; just before taking up the soup, beat up an egg and stir in with pepper and salt.

TURTLE BEAN SOUP.

Mrs. A. N. Arnold.

Take a quart of black beans, wash them and put them in a pot with three quarts of water; boil until thoroughly soft; rub the pulp through a colander and return it to the pot; add some thyme in a clean cloth, and let it boil a few minutes for flavour; slice some hard boiled eggs and drop them into the soup; add a little butter, pepper and salt.

BEAN SOUP.

Mrs. Whitehead.

One pint beans, four quarts water, small piece fat beef; boil three hours and strain. If too thin add one tablespoon flour.

POTATO SOUP.

M. A. T.

Boil five or six potatoes with a small piece of salt pork and a little celery; pass through a colander and add milk or cream (if milk, a little butter,) to make the consistency of thick cream; chop a little parsley fine and throw in; let boil five minutes; cut some dry bread in small dice, fry brown in hot lard; drain them and place in the bottom of soup tureen, and pour the soup over; chop two onions and boil with the soup, if liked.

FORCE MEAT BALLS.

Mrs. James S. Gibbs.

Mix with one pound of chopped veal or other meat, one egg, a little butter or raw pork chopped fine, one cup or less of bread crumbs; the whole well moistened with warm water, or what is better, the water from stewed meat; season with salt and pepper; make in small balls and fry them brown.

EGG BALLS FOR SOUP.

M. A. T.

Boil four eggs; put into cold water; mash yolks with yolk of one raw egg, and one teaspoon of flour; pepper, salt and parsley; make into balls and boil two minutes.

NOODLES FOR SOUP.

Mrs. F. D. J.

Rub into two eggs as much sifted flour as they will absorb; then roll out until thin as a wafer; dust over a little flour, and then roll over and over into a roll; cut off thin slices from the edge of the roll and shake out into long strips; put them into the soup lightly and boil for ten minutes; salt should be added while mixing with the flour—about a saltspoonful.

CARAMEL, OR BURNED SUGAR.

Put two ounces of brown or white sugar in an old tin cup over a brisk fire, stir this until it is quite dark and gives forth a burned smell, then add half a cup of cold water; let it boil gently a few minutes, stirring well and all the while. Take off, and when cold bottle for use. This keeps well, and may be used for flavoring gravies and soups.

CROUTONS.

These are simply pieces of bread fried brown and crisp to be used in soups.

FISH.

> "The silvery fish,
> Grazing at large in meadows submarine,
> Fresh from the wave now cheers
> Our festive board."
> —Anon.

Fish are good, when the gills are red, eyes are full, and the body of the fish is firm and stiff. After washing them well, they should be allowed to remain for a short time in salt water sufficient to cover them; before cooking, wipe them dry, dredge lightly with flour, and season with salt and pepper. Salmon trout and other small fish are usually fried or broiled; all large fish should be put in a cloth, tied closely with twine, and placed in cold water, when they may be put over the fire to boil. When fish are baked, prepare the fish the same as for boiling, and put in the oven on a wire gridiron, over a dripping pan.

SUGGESTIONS AS TO FISH, POULTRY, &c.

Miss Riley.

Cod-Fish—requires great care in cleaning, particularly in cleansing the back-bone from blood which spoils its appearance, and sometimes renders it too unsightly for the table. Fishes that are to be dressed in their scales, should be dipped in water, and rubbed with a coarse towel to remove the shine. All salt fish should be properly soaked in water, previous to cooking. It is asserted that a small proportion of sugar will keep fish perfectly fresh for several days; it also cures salmon and white fish with a little salt added to please the taste. Fresh water fish has often a muddy smell and taste; to take this off, soak it in strong salt and water after it is nicely cleansed, then dry and dress it.

BOILED WHITE FISH.

Mrs. Andrews.

Lay the fish open; put it in a dripping pan, with the back down; nearly cover with water; to one fish put two tablespoons salt; cover tightly and simmer (not boil) one-half hour; dress with gravy, butter and pepper; garnish with sliced eggs.

For sauce use a piece of butter the size of an egg, one tablespoon of flour, one-half pint boiling water; boil a few minutes, and add three hard boiled eggs, sliced.

FISH A LA CREME.

Mrs. J. A. Ellis.

Take any firm salt water fish, rub it with salt and put it in a kettle with enough boiling water to cover it. As soon as it boils set it back where it will simmer, let it stand for an hour, then take it up and draw out all the bones. Put one ounce of flour into a sauce-pan, to which add by degree one quart of cream or new milk, mixing it very smoothly, then add the juice of one lemon, one onion chopped fine, a bunch of parsley, a little nutmeg, salt and pepper. Put this on the fire, stirring it till it forms a thick sauce; stir in a quarter of a pound of butter; strain the sauce through a sieve. Put a little on a dish, then lay the fish on it and turn the remainder of the sauce over it. Beat to a froth the whites of six eggs, spread over the whole, and bake half an hour a light brown.

SAUCE FOR BOILED FISH.

To one teacup of milk, add one teacup of water; put it on the fire to scald, and when hot stir in a tablespoon of flour, previously wet with cold water; add two or three eggs; season with salt and pepper, a little celery, vinegar and three tablespoons of butter. Boil four or five eggs hard, take off the shells, and cut in slices, and lay over the dish. Then pour over the sauce and serve.

BAKED HALIBUT OR SALMON.

Let the fish remain in cold water, slightly salted, for an hour before it is time to cook it; place the gridiron on a dripping pan with a little hot water in it and bake in a hot oven; just before it is done, butter it well on the top, and brown it nicely. The time of baking depends upon the size of the fish. A small fish will bake in about half an hour, and a large one in an hour. They are very nice when cooked as above and served with a sauce which is made from the gravy in the dripping pan, to which is added a tablespoon of catsup and another of some pungent sauce and the juice of a lemon. Thicken with brown flour moistened with a little cold water. Garnish handsomely with sprigs of parsley and currant jelly.

BAKED BLACK BASS.

Mrs. P. B. Ayer.

Eight good sized onions chopped fine; half that quantity of bread crumbs; butter size of hen's egg; plenty of pepper and salt, mix thoroughly with anchovy sauce until quite red. Stuff your fish with this compound and pour the rest over it, previously sprinkling it with a little red pepper. Shad, pickerel and trout are good the same way. Tomatoes can be used instead of anchovies, and are more economical. If using them, take pork in place of butter and chop fine.

BROILED WHITE FISH—FRESH.

Mrs. G. E. P.

Wash and drain the fish; sprinkle with pepper and lay with the inside down upon the gridiron, and broil over fresh bright coals. When a nice brown, turn for a moment on the other side, then take up and spread with butter. This is a very nice way of broiling all kinds of fish, fresh or salted. A little smoke under the fish adds to its flavour. This may be made by putting two or three cobs under the gridiron.

SALT MACKEREL.

Mrs. F. D. J.

Soak the fish for a few hours in lukewarm water, changing the water several times; then put into cold water loosely tied in cloths, and let the fish come to a boil, turning off the water once, and pouring over the fish hot water from the tea kettle; let this just come to a boil, then take them out and drain them, lay them on a platter, butter and pepper them, and place them for a few moments in the oven. Serve with sliced lemons, or with any nice fish sauce.

BOILED CODFISH—SALT.

Soak two pounds of codfish in lukewarm water over night or for several hours; change the water several times; about one hour before dinner put this into cold fresh water, and set over the fire; let it come to a boil, or just simmer, for fifteen minutes but not to boil hard, then take out of the water, drain and serve with egg sauce, or with cold boiled eggs sliced and laid over it, with a drawn butter or cream gravy poured over all.

EELS.

Mrs. P. B. Ayer.

Skin and parboil them; cleanse the back bone of all coagulations; cut them in pieces about three inches in length; dip in flour and cook in pork fat, brown.

CHOWDER.

Mrs. P. B. Ayer.

Five pounds of codfish cut in squares; fry plenty of salt pork cut in thin slices; put a layer of pork in your kettle, then one of fish; one of potatoes in thick slices, and one of onions in slices; plenty of pepper and salt;

repeat as long as your materials last, and finish with a layer of Boston crackers or crusts of bread. Water sufficient to cook with, or milk if you prefer. Cook one-half hour and turn over on your platter, disturbing as little as possible. Clams and eels the same way.

POTTED FISH.

Mrs. Gridley.

Take out the backbone of the fish; for one weighing two pounds take a tablespoon of allspice and cloves mixed; these spices should be put into little bags of not too thick muslin; put sufficient salt directly upon each fish; then roll in a cloth, over which sprinkle a little cayenne pepper; put alternate layers of fish, spice and sago in an earthern jar; cover with the best cider vinegar; cover the jar closely with a plate and over this put a covering of dough, rolled out to twice the thickness of pie crust. Make the edges of paste, to adhere closely to the sides of the jar, so as to make it air-tight. Put the jar into a pot of cold water and let it boil from three to five hours, according to quantity. Ready when cold.

Sauces for "Fish and Meat" will follow "Meats."

SHELL FISH.

OYSTERS ON THE SHELL.

Wash the shells and put them on hot coals or upon the top of a hot stove, or bake them in a hot oven; open.

the shells with an oyster knife, taking care to lose none of the liquor, and serve quickly on hot plates, with toast. Oysters may be steamed in the shells, and are excellent eaten in the same manner.

BROILED OYSTERS.

Drain the oysters well and dry them with a napkin. Have ready a griddle hot and well buttered; season the oysters; lay them to griddle and brown them on both sides. Serve them on a hot plate with plenty of butter.

CREAMED OYSTERS.

Clara E. Thatcher.

To one quart of oysters take one pint of cream or sweet milk; thicken with a little flour, as for gravy; when cooked pour in the oysters with liquor; pepper, salt and butter the mixture. Have ready a platter with slices of nicely browned toast, pour creamed oysters on toast and serve hot.

OYSTERS A LA CREME.

Mrs. J. B. Lyon.

One quart of oysters, one pint of cream; put the oysters in a double kettle, cook until the milk juice begins to flow out; drain the oysters in a colander; put the cream on the same way; when it comes to a boil, thicken with flour wet with milk as thick as corn starch ready to mould; then put in the oysters and cook five minutes. Serve hot on toast.

PANNED OYSTERS.

Mrs. J. B. Lyon.

Drain the oysters from the liquor; put them in a hot pan or spider; as soon as they begin to curl, add butter, pepper and salt. Serve on toast, or without, if preferred.

STEWED OYSTERS.

Mrs. Andrews.

In all cases, unless shell oysters, wash and drain; mix half a cup of butter and a tablespoon of corn starch; put with the oysters in a porcelain kettle; stir until they boil; add two cups of cream or milk; salt to taste; do not use the liquor of the oysters in either stewing or escaloping.

ESCALOPED OYSTERS.

Mrs. Andrews.

Butter the dish, (common earthern pie-plates are the best,) cover the bottom of the dish with very fine bread crumbs; add a layer of oysters; season with pepper and salt; alternate the crumbs and oysters until you have three layers; finish with crumbs; cover the top with small pieces of butter; finish around the edge with bread cut into small oblong pieces dipped in butter; bake half an hour; unless shell oysters, wash them thoroughly and strain.

OYSTER PATTIES.

Aunt Maggie.

Make some rich puff paste and bake it in very small tin patty pans; when cool, turn them out upon a large dish; stew some large fresh oysters with a few cloves, a little mace and nutmeg; then add the yolk of one egg, boiled hard and grated; add a little butter, and as much of the oyster liquor as will cover them. When they have stewed a little while, take them out of the pan and set them to cool. When quite cold, lay two or three oysters in each shell of puff paste.

TO FRY OYSTERS.
Mrs. D. Wadskier.

Use the largest and best oysters; lay them in rows upon a clean cloth and press another upon them, to absorb the moisture; have ready several beaten eggs; and in another dish some finely crushed crackers; in the frying pan heat enough butter to entirely cover the oysters; dip the oysters first into the eggs, then into the crackers, rolling it or them over that they may become well incrusted; drop into the frying pan and fry quickly to a light brown. Serve dry and let the dish be warm. A chafing dish is best.

FRICASSEED OYSTERS.
Mrs. W. P. Brown.

For a quart can, drain the oysters dry as possible; put a piece of butter the size of an egg into your spider, and let it get quite brown; put in your oysters and as soon as they commence to cook, add as much more butter, which has been previously well mixed with a tablespoon of flour; let it cook a moment and add one egg, beaten with a tablespoon of cream; let this cook a moment and pour all over toasted bread.

STEWED OYSTERS.

Mrs. T. McMish.

Drain the liquor from two quarts of firm, plump oysters, mix with it a small teacup of hot water, add a little salt and pepper, and set over the fire in a saucepan. When it boils, add a large cupful of rich milk. Let it boil up once, add the oysters, let them boil five minutes. When they ruffle, add two tablespoons butter, and the instant it is melted, and well stirred in, take off the fire.

BEEFSTEAK AND OYSTER PIE.

Miss Riley.

Beat the steak gently with a rolling pin, and season with pepper and salt. Have ready a deep dish lined with not too rich a pastry. Put in the meat with layers of oysters; then the oyster liquor with a little mace, and a teaspoon catsup; cover with top crust and bake. Veal will do as well as beef.

SCALLOPED OYSTERS.

Crush and roll several handfuls of Boston crackers; put a layer in the bottom of a buttered pudding-dish. Wet this with a mixture of the oyster liquor and milk slightly warmed. Next a layer of oysters sprinkled with salt, pepper, and small bits of butter; then another layer of the moistened crumbs, then a layer of oysters, and so on till the dish is full. Let the top layer be of crumbs, and beat an egg into the milk, which you pour over them. Stick bits of butter thickly over it, and bake half an hour.

PICKLED OYSTERS.
Mrs. C. G. Smith.

Wash them from their liquor and put them into a porcelain lined kettle, with strong salt and water to cover them; let them come to a boil, and then skim them into cold water; scald whole peppers, mace, and cloves in a little vinegar; the quantity of these must be determined by the number of oysters; when the oysters are cold, put them into a stone jar with layers of spice between them, and make liquor enough to cover them from the liquor in which they were cooked; spice your vinegar and cold water to taste.

LOBSTER CHOWDER.
Mrs. Lambkin.

Four or five pounds of lobster, chopped fine; take the green part and add to it four pounded crackers; stir this into one quart of boiling milk; then add the lobster, a piece of butter one-half the size of an egg, a little pepper and salt, and bring it to a boil.

LOBSTER CROQUETTES.
M. A. T.

The same mixture as given for stuffed lobster, without the cream; made into pointed balls, dipped in egg, and then rolled in cracker and fried in very hot lard; served dry and garnished with parsley.

CLAM STEW.
Mrs. M. L. S.

Lay the clams on a gridiron over hot coals, taking them out of the shells as soon as open, saving the juice; add a little hot water, pepper, a very little salt and butter rolled in flour sufficient for seasoning; cook for five minutes and pour over toast.

CLAM FRITTERS.
M. A. T.

Twelve clams chopped or not; one pint milk; three eggs; add liquor from clams; salt and pepper, and flour enough for thin batter. Fry in hot lard.

TRIPE A LA LYONNAISE (LYONS FASHION).

When any cold tripe remains, cut it in thin slices about an inch square, and wipe it very dry. Mince two onions, put some butter (in the proportion of 3 oz. to 1 lb. of tripe) into a frying-pan with the onions; when they are about half done put in the tripe, and let all fry for about ten minutes; season with pepper and salt, and three tablespoonfuls of vinegar to each pound of tripe. Serve very hot.

TRIPE.
From Lady Harriet St. Clair's Dainty Dishes.

Stewed Tripe.—Select two pounds of double tripe well cleaned and blanched, cut in pieces of rather less than a quarter of a pound each, put in a clean stew-pan with a pint of milk and one of water, two teaspoonfuls of salt, one of pepper, eight middle-sized onions carefully peeled; set it on to boil, which it should do at first rather fast, then simmer till done, which will be in rather more than half an hour. Put it into a deep dish or tureen and serve with the milk and onions.

POULTRY AND GAME.

> "Whoso seeks an audit here,
> 1 copitious pays his tribute—game or fish,
> Wild fowl or venison, and his errand speed."
> —Cowper.

POULTRY.

When poultry is brought into the kitchen for use it should be kept as cool as possible. The best position in which to place it is with the breast downwards on a shelf or marble slab. The crop should be taken out. Choose fowls with a thin, transparent skin, white and delicate. Time required to boil poultry: a chicken will take about 20 minutes; a fowl about 40 minutes; a small turkey an hour and a half; a large turkey two hours or more.

BOILED FOWL.

Take a young fowl and fill the inside with oysters; place in a jar and plunge into a kettle of water; boil for one and one-half hours; there will be a quantity of gravy in the jar from the juice of the fowl and the oysters; make this into a white sauce with the addition of egg, cream, or a little flour and butter; add oysters, or serve up plain with the fowl. This is very nice with the addition of a little parsley to the sauce.

ROAST TURKEY OR CHICKEN.

Having picked and drawn the fowls, wash them well in two or three waters; wipe them dry; dredge them with a little flour inside and out, and a little pepper and salt; prepare a dressing of bread and cracker crumbs, fill the bodies and crops of the fowls and then bake them from two to three hours; baste them frequently while roasting; stew the giblets in a saucepan; just before serving, chop the giblets fine; after taking up the chicken, and the water in which the giblets were boiled, add the chopped giblets to the gravy of the roast fowl; thicken with a little flour, which has been previously wet with the water; boil up, and serve in a gravy-dish. Roast chickens and turkey should be accompanied with celery and jellies.

TO BOIL A TURKEY.

Mrs. Robert Beaty.

Make a stuffing for the craw of chopped bread and butter, cream, oysters, and the yolks of eggs; sew it in, and dredge flour over the turkey, and put it to boil in cold water, with a spoonful of salt in it, and enough water to cover them well; let it simmer for two hours and a half, or, if small, less time; skim it while boiling; it looks nicer if wrapped in a cloth dredged with flour; serve it with drawn butter, in which put some oysters.

ROAST CHICKENS.

Mrs. Jas. Beaty.

Wash them clean outside and inside; stuff them as

directed for turkeys; baste them with butter, lard, or drippings, and roast them about an hour. Chickens should be cooked thoroughly. Stew the inwards till tender, and till there is but little water; chop them and mix in gravy from the dripping-pan; thicken with brown flour; season with salt, pepper, and butter. Cranberry or new made apple sauce, is good with them.

TO STEW BIRDS.

Mrs. Jas. Beaty.

Wash and stuff them with bread crumbs, seasoned with pepper, salt, butter or chopped salt pork, and fasten them tight. Line a stew pan with slices of bacon, add a quart of water and a bit of butter the size of a goose egg, or else four slices of salt pork. Add if you like sliced onions, and sweet herbs and mace. Stew till tender, then take them up and strain the gravy over them. Add boiling water if the liquor is too much reduced.

ON THE PREPARATION OF HASHES, GRAVIES, AND SAUCES.

Mrs. Jas. Beaty.

There is nothing worse for the health, or for the palate, than *a poor hash*, while a *good* hash is not only a favourite dish in most families, but an essential article of economy and convenience. For this reason a separate article is devoted to this subject. The following are the ways in which hashes are spoilt. The first is by *cooking* them. Meat, when once cooked, should only be *heated*. If it is again stewed or fried, it tends to make it hard or tough, and diminishes its flavour. The second is by frying the *butter* or *gravy* in which they are prepared. It has been shown that this is very injurious to the healthfulness of food. Butter and oils may be *melted* without changing their nature, but when *cooked*, they become much more indigestible and injurious to weak stomachs. The third mode of injuring hashes is by putting in flour in such ways that it is not properly cooked. Flour dredged on to hashes while they are cooking imparts the raw taste of dough. The fourth mode, is by putting in so much water as to make them vapid, or else so much grease as to make them gross. The fifth is by seasoning them with so little care, that they either have very little savory taste, or else are so hot with pepper and spice as to be unhealthy. If a housekeeper will follow these directions, or give them to a cook who will follow them exactly, she will always have good and healthful hashes.

TO CURRY CHICKEN.

Mrs. W. Arthurs.

Slice an onion and brown in a little butter; add a spoonful of curry powder; allow it to remain covered for a few minutes to cook; add a little more butter and put in chicken, veal, &c., &c.; cut up small, thicken with a little flour. This is excellent.

BAKED CHICKEN.

Anonymous.

Cut the fowls open and lay them flat in a pan, breaking down the breast and the back bones; dredge with flour and season well with salt and pepper, with bits of butter; put in a very hot oven until done, basting frequently with melted butter; or when half done take out the chicken and finish by broiling it upon a gridiron over bright coals; pour over it melted butter and the juices in the pan in which it was baked.

CHICKEN FRICASSEE.

Sarah Page.

Cut up the chickens and put on the fire in a kettle with cold water sufficient to cover, add a little salt or salt pork sliced, if you like; boil until tender, and cut up and put in part of a head of celery. When tender have ready hot baking-powder biscuits broken open and laid on a platter; on this place the chicken; thicken the gravy with flour moistened with water or milk, and pour it over the chicken and biscuits. If you prefer, use a good-sized piece of butter to season instead of the salt pork. Oysters are an addition.

FRIED CHICKEN.

Mrs. Dausher.

Cut the chicken in pieces, lay it in salt and water, which change several times; roll each piece in flour; fry in very hot lard or butter, season with salt and pepper; fry parsley with them also. Make a gravy of cream seasoned with salt, pepper and a little mace, thickened with a little flour in the pan in which the chickens were fried, pouring off the lard.

DRESSING FOR CHICKENS OR TURKEY.

Mrs. F. D.

Chop bread crumbs quite fine, season well with pepper, salt, and plenty of butter; moisten with a very little water, and add a few oysters with a little of the liquor, if you please. The best authorities say the dressing is the finest when it crumbles as the fowl is cut.

DRESSING FOR TURKEY.

C. Kennicot.

One pint of soaked bread, two tablespoons of sage, two tablespoons of summer savory, two teaspoons of salt, two teaspoons pepper, butter size of an egg.

CHICKEN CHEESE.

Two chickens boiled tender, chop, but not too fine; salt and pepper; three or four eggs boiled and sliced; line dishes or moulds with them; pour in the chicken and the liquor they were boiled in; when cold slice. Should be boiled in as little water as possible.

CURRY.

Miss Brokovski.

To make curry with rabbit, chicken, or any other meat, flour the meat and fry it a nice light brown; fry also two large onions in the same way; mix a tablespoonful of curry powder, and a small quantity of cayenne in a tea cup, with warm water in the consistency of cream, and cover every part of the meat with the mixture; have ready some nice stock or thin gravy; put all together into a stew-pan, and let it stew gently for twenty minutes; before serving slice two or three apples, let them stew away; this addition is thought to be a great improvement, as it makes the curry milder; rice to be boiled very dry and served around the dish.

JELLIED CHICHEN.

M. A. T.

Boil a fowl until it will slip easily from the bones; let the water be reduced to about one pint in boiling; pick the meat from the bones in good sized pieces, taking out all gristle, fat, and bones; place in a wet mould; skim the fat from the liquor; a little butter; pepper and salt to the taste and one half ounce of gelatine. When this dissolves, pour it hot over the chicken. The liquor must be seasoned pretty high, for the chicken absorbs.

CHICKEN PIE.

Mrs. H.

Stew chickens until tender; line the sides of a deep pie dish with nice pastry; put in the chicken, and the water in which it has boiled, (which should be but half a pint); season with a large piece of butter, salt and pepper, and then cover loosely with crust. While this is baking, have ready a quart can of fine oysters; put on the fire a pint of rich milk, (or the liquor of the oysters will do); let it come to a boil; thicken with a little flour, and season with butter, pepper, and salt; pour this over the oysters boiling hot, and about fifteen minutes before the pie is done, lift the crust and pour the oysters and all into the pie; then return to the oven to finish.

CHICKEN LOAF.

Mrs. W. H. Low.

Take two chickens, boil them in as little water as possible until the meat will drop from the bones; cut it with a knife and fork, then put it back into the kettle; put in plenty of butter, pepper and salt; heat it thoroughly; boil an egg hard and slice it and place it in the bottom of a dish; pour it in hot, place a weight upon it, and put it away to cool; it will come out in form.

CHICKEN CROQUETTES.

Marion Harland.

Minced chicken; about one-quarter as much fine bread crumbs as you have of meat; one egg beaten light to each cup of meat; gravy enough to moisten the crumbs and chicken; or, if you have no gravy, a little drawn butter; pepper and salt and chopped parsley to taste; yolks of two hard boiled eggs rubbed fine with the back of a silver spoon, added to the meat; mix up into a paste with as little handling as may be; nor must the paste be too wet to mould readily; make with floured hands into llsro or ovate balls, roll in flour until well coated, and fry a few at a time, lest crowding should injure the shape, in nice dripping, or a mixture half lard and half butter. As you take them out lay in a hot colander, that every drop of fat may be drained off. Serve in a heated dish with cresses or parsley.

CHICKEN CROQUETTES.

Mrs. J. A. Ellis.

Four and one-half pounds chicken boiled and chopped very fine; moisten to a thick pulp with the liquor in which it has been boiled. Mix with this a pint and a half of mashed potatoes, beaten to a cream; three eggs, one teaspoon of mustard, sweet majoram, salt and pepper to taste; a little celery chopped very fine; soften with milk till very soft, and add a quarter of a pound of butter. Mould into forms, dip in egg and cracker dust, and fry in boiling lard.

CHICKEN PATES.

Mince chicken that has been previously roasted or boiled, and season well; stir into this a sauce made of half a pint of milk, into which while boiling a teaspoonful of corn starch has been added to thicken, season with butter, about a teaspoonful, and salt and pepper to taste. Have ready small pate pans lined with a good puff paste. Bake the crust in a brisk oven; then fill the pans and set in the oven a few minutes to brown very slightly.

DUCKS.

Miss S. P.

When roasted, use dressing as for turkey, with the addition of a few slices of onion. Many cooks lay over the game slices of onions, which take away the fishy flavour, removing the onion before serving. Make a sauce with the drippings in the pan in which the game is roasted, and to which are put the chopped giblets, which are previously well cooked; thicken the gravy with brown flour, moistened with water. Serve with currant jelly.

ROAST GOOSE.

Stuff and roast in the same manner as ducks. Many cooks cover poultry with a paste of flour and water while baking, removing it before it is served.

TO ROAST WILD FOWL.

M. A. T.

Put an onion, salt and hot water into a pan, and baste for ten or fifteen minutes; change the pan; put in a slice of salt pork and baste with butter and pork drippings very often; just before serving dredge lightly with flour and baste. Ducks take from twenty-five to thirty-five minutes to roast, and woodcock and snipes fifteen to twenty-five.

Do not draw or take off the heads of either. Garnish with fried or toasted bread, lemon, parsley, and currant jelly.

PRAIRIE CHICKENS, PARTRIDGES, AND QUAILS.

Miss Sarah Page.

Clean nicely, using a little soda in the water in which they are washed; rinse them and dry, and then fill them with dressing, sewing them up nicely, and binding down the legs and wings with cords. Put them in a steamer over hot water, and let them cook until just done. Then place then in a pan with a little butter; set them in the oven and baste them frequently with melted butter until of a nice brown. They ought to brown nicely in about fifteen minutes. Serve them on a platter, with sprigs of parsley alternating with currant jelly.

QUAIL ON TOAST.

After the birds are nicely cleaned, cut them open down the back; salt and pepper them, and dredge with flour. Break down the breast and back-bones, so they will lie flat, and place them in a pan with very little water and butter in a hot oven, covering them up tightly until nearly done. Then place them in a spider in hot butter, and fry a moment to a nice brown. Have ready slices of baker's bread toasted, and slightly buttered upon a platter. The toast should be broken down with a carving knife, so that it will be tender. On this place the quail; make a sauce of the gravy in the pan, thicken lightly with browned flour, and pour over each quail and the toast.

A SUGGESTION.

M. A. T.

Singe all poultry with alcohol, and dip quails into clarified butter for broiling.

PRESSED CHICKEN.

Mrs. C. Belford.

Cut up the fowls and place in a kettle with a tight cover, so as to retain the steam; put about two teacups of water and plenty of salt and pepper over the chicken, then let it cook until the meat cleaves easily from the bones, cut or chop all the meat (freed from skin, bone and gristle) about as for chicken salad; season well, put into a dish and pour the remnant of the juice in which it was cooked over it. This will jelly when cold, and can then be sliced or set on the table in shape. Nice for tea or lunch. The knack of making this simple dish is not having too much water; it will not jelly if too weak, or if the water is allowed to boil away entirely while cooking.

PIGEON PIE.

Mrs. L.

Make a fine puff paste; lay a border of it around a large dish, and cover the bottom with a veal cutlet, or a very tender steak free from fat and bone; season with salt, cayenne pepper, and mace. Prepare as many pigeons as can be put in one layer of the dish; put in each pigeon a small lump of butter, and season with pepper and salt; lay them in the dish breast downwards, and cut in slices a half dozen of hard boiled eggs, and lay in with the birds; put in more butter, some veal broth, and cover the whole with crust. Bake slowly for an hour and a half.

MEATS.

—" Cook, see all your sawces
Be sharp and poynant in the palate, that they may
Commend you; look to your roast and baked meats handsomely,
And what new kickshaws and delicate made things."

—BEAUMONT AND FLETCHER.

GENERAL RULES FOR COOKING MEATS.

All salt meat should be put on in cold water, that the salt may be extracted while cooking. Fresh meat, which is boiled to be served with sauces at the table, should be put to cook in boiling water; when the outer fibres contract, the inner juices are preserved.

For making soup, put the meat over in cold water, to extract the juices for the broth.

In boiling meats, if more water is needed, add that which is hot, and be careful to keep the water on the meat constantly boiling.

Remove the scum when it first begins to boil. The more gently meat boils, the more tender it will become. Allow twenty minutes for boiling each pound of fresh meat.

Roast meats require a brisk fire. Baste often. Twenty minutes is required for roasting each pound of fresh meat. The variation in roasted meats consists simply in the method of preparing them to cook, before putting them in the oven. Some are to be larded, some stuffed with bread dressing, and others plain, only seasoning with pepper and salt.

A piece of red pepper, cooked in a boiled dinner, is very nice.

ROAST BEEF.

Mrs. C. Belford.

Prepare for the oven by dredging lightly with flour, and seasoning with salt and pepper; place in the oven, and baste frequently while roasting. Allow a quarter of an hour for a pound of meat, if you like it rare; longer if you like it well done. Serve with a sauce, made from the drippings in the pan, to which has been added a tablespoon of Harvey or Worcestershire sauce, and a tablespoon of tomato catsup.

YORKSHIRE PUDDING.

Mrs. W. Gale.

One and a half pints milk, six large tablespoonfuls flour, three eggs, one saltspoonful salt; bake under the meat for one hour and a half.

YORKSHIRE PUDDING.

Mrs. Joseph B. Leake.

To be eaten with roast beef, instead of a vegetable. Three tablespoons flour, mixed with one pint of milk, three eggs and a little salt. Pour into a shallow tin baking pan; put into oven, an hour before dinner, for ten minutes; then put it under the roasting beef and leave it till you take up the beef; leave it in about five minutes after you take up the beef; then pour off the fat and send it to the table.

BEEFSTEAK AND MUSHROOMS.

Mrs. Perry H. Smith.

Put in a saucepan one ounce of butter, a small onion chopped fine, a little ground sage, and a little thyme, and put it over the fire; when hot, shake in two tablespoons of flour, and when it becomes brown, put in one gill of water, and let it boil for half an hour. Then add three tablespoons of beef stock, a little salt, a little nutmeg and one wine glass of sherry wine. Put in one can of mushrooms, and let it boil for ten minutes. Pour this over a nicely broiled beefsteak.

BROILED BEEFSTEAK.

Lay a thick tender steak upon a gridiron over hot coals, having greased the bars with butter before the steak has been put upon it; (a steel gridiron with slender bars is to be preferred, the broad flat iron bars of gridirons commonly used fry and scorch the meat, imparting a disagreeable flavour). When done on one side, have ready your platter warmed, with a little butter on it; lay the steak upon the platter with the cooked side down, that the juices which have gathered may run on the platter, but do not press the meat; then lay your beefsteak again upon the gridiron quickly and cook the other side. When done to your liking, put again on the platter, spread lightly with butter, place where it will keep warm for a few moments, but not to let the butter become oily, (over boiling steam is best); and then serve on hot plates. Beefsteak should never be seasoned with salt and pepper while cooking. If your meat is **tough**, pound *well* with a steak mallet on both sides.

BEEF LOAF.

Mrs. Carson.

Three and a half pounds veal or beef, minced very fine, and uncooked; four large crackers, crushed very fine; one egg, one cup of milk, butter size of an egg, one tablespoon salt, one of pepper; mix in shape of a loaf, and bake in a slow oven two hours and a half, basting often; to be eaten cold; very nice for tea or lunch.

BEEF EN MIROTON.

Mrs. S. McMaster.

Cut thin slices of cold roast beef, and put them into a frying pan with some butter and six onions, turn the pan frequently, then mix a little broth, add pepper and salt, and after a few boils serve up hot.

BEEF WITH TOMATOES.

Mrs. P. B. Ayer.

Eight pounds fresh plate beef, second cut broiled; boil tender two quarts tomatoes, three cloves, plenty butter, pepper and salt; when cooked nicely and thick, strain through a colander and pour over your beef and serve hot or cold.

TO BOIL CORNED BEEF.

Mrs. J. Beaty.

Put the beef in water enough to cover it, and let it heat slowly, and boil slowly, and be careful to take off the grease. Many think it much improved by boiling potatoes, turnips, and cabbages with it. In this case the vegetables must be pealed and *all* the grease carefully skimmed as fast as it rises. Allow about twenty minutes of boiling for each pound of meat.

BFEF OR VEAL STEWED WITH APPLES.

Mrs. James Beaty.

Rub a stewpan with butter; cut the meat in thin slices, and put in with pepper, salt, and apple, sliced fine; some would add a little onion. Cover it tight, and stew till tender.

DOMESTIC RECEIPTS.

TO COOK A HAM (VERY FINE).
Mrs. J. Beaty.

Boil a common-sized ham four or five hours, then skin the whole, and fit it for the table; then set it in an oven for half an hour, then cover it thickly with pounded rusk or bread crumbs, and set it back for half an hour. Boiled ham is always improved by setting it into an oven for nearly an hour, till much of the fat fries out; and this also makes it more tender.

TO BOIL A LEG OF VEAL OR MUTTON.
Miss Kate Beaty.

Make a stuffing of bread and a quarter as much of salt pork, chopped fine and seasoned with sweet herbs, pepper and salt. Make deep gashes, or, what is better, take out the bone with a carving-knife and fill up with stuffing, and sew up the opening with strong thread. When there is a flap of flesh lap it over the opening and sew it down. Put it into a large pot and fill it with water, putting in a tablespoonful of salt, and let it simmer slowly three hours. If it is needful to add water pour in *boiling* water.

SALLIE MUNDER'S WAY OF DRESSING COLD MEAT.

Mince beef or mutton, small, with onions, pepper and salt; add a little gravy, put into scallop shells or smal cups, making them three parts full, and fill them up with potatoes mashed with a little cream, put a bit of butter on the top and brown them in an oven.

BOILED BEEF (COLD).
Madame E. Pernet.

To use next day or when you like, for breakfast.

Melt a good lump of butter, about two ounces, over a slow fire, into a tablespoonful of flour; when it has simmered a little add some chopped onion (to taste) and a dessert spoonful of chopped parsley when brown; season with pepper and add a little stock or gravy, or water; mince the meat, put it in with the rest, and let it heat gradually; when nearly boiling thicken with a teaspoonful of flour. Add a little catsup or sauce of any kind.

A LA MODE BEEF.
Miss Sarah Page.

Take a piece of beef four or five inches thick, and with a knife make small holes entirely through it at slight distances apart. Then take strips of fat salt pork, roll them in pepper and cloves. Lay on a pan, cover closely, and put over in a steamer, and steam for three hours. When done thicken the gravy in the pan with a little flour. This is excellent when eaten as cold meat.

MOCK DUCK.
Mrs. C. C. Stratton.

Take the round of beefsteak, salt and pepper either side; prepare bread or crackers with oysters or without, as for stuffing a turkey; lay your stuffing on the meat; sew up and roast about an hour; and if you do not see the wings and legs you will think you have roast duck.

BEEF OMELET.
Mrs. S. B. Adams.

Four pounds of round beef, uncooked, chopped fine; six eggs beaten together; five or six soda crackers rolled fine, little butter and suet, pepper, salt, and sage, if you choose; make two loaves, roll in cracker; bake about an hour; slice when cold.

SPICED BEEF.
Mrs. E. B. Harmon.

Four pounds of round of beef chopped fine; take from it all fat; add to it three dozen small crackers rolled fine, four eggs, one cup of milk, one tablespoon ground mace, two tablespoons of black pepper, one tablespoon melted butter; mix well and put in any tin pan that it will just fill, packing it well; baste with butter and water, and bake two hours in a slow oven.

MEAT FROM SOUP BONES.
Mrs. DeForest.

Before thickening the soup or putting in the vegetables, take out a large bowl of the liquor; take the meat from the bones, chop it fine, season with catsup and spices; pour over the liquor, which should be thick enough to jelly when cold; put into moulds and serve cold in slices.

BEEF CROQUETTES.

Mrs. J. B. R.

Chop fine some cold beef; beat two eggs and mix with the meat and add a little milk, melted butter, and salt and pepper. Make into rolls and fry.

BEEF CAKES FOR A SIDE DISH OF DRESSED MEAT.

Mrs. S. McMaster, Toronto.

Pound some beef that is underdone with a little fat bacon or ham; season with pepper and salt, and a little shalot or garlic. Mix them well, and make into small cakes three inches long and half as wide and thick; fry them a light brown, and serve them in a good thick gravy.

BEEF OR VEAL LOAF.

Three pounds of meat chopped fine with one-fourth of a pound of salt pork, six Boston crackers powdered fine, one sheet of Cooper's isinglass dissolved in a coffee-cup of warm water, one tablespoon of butter, one teaspoon of salt, and one of pepper, one of powdered cloves, or a nutmeg grated. Mix well together with two eggs; bake one hour. This will slice well when cold.

PRESERVED BEEF.

Mrs. Carter.

For preserving one hundred pounds beef: Six pounds salt, two ounces salt-petre, two tablespoons soda, two pounds sugar, four gallons water; mix well together; sprinkle the bottom of the barrel with salt; put in the beef with very little salt between each layer; pour over the brine and put on a weight to keep all well covered.

TO CORN BEEF.

Mrs. A. M. Gibbs.

To each gallon of cold water, put one quart of rock salt, one ounce of salt-petre and four ounces of brown sugar, (it need not be boiled), as long as any salt remains undissolved, the meat will be sweet. If any scum should rise, scald and skim well; add more salt, salt-petre and sugar; as you put each piece of meat into the brine, rub over with salt. If the weather is hot, gash the meat to the bone, and put it in salt. Put a flat stone or some weight on the meat to keep it under the brine.

Or this: To every four gallons of water allow two pounds of brown sugar and six pounds of salt, boil about twenty minutes, taking off the scum; the next day turn it on the meat packed in the pickling tub; pour off this brine; boil and strain every two months, adding three ounces of brown sugar and half a pound of common salt. It will keep good a year. Sprinkle the meat with salt the next day, wipe dry before turning the pickle over it. Let it entirely cover the meat; add four ounces salt-petre. Canvas lids are excellent for covering, as they admit the air and exclude flies. Mutton and beef may be kept sweet several weeks by simply rubbing well with dry salt and closely covering. Turn the pieces whenever the vessel is uncovered.

BOILED TONGUE WITH TOMATO SAUCE.

Mrs. J. Ellis.

Half boil a tongue, then stew it with a sauce made of a little broth, flour, parsley, one small onion, one small carrot, salt and pepper, and one can of tomatoes cooked and strained. Lay the tongue on a dish and strain the sauce over it.

VEAL CAKE.

Miss Brokovski.

Butter your mould, then put in a layer of veal and ham, cut in thin slices, season it with cayenne, salt, a little beaten mace, some parsley, and a very little shalot, some eggs boiled hard and cut in slices; press it down and bake it, make a little veal gravy with a few shreds of Isinglass, strain it, and add a small quantity of catsup, pour it over hot, when cold turn it out.

PICKLED PORK (EQUAL TO FRESH).

Mrs. Dr. Oliphant.

Let the meat cool thoroughly, cut into pieces four to six inches wide, weigh them and pack as tight as possible, salting lightly. Cover the meat with brine as strong as possible. Next day pour off a gallon of the brine and mix with it a tablespoonful of saltpetre for every hundred pounds of meat, and return it to the barrel. Let it stand one month, take out the meat and let it drain twelve hours. Put the brine into an iron kettle, add a quart of molasses or two pounds sugar, and boil till clear. When cold return the meat to the barrel and pour on the brine. Cover it close, and you will have the sweetest meat you ever tasted.

STEWED TONGUE.

Mrs. J. Ellis.

Cut square fillets of bacon, which dredge with a mixture of chopped parsley, salt, pepper, and a little allspice. Lard the tongue with the fillets; put in a sauce-pan two ounces of bacon cut in slices, four sprigs of parsley, two of thyme, a little garlic, two cloves, two carrots cut in small pieces, two small onions, salt and pepper. Lay the tongue on the whole; wet with a glass of white wine and a glass of broth. Set it on a moderate fire and simmer about five hours, keeping it well covered. Put the tongue on a dish and strain the sauce over it.

BOILED LEG OF MUTTON.

Mrs. G. Brown.

Boil well in clear water until tender, seasoning the water with salt; serve with egg sauce, and garnish with parsley, sliced lemons, or some sour jelly.

MUTTON A LA VENISON.

Mrs. J. B. L.

Take a leg of mutton and lard it well with strips of

salt pork inserted in deep slits in the meat, which has been previously rolled in pepper and cloves; bake two hours or according to the size of the roast, basting frequently while in the oven; about an hour before serving, spread over it currant jelly, return to the oven and let it brown.

MUTTON CHOPS.

Cut them nicely, clearing away all ragged ends and edges; fry for a few moments covered closely, and then dip each piece in cracker crumbs and beaten egg, or you may prepare them as for frying; then, lay them in a dripping pan, and put into the oven to bake; baste frequently with a little melted butter and water.

ROAST VEAL.

Mrs. D. S. F.

Prepare a leg of veal for the oven, by washing, drying, and larding it with strips of fat bacon or ham, and dredging it well with flour, and seasoning with salt and pepper; baste frequently and serve with the gravy thickened. A roast fillet of veal should be prepared by stuffing it with bread crumbs, seasoned with chopped ham, summer savory, pepper and salt. Dredge lightly with flour and bake.

NECK PIECE OR SHOULDER OF VEAL.

Mrs. C. C. Stratton.

Put a piece of butter the size of an egg into a kettle; put it on the stove; when it begins to fry, put in the veal, season it and let it fry until brown; then add water sufficient to cook it. When done take cream and flour well stirred, and thicken as for fricasseed chicken, and you have a nice dinner, very like chicken and much cheaper. Two pounds of veal will make a dinner for six or eight, providing it is not all bone.

VEAL PATES.

Mrs. H. Baird.

Chop some cold veal fine, moisten with cream and an egg, beaten; season with salt, sweet marjoram, and powdered mace; then make up with the hands in the shape of cones or patty-cakes, and roll in crumbs. Either fry in a buttered pan or bake in a hot oven.

PATE OF VEAL.

Mrs. L. J. Tilton.

Three and one-half pounds of the leg of veal, fat and lean, chopped fine; six or eight small crackers rolled fine; two eggs, piece of butter the size of an egg, one tablespoon of salt, one of pepper, and one of nutmeg; a slice of salt pork chopped fine. Work all together in the form of a loaf; put bits of butter and grate bread crumbs over the top. Bake two hours; to be cut in slices when cold.

VEAL CUTLETS, A LA FRIED OYSTERS.

Mrs. A. M. Gibbs.

Cut the veal in small pieces three or four inches square; dry with a towel; season to taste; have ready a beaten egg and crackers rolled fine, each on separate dishes; dip each piece of the cutlet in the egg, then in the rolled cracker; have enough lard or butter hot in your spider so that it will nearly cover the cutlets when you put them in. A rich gravy can be made after the meat is done by adding a little boiling water.

HASHED LAMB OR MUTTON—COLD MEAT COOKERY.

Madame E. Pernet.

Take your bones, and stew them in a little water with an onion, some salt and pepper, and, if you like, a little savoury herbs; when the goodness is all out of the bones, and it tastes nice, thicken the gravy with a teaspoonful of corn starch, and if it is not very strong put in a bit of butter, then place your stew pan on the hot hearth, and put in your slices of meat. Warm but not boil. Serve with toasted bread.

SPICED VEAL.

Mrs. C. E. Brown.

Take four pounds veal, chop it fine and season highly with salt, pepper, cloves, and cinnamon; add four small crackers rolled out, one egg, and a lump of butter nearly the size of an egg; mix thoroughly together and press it in a baking tin, and bake two and a half hours. When thoroughly cold, slice for tea. Some prefer it in rolls, convenient for slicing, and baked from one-half to three quarters of an hour.

JELLIED VEAL.

M. A. T.

Boil the veal tender, pick it up fine, put in a mould, add the water it was boiled in, and set it in a cold place; season with salt and pepper to taste; a layer of hard boiled eggs improves it.

FRICANDEAU.

Mrs. J. M. Brown and Mrs. M. L.

Three and one-half pounds of cold roast veal chopped fine, one tablespoon of salt and one of pepper, one-half of a nutmeg, four or five rolled crackers, three eggs. If the veal is thin, add a piece of butter half as large as an egg, and tablespoon of cream. Form all this in a large roll, and spot the roll over with bits of butter; then strew over it the pounded crackers, (a little of the cracker should be mixed with the meat), put it in the oven, and from time to time add a little water. Cook slowly two hours. When cold, slice thin, and it makes an excellent relish.

SWEET BREADS.

Scald in salt and water, take out the stringy parts; then put in cold water a few minutes; dry in a towel; dip in egg and bread crumbs, and fry brown in butter; when done place in a hot dish; pour into the pan a cup of sweet cream, a little pepper and salt, and a little parsley chopped fine; add flour, and when boiling pour over the sweet breads; add mushrooms, if desired.

SWEET BREADS—BROILED.

Mrs. Bates.

Parboil, rub them well with butter, and broil on a clean gridiron; turn them often, and now and then roll them over in a plate containing hot melted butter, to prevent them from getting hard and dry.

CALF'S LIVER—FRIED.

Cut in thin slices; wash and drain them, roll them in corn meal or cracked crumbs, and fry in fresh or salt pork gravy or butter.

CALF'S LIVER—STEWED.

Boil till partly done; take out of the sauce-pan; chop in small pieces; put back in the sauce-pan; skim well; stew until tender; season with butter, pepper and salt; thicken with a little flour, and serve over slices of toasted bread.

CALF'S LIVER—MARINE.

Mrs. J. M. Ayer.

Lard the liver; add pepper and salt sufficient to season it, then roll and tie it; cut two onions in thin slices and lay in the bottom of an earthen crock; add two slices of salt pork cut thin, and lay the liver on that; add more pepper and salt, a little vinegar and salad oil, and set in a cool place for twenty-four hours. Cook over a slow fire from half-past two until six; a wine-glass of claret added at half-past four is excellent.

This is arranged for dinner at night; of course the rule for time will do for noon dinner. Easily mistaken for canvas-back duck.

TO ROAST VENISON.
Mrs. Porter.

Wash a saddle of venison thoroughly in several waters, then rub it over with vinegar, red pepper, and a little salt; lard with strips of salt pork rolled in seasoned bread crumbs; season if you like, with sweet marjoram and sweet basil, one teaspoon each, also pepper; then rub the whole with currant jelly, and pour over it one bottle of claret wine. Let it stand all night, and next morning cover the venison with a paste made of flour and water half an inch thick; then cover with soft paper, and secure well with strings; place it in the dripping-pan with some claret, butter, and water, and baste very often; half an hour before you take it up, remove paste and paper, baste it with butter and dredge with flour to make it brown.

FOR SAUCE.—Take a pound and a half of scraps of venison, with three pints of water, a few cloves, a few blades of mace, one-half a nutmeg, and salt and cayenne pepper to taste; boil it down to a pint, skim off the fat and strain; add half a pint of currant jelly, one pint of claret and one-quarter pound of butter, divided into bits and rolled in flour.

TO COOK SLICED HAM (VERY NICE).
Madame E. Pernet.

Cut raw ham in slices, soak in scalding water half an hour, lay your slices in a frying pan, pepper each, and lay on each slice a little made mustard; pour in half a teaspoonful of vinegar to each slice; fry quickly, turn often. When done take out, serve on a dish; add to the gravy a spoonful of wine, (if you have any handy), and a teaspoonful of sugar. Boil up once; pour over your ham, and serve.

OXFORD SAUSAGE.

M. A. Sadler.

Take one pound of young pork, fat and lean, without skin or gristle, one pound of lean veal, one pound of beef suet chopped very fine together. Put in half a pound of bread crumbs, six sage leaves, a teaspoon of pepper and two of salt, some thyme, marjoram and savoury shred fine. Mix well together.

SAUSAGES.

Mrs. O. Bradley and others.

Six pounds of lean fresh pork, twelve teaspoons of sage, and six teaspoons of pepper, six teaspoons of salt, (and two of cloves, and one nutmeg, if you prefer), grind or chop very fine; mix these ingredients thoroughly, and pack in a jar, and pour hot lard over the top.

HAM SANDWICHES.

Mrs. W. Butterfield.

Chop fine some cold boiled ham, a little fat with the lean; add tongue and chicken also chopped fine; make a dressing of one half a pound of butter, three tablespoons of salad oil, three of mustard, the yolk of one egg, and a little salt; mix well together and spread over the meat smoothly on thin slices of bread. Very nice.

TRAVELLING LUNCH.

Mrs. J. L. B.

Chop sardines, ham, and a few pickles quite fine; mix with mustard, pepper, catsup, salt, and vinegar; spread between bread nicely buttered. This is to be cut crosswise, like jelly cake.

BAKED HAM.

Mrs. W. G. Davis.

Most persons boil ham. It is much better baked, if baked right. Soak it for an hour in clean water and wipe it dry, next spread it all over with thin batter, and then put it into a deep dish with sticks under it to keep it out of the gravy. When it is fully done and the batter crusted on the flesh side, take off the skin and set it away to cool.

BOILED HAM.

Mrs. C. Waggoner.

Take a ham weighing about eight or ten pounds; soak it for twelve or twenty-four hours in cold water; then cover it with boiling water, add one pint of vinegar, two or three bay-leaves, a little bunch of thyme and parsley, (the dried and sifted will do, or even the seeds of parsley may be used, if the fresh cannot be procured); boil very slowly two hours and a half, take it out, skim it, remove all the fat, except a layer half an inch thick; cut off with a sharp knife all the black-looking outside; put the ham into your dripping pan, fat side uppermost, grate bread crust over it and sprinkle a teaspoon of powdered sugar over it; put it in the oven for half an hour, until it is a beautiful brown. Eat cold; cut the nicest portion in slices; the ragged parts and odds and ends can be chopped fine and used for sandwiches; or, by adding three eggs to one pint of chopped ham, and frying brown, you have a delicious omelet for breakfast or lunch. The bones should be put in a soup-kettle, the rind and fat should be rendered and strained for frying potatoes and crullers. Ham cooked in this way will go much farther than when cooked in the ordinary manner.

BOILED AND BAKED HAM.

Mrs. P. B. Ayer.

Boil your ham tender; cover it with the white of a raw egg, and sprinkle sugar or bread crumbs over it; put it in the oven and brown; it is delicious also covered with a regular cake icing and browned.

TO BOIL A HAM.

M.

Wash and scrape the ham clean; put it on in cold water enough to cover it; put into the water two onions, two carrots, a head of celery, a dozen cloves and a handful of timothy hay; boil without stopping until the skin will readily peel from the ham; cover the ham with rolled crackers, or bread crumbs that have been browned and rolled, and bake in a slow oven for two hours.

SALTING PORK.

A. M. G.

Cover the bottom of the barrel with salt an inch deep; put down one layer of pork and cover that with salt half an inch thick; continue this until all your pork is disposed of; then cover the whole with strong brine; pack as tight as possible, the rind side down or next to the barrel; keep the pork always under the brine by using an inner cover and clean stones. Should any scum arise, pour off the brine, scald it, and add more salt. Old brine can be boiled down, well skimmed, and used for a fresh supply.

CURING HAMS.

Mrs. Mulford.

Hang up the hams a week or ten days, the longer the tenderer and better, if kept perfectly sweet; mix for each good-sized ham, one teacup of salt, one tablespoon of molasses, one ounce of salt-petre; lay the hams in a clean dry tub; heat the mixture and rub well into the hams, especially around the bones and recesses; repeat the process once or twice, or until all the mixture is used; then let the hams lie two or three days, when they must be put for three weeks in brine strong enough to bear an egg; then soak eight hours in cold water; hang up to dry in the kitchen or other more convenient place for a week or more; smoke from three to five days, being careful not to heat the hams. Corn cobs and apple-tree wood are good for smoking. The juices are better retained if smoked with the hock down. Tie up carefully in bags for the summer.

SALADS, SAUCES, AND PICKLES.

" To make this condiment, your poet begs
   The powdered yellow of two hard-boiled eggs;
   Two boiled potatoes, passed through the kitchen sieve,
   Smoothness and softness to the salad give ;
   Let onions atoms lurk within the bowl,
   And, half suspected, animate the whole;
   Of mordant mustard, add a single spoon;
   Distrust the condiment that bites so soon ;
   But, deem it not, thou man of herbs, a fault
   To add a double quantity of salt ;
   Four times the spoon with oil from Lucca crown,
   And twice with vinegar, procured from town ;
   And lastly, o'er the flavoured compound toss
   A magic *soupçon* of anchovy sauce.
   O, green and glorious! O, herbaceous treat !
   'Twould tempt the dying anchorite to eat ;
   Back to the world he'd turn his fleeting soul,
   And plunge his fingers in the salad bowl ;
   Serenely full, the epicure would say,
' Fate cannot harm me, I have dined to-day.' "
—SIDNEY SMITH.

CHICKEN SALAD.

Mrs. Morgan.

Cut the white meat of chickens into small bits, the size of peas, (also the dark meat, if you like), chop the whole parts of celery nearly as small. Prepare a dressing thus: Rub the yolks of hard boiled eggs smooth; to each yolk put half a teaspoon of mustard, the same quantity of salt, a tablespoon of oil, and a wine glass of vinegar; mix the chicken and celery in a large bowl and pour over this dressing with a little cream added. The dressing must not be put on till just before it is served.

CHICKEN SALAD.

Mrs. Higgins.

Two chickens, chopped coarse; eight heads of celery, three eggs, one pint vinegar, one tablespoon flour, one tablespoon sugar, rub the yolks of the eggs to a fine powder, then add the salt, mustard, and oil, mixing well together; then add the cream; and after that the vinegar and raw egg.

CHICKEN SALAD.

Mrs. Hobbs.

Three chickens chopped fine, both light and dark meat; the juice of two lemons; eight or ten eggs boiled hard; the whites chopped fine and the yolks mashed fine, moisten with six teaspoons melted butter, two of sweet oil; to which add one tablespoon of mustard, one of pepper, one of salt, one of sugar, three of cream; and last, add six large bunches of celery chopped fine, with sufficient vinegar to moisten the whole.

FRENCH POTATO SALAD.

Slice some cold boiled potatoes into a salad bowl, sprinkle over them some parsley and a small quantity of onions cut very fine, and then pour over a sauce made of the following ingredients: mustard, pepper, and salt, and a small quantity of vinegar, rub well together before pouring in some fine olive oil, whip all till the sauce looks creamy.

CHICKEN SALAD.

Mary Norton.

Take the breasts of four well boiled chickens, cut in small pieces, but not too fine; mix with the chicken eight teacups of celery cut also in small pieces, and, with the above, the chopped whites of twelve hard-boiled eggs. For dressing, the yolks of four raw eggs; beat into them half of an ordinary sized bottle of olive oil, beginning with a teaspoon, and adding no more than that at a time, until it is thoroughly mixed; then add the well-mashed and pulverized yolks of twelve eggs, salt and pepper, three tablespoons mustard, a pinch of cayenne pepper, and a gill of vinegar; then stir this dressing thoroughly into the mixed chicken celery and whites of eggs.

CHICKEN SALAD.

Mrs. Parmelee.

Boil one chicken tender, then take the meat and chop up, take two tablespoons of mustard, 3 eggs boiled hard, chop the whites with the chickens, the yolks rub up fine with the mustard, one tablespoon of salt, three tablespoons melted butter, one tablespoon black pepper, vinegar enough to moisten it, chop three heads of celery to one chicken, mix all together and serve.

SALAD DRESSING FOR CABBAGE OR LETTUCE.

Mrs. Parmelee.

Three eggs, two teaspoons black pepper, one teaspoon salt, one tablespoon mustard, three of melted butter, six teaspoons sweet cream, one coffee cup of vinegar; put all together, on stove, and cook till it looks smooth like cream, stirring all the time to keep from burning; then, when cold, put over cabbage chopped fine.

SALAD.

Miss Ada King.

Two eggs boiled hard, one teaspoon mustard, two tablespoons vinegar, one cup milk, two heads celery, and one-half cup sugar.

FISH SALAD.

M. A. T.

Boil tender a white-fish or trout; chop fine; add same quantity chopped celery, cabbage or lettuce; season same as chicken salad.

VEGETABLE SALAD.

Anonymous.

Take cold vegetables left from dinner, such as potatoes, peas, string beans, shell beans, beets, etc., and chill them on the ice; cover with mayonaise, and serve You may use for this any salad dressing.

POTATO SALAD.

M. A. T.

Sliced cold boiled potatoes; almonds blanched and quartered; hickory nuts, also, if liked (both of these may be omitted). A very small quantity of chopped onions; pour over this any good salad dressing, not too much, and garnish with chopped parsley; cold boiled beets, sliced lemon, and anchovies, may be added to the salad, if liked.

ASPARAGUS SALAD.

Boil the asparagus in water until tender; cut off the hard ends, and set the rest away. When cool, cut in inch long pieces, and put it in your salad dish. Pour over a mayonaise dressing, and garnish with a few capers.

CUCUMBER SALAD.

Mrs. King.

Take a dozen ripe "white spine" cucumbers; wash, pare, and cut into strips, taking out the seeds; cut into pieces, like small dice; to each dozen cucumbers take twelve large white onions chopped; six large green peppers, also chopped; one-quarter pound each of black and white mustard seed, and a gill of celery seed; mix all well together; add a teacup of salt, and hang up in a cotton bag to drain for twenty-four hours. Then add enough clear cold vinegar to cover it; put into stone jars and fasten nearly air-tight. In six weeks it will be fit for use. Excellent.

CABBAGE SALAD.

Mr. J. H. Mead.

First prepare the cabbage by letting it stand for some time in cold water, in order to make it crisp; dry well and shave as finely as possible. Choose a firm white cabbage. Dressing: Rub together a piece of butter the size of a walnut, and one tablespoon of flour; stir in two tablespoons of vinegar, and scald for a minute; then add the yolk of an egg (beaten) and two tablespoons of cream; salt and pepper to taste.

SALAD DRESSING FOR CHOPPED CABBAGE OR LETTUCE.

Mrs. S. McMaster.

Three eggs, two teaspoons black pepper, one teaspoon salt, one tablespoon mustard, three tablespoons melted butter, six teaspoons sweet cream, one coffee-cup of good vinegar. Put all on the stove and cook until it looks like cream, taking care to stir it all the time.

DRESSING FOR SALAD.

Mrs. Hoge.

Two raw eggs, one tablespoon of butter, eight tablespoons of vinegar; one-half teaspoon of mustard; put in a bowl over boiling water and stir until it becomes like cream; pepper and salt to your taste.

SALAD DRESSING.

Mrs. A. A. Carpenter.

The yolks of four eggs, two-thirds of a cup of oil, **red**

pepper, salt and mustard to taste, the juice of two lemons, and last of all, one cup of thick cream. If the dressing is for chicken salad, use the oil or fat from the chicken instead of sweet oil. Be sure and put the cream in last, just before sending to table.

SAUCES FOR MEAT OR FISH.

DRAWN BUTTER.

Drawn butter forms the basis of most sauces. From this a great variety may be made, by adding to this different flavours—anchovies, ochra, onions, celery, parsley, mint, and relishes—using those flavours, which are suitable for the meat, game, or fish, with which the sauces are to be served. A good standard receipt for drawn butter is as follows:

Rub one tablespoon of flour with one-quarter of a pound of butter; when well mixed, put in a saucepan with a tablespoon of milk or water; set it in a dish of boiling water, shaking it well until the butter melts and is near boiling. It should not be set directly on the stove or over the coals, as the heat will make the butter oily and spoil it.

MELTED BUTTER OR PARSLEY SAUCE.

Miss A. C.

One tablespoon of butter, one teaspoon of flour, rubbed together, one tablespoon chopped parsley, first boiled five minutes in water and squeezed out; two tablespoons water; shake over a clear fire, *one way*, until it boils; add the parsley gradually.

MINT SAUCE.

Mrs. J. Salter.

Mix one tablespoon of white sugar to half a teacup of good vinegar; add the mint and let it infuse for half an hour in a cool place before sending to the table. Serve with roast lamb or mutton.

CELERY SAUCE.

Mrs. J. B. L.

Mix two tablespoons of flour with half a teacup of butter; have ready a pint of boiling milk; stir the flour and butter into the milk; take three heads of celery, cut into small bits, and boil for a few minutes in water, which strain off; put the celery into the melted butter, and keep it stirred over the fire for five or ten minutes. This is very nice with boiled fowl or turkey.

CREAM SAUCE.

Anonymous.

Cream together a large tablespoon of butter with a little flour, and put over a gentle heat; add a little chopped parsley, a little grated onion, pepper, salt, and nutmeg; when these ingredients are well mixed, add half a pint of cream or milk and let it boil for fifteen minutes. If used with fresh fish, a little horse radish may be added.

EGG SAUCE.

Miss Hattie Buck.

Take the yolks of two eggs boiled hard; mash them with a teaspoon of mustard, a little pepper and salt, three tablespoons of vinegar, and three of salad oil. A tablespoon of catsup improves this for some. Nice for boiled fish.

EGG SAUCE.

Mrs. C. Belford.

Prepare drawn butter, and to this add three or four hard-boiled eggs sliced or chopped.

FISH SAUCE.

One-quarter of a pound of fresh butter; one tablespoon of finely chopped parsley, a little salt and pepper and the juice of two lemons. Cream the butter; mix all well together, adding at the least a teaspoon of mayonaise. Less lemon juice may be used if preferred.

WHITE SAUCE FOR FOWLS.

Miss Brokovski.

Take half a pint of cream, and put some flour and butter mixed together to thicken it, some nutmeg grated, cayenne pepper, and some oyster or cucumber catsup— or a little of both; stir it over the fire till it thickens.

GOVERNOR'S SAUCE.

Mrs. Midgley.

Slice a peck of green tomatoes, sprinkle salt over them, say about a cupful, and let them stand one night; in the morning pour off the liquor, and put them in a kettle with vinegar enough to cover them, add six green or red peppers, (moderate size), four large onions chopped fine, one cup of brown sugar, one cup of scraped horse-radish, a tablespoonful of cloves, one of allspice, a teaspoonful of cayenne, one of white pepper; let it simmer till soft, put into jars and always keep it air tight.

TOMATO SAUCE.

Mrs. O. S. Horseman.

Thirty-six ripe tomatoes, six green peppers, two onions chopped fine, two cups of sugar, two tablespoons salt, two teaspoons of ground cloves, two teaspoons mustard, two teaspoons of cinnamon, two cups of vinegar, and boil half a day.

TOMATO CHILI SAUCE.

Mrs. H. Baird.

Nine ripe tomatoes, peeled and cut small, red peppers and one onion chopped fine, one teacup vinegar, two tablespoons brown sugar, one tablespoon salt, one teaspoon ginger, one of cloves, one of allspice, vinegar in last; stew one hour.

GOVERNOR'S SAUCE.

Mrs. H. Baird.

One peck green tomatoes, four large onions, six red peppers, one teacup grated horse-radish, one teaspoon cayenne and one of black pepper, one teaspoon mustard, half cup sugar; slice the tomatoes and sprinkle one teacup salt on, and lay all night; drain well in the morning, then simmer all together till cooked through.

SHIRLEY SAUCE.

Mrs. H. Baird.

Wash, peel, and slice two dozen ripe tomatoes, four large onions, and four green peppers, not too large; add four tablespoons sugar, one pint vinegar; boil tomatoes and onions first, strain, then boil all slowly till done.

CHILI SAUCE.

Mrs. H. Baird.

Twelve large ripe tomatoes, six green peppers, one large onion, all chopped fine, one tablespoon salt, one teaspoon ginger, one of cinnamon, one of allspice, one of cloves, one tablespoon sugar, two cups vinegar; boil thick.

WINTER SAUCE.

Mrs. Snider.

One peck green tomatoes chopped fine, two dozen large onions peeled and chopped, one dozen green or red peppers chopped fine; salt, pepper, and spice to suit taste;

one cup brown sugar, vinegar to cover; pour the vinegar over all boiling hot, and bottle for winter use.

ENGLISH SAUCE.

Mrs. Snider.

One pound brown sugar, half-pound salt, half-pound garlic, half-pound onions, quarter-pound pepper, quarter-pound ground ginger, half-pound mustard seed, one pound raisins, two pounds apples, half-ounce cayenne, two quarts vinegar. The raisins to be chopped, apples to be pealed and cut and boiled in one pint of the vinegar; garlic and onions must be chopped fine and well bruised; the sugar made into a syrup with one pint of the vinegar. When the apples are cool, mix the whole, including the remainder of the vinegar; blend well together and jar.

TOMATO MUSTARD.

M. R. Beard.

One peck of ripe tomatoes; boil with two onions, six red peppers, four cloves of garlic, for one hour; then add a half-pint or half-pound salt, three tablespoons black pepper, half-ounce ginger, half-ounce allspice, half-ounce mace, half-ounce cloves; then boil again for one hour longer, and when cold add one pint of vinegar and a quarter-pound of mustard; and if you like it very hot, a tablespoonful of cayenne.

CHILI SAUCE.

Mrs. E. H. Dennison.

To nine large ripe tomatoes and three green peppers,

add one onion chopped fine, two cups of vinegar, two tablespoons of sugar, and one of salt; steam one hour, then add one teaspoon of ginger, one of allspice, and one of cloves.

HORSE-RADISH SAUCE.

Two teaspoons of made mustard, two of white sugar, half a teaspoon of salt, and a gill of vinegar; mix and pour over grated horse-radish. Excellent with beef.

MADE MUSTARD.

Pour a very little boiling water over three tablespoons of mustard; add one saltspoon of salt, a tablespoon of olive oil, stirred slowly in, and one teaspoon of sugar; add the yolk of an egg, beaten well, and pour in vinegar to taste. It is best eaten next day.

CELERY VINEGAR.

Soak one ounce of celery seed in half a pint of vinegar; bottle it and use to flavour soups and gravies.

SPICED CURRANTS.

Mrs. H. Baird.

Six pounds currants or gooseberries, five pounds sugar half a pint of vinegar; spices, cloves, and cinnamon. Boil till thick.

GOOSEBERRY CATSUP.

Mrs. H. Baird.

Five pints vinegar, four pounds green gooseberries,

one-half pound brown sugar, one-half pound raisins, one-quarter pound currants, one-quarter pound common salt, two ounces mustard, two ounces onions, one-half ounce chilies, one-half ounce allspice, one-half ounce ground ginger, one-half ounce ground mace, one-half ounce turmeric, one nutmeg. Boil the vinegar, currants, raisins, onions, gooseberries, and chilies till quite soft, then pour through a fine sieve on the remaining ingredients.

FRENCH PUDDING SAUCE.

Mrs. J. H. Mead.

Beat four ounces butter to a cream; stir in one-quarter ounce brown sugar; add the yolk of one egg and one gill of wine; put it on the stove, stirring all the time till it simmers. Grate nutmeg over it before sending it to table.

TOMATO CATSUP.

Miss Brokovski.

Boil the tomatoes until quite soft, and rub them well through a sieve; to every quart add two ounces shalots and large red peppers, or one teaspoonful cayenne pepper, one ounce bruised ginger, one spoonful salt, a few cloves; boil until reduced one-third; ten minutes before taking off the fire add a half-pint vinegar to each quart.

TOMATO CATSUP.

Mrs. George Simpson.

Take a bushel of nice ripe tomatoes, and split, and

sprinkle with salt, and lay twenty-four hours; mash them up and run through a sieve so as to waste nothing but seed and skin, and season to taste with red pepper and cloves; boil until it begins to settle at the bottom of the kettle, then add one quart of vinegar, then bottle and seal up tight.

TOMATO MUSTARD.

Mrs. Spence.

Boil one peck tomatoes for one hour with six red peppers, strain through a colander, and add a half pound salt, three tablespoons of black pepper ground, one ounce ginger ground, one ounce allspice round, half ounce cloves ground, two onions; boil for another hour, then add quarter pound mustard and half pint of vinegar, then bottle.

GOOSEBERRY CATSUP.

Mrs. J. B. Adams, Mrs. Henry Stevens, and Mrs. R. Harris.

Eight pounds of ripe or partially ripe fruit, four pounds brown sugar, one pint of good vinegar, two ounces each fine cloves and cinnamon tied in a bag; boil the berries and sugar for three or four hours, then add spice; boil a little more; put in a jar and cover well. Will keep two years by occasionally scalding and adding a little vinegar and spice.

SWEET PICKLES.

PICKLED CHERRIES.

Five pounds of cherries, stoned or not; one quart of vinegar, two pounds of sugar, one-half ounce of cinnamon, one-half ounce of cloves, one-half ounce of mace; boil the sugar and vinegar and spices together, (grind the spices and tie them in a muslin bag), and pour hot over the cherries.

PICKLED PLUMS.

Mrs. Meek.

To seven pounds plums, four pounds sugar, two ounces stick cinnamon, two ounces cloves, one quart vinegar, add a little mace; put in the jar first a layer of plums, then a layer of spices alternately; scald the vinegar and sugar together, pour it over the plums; repeat three times for plums, (only once for cut apples and pears), the fourth time scald all together; put them into glass jars and they are ready for use.

PICKLED APPLES.

Mrs. Watson.

For one peck of sweet apples take three pounds of sugar, two quarts of vinegar, one-half ounce of cinnamon, one-half ounce cloves; pare the apples, leaving them whole; boil them in part of the vinegar and sugar until you can put a fork through them; take them out; beat the remainder of vinegar and sugar and pour over them. Be careful not to boil them too long or they will break.

SPICED CURRANTS TO BE EATEN WITH MEATS.

Mrs. Carson.

Four quarts currants, one pint of vinegar, three pounds sugar, one tablespoon cinnamon, one of allspice, one of cloves, one of nutmeg; cook one hour; keep in cool place, tightly covered.

PICKLED PEACHES.

Mrs. C. D. Howard.

Take five pounds of brown sugar to one gallon of pure cider vinegar; boil it hard for thirty minutes, skimming off the scum till clear; rub off the peaches in the meantime out of boiling water (quickly) with a flannel cloth, sticking four cloves in each peach; and put a bag of cinnamon into the boiling syrup. If the peaches are clingstones, put them into the boiling syrup for fifteen or twenty minutes; if freestones, lay them in the jar in layers, and pour the syrup over them while hot; then put a small plate over to keep them from rising, and cover tightly with cloth or paper. In four days look at them, and if necessary, boil the syrup again, and pour on while hot; keep them in a cool place while the weather is hot to prevent their souring. The White Sugar Cling is nice for pickling, and the Blood Peach is very rich, but dark. Small pears can be pickled in the same manner, if the skin is taken off.

SOUR PICKLES.

" Who peppered the highest was surest to please."
PREPARED MUSTARD.

C. D. Adams.

Two tablespoons mustard, one teaspoon sugar, one-half teaspoon salt, boiling water enough to mix it; when cold, add one tablespoon salad oil and vinegar enough to thin it. This will keep a week or two.

GREEN TOMATO PICKLE.

Mrs. Joseph Saulter.

Cut half-peck of green tomatoes and six large onions into thin slices; let them remain in salt and water over night; then pour off the brine and put them in a preserving kettle with four tablespoonsful of sugar, four of the best mustard, two teaspoonsful of ground cloves, two of cinnamon, one of cayenne pepper, and one of curry powder, and let them simmer for one hour; then put them in stone or glass jars.

GREEN TOMATO PICKLES.

Mrs. Spence.

Slice one peck of tomatoes into a jar, sprinkle a little salt over each layer; let them stand twenty-four hours, drain off the liquor; put the tomatoes into a kettle with a teaspoonful of each of the following spices: ground ginger, allspice, cloves, mace, cinnamon, a teaspoonful of scraped horse-radish, twelve small or three large red peppers, three onions, a cup full of brown sugar; cover all with vinegar; boil slowly for three hours.

Neither add to nor take from any of the ingredients or quantities given in the recipe, as it is perfect.

OUDE SAUCE.

C. Kennicott.

One pint green tomatoes, six peppers (not large); four onions, chop together; add one cup salt, and let it stand over night; in the morning, drain off the water; add one cup sugar, one cup horse-radish, one tablespoon ground cloves, one tablespoon cinnamon, cover with vinegar, and stew gently all day.

MY MOTHER'S FAVOURITE PICKLES.

Mrs. Savage.

One quart raw cabbage chopped fine; one quart boiled beets chopped fine; two cups of sugar, tablespoon of salt, one teaspoon black pepper, one-fourth teaspoon red pepper, one teacup of grated horse-radish; cover with cold vinegar, and keep from the air.

MIXED PICKLES.

Mrs. F. M. Cragin.

Three hundred small cucumbers, four green peppers sliced fine, two large or three small heads cauliflower, three heads of white cabbage shaved fine, nine large onions sliced, one large root horse-radish, one quart of green beans cut one inch long, one quart green tomatoes sliced; put this mixture in a pretty strong brine twenty-four hours; drain three hours, then sprinkle in one-fourth pound black and one-fourth pound of white mustard seed; also one tablespoon black ground pepper; let it come to a good boil in just vinegar enough to cover it, adding a little alum. Drain again, and when cold, mix in one-half pint of ground mustard; cover the whole with good cider vinegar; add turmeric enough to colour, if you like.

PICKLED CABBAGE.

Mrs. A. N. Arnold.

Select solid heads, slice very fine, put in a jar, then cover with boiling water; when cold, drain off the water, and season with grated horse-radish, salt, equal parts of black and red pepper, cinnamon, and cloves whole; cover with strong vinegar. This is convenient and always good.

INDIA PICKLE.

Mrs. George Simpson.

Take three quarts vinegar, quarter pound mustard, half ounce black pepper, one ounce cloves, one ounce allspice, one ounce turmeric, one ounce ginger, one ounce cayenne pepper, handfull salt, same of sugar; boil for twenty minutes. When cold put in the vegetables and cover closely; if the liquid should become thin, boil again and add more mustard in three weeks after making.

TOMATO MUSTARD.

Mrs. George Simpson.

Slice and boil for an hour, with six small red peppers, half bushel of ripe tomatoes strain through a colander and boil for an hour, with two tablespoonsful of black pepper, two ounces ginger, one ounce allspice, half ounce cloves, one-eighth ounce mace, quarter pound salt. When cold add two ounces mustard, two ounces currie powder, and one pint of vinegar.

PICKLED CAULIFLOWER.

After cutting off all the green leaves, put the cauliflower into boiling water, with a good supply of salt, and boil from three to five minutes; take them out of the salt and water, dip them in clear cold water one minute to send the heat to the heart of the cauliflower, cut them in pieces convenient to put in jars, then make a mixture of one tablespoonful of mace, one of cloves, one of allspice, one of ginger, two of white mustard seed, and a red pepper pod; with each a gallon of vinegar. Let the mixture boil and pour it upon the cauliflower; cover it closely and let it stand one week; then pour off the vinegar, scald it, and return it hot again to the cauliflower; then put it in jars ready for use. The best cider vinegar should be used, and if it is not perfectly clear it will dissolve the cauliflower.

PICKLES.

Mrs. H. Baird.

Slice one peck green tomatoes, and one quart small

white onions, each in a separate dish, with a small teacup of salt on them; to stand over night. Drain well, then take two quarts vinegar, one pound brown sugar, a few pepper pods, capsicums, some mace and ginger root, and put all together and simmer until tender. A very nice pickle.

ANOTHER GOOD PICKLE.

Two quarts small cucumbers, one quart small onions, two small cauliflowers, one quart beans; let them lie over-night, with a small teacup of salt in a gallon of water; in the morning put them on the stove and let them come to a scald, then take out and let them cool. To two quarts of vinegar put one ounce of curry powder, one ounce turmeric, one ounce ground ginger, two ounces mustard, one teaspoon cayenne pepper, two or three tablespoons salad oil; mix all together, and let it just come to a boil and pour over the vegetables.

FRENCH TOMATO PICKLE.

One peck green tomatoes, six onions nicely sliced; sprinkle one teacup salt over and stand all night; then drain well and scald in weak vinegar ten or fifteen minutes; drain again and scald with two quarts strong vinegar, one pound sugar, two tablespoons curry powder, two tablespoons turmeric, two teaspoons cinnamon, two teaspoons cloves, two teaspoons allspice, two teaspoons mustard; simmer all together slowly a few minutes. It is a beautiful rich pickle.

SPICED TOMATOES.

Mrs. Stotesbury.

To four pounds of large red tomatoes, take two pounds of good brown sugar, one pint of cider vinegar, half ounce of cloves, and half ounce of stick cinnamon; stew all together in a preserving kettle until the tomatoes are cooked; take the tomatoes out and put them on dishes to cool, letting the syrup go on simmering slowly; when the tomatoes are cold return them to the syrup for a little while; let them become cold before putting them in the jars. The syrup must be boiled down as thick as molasses, and poured cold over the tomatoes; tie them down with bladder or waxed paper.

PICKLED CUCUMBERS.

Mrs. Packard.

Wash with care your cucumbers, and place in jars. Make a weak brine (a handful of salt to a gallon and a half of water). When scalding hot, turn over the cucumbers and cover; repeat this process three mornings in succession, taking care to skim thoroughly. On the fourth day have ready a porcelain kettle of vinegar, to which has been added a piece of alum the size of a walnut. When scalding hot, put in as many cucumbers as may be covered with the vinegar; do not let them boil, but skim off as soon as scalded through, and replace with others, adding each time a small piece of alum. When this process is through, throw out the vinegar and replace with good cider or white wine vinegar; add spices, mustard seed, and red peppers. Sort the pickles and place in stone or glass jars, turn-over the hot spiced vinegar; seal and put away the jars not needed for immediate use. Pickles thus prepared are fine and crisp at the expiration of a year. Those that are kept in open-mouth jars may be covered with a cloth, which will need to be taken off and rinsed occasionally. I prefer green peppers, and prepare them with cucumbers in brine. They are not as apt to become soft.

DRESSING SALAD.

Mrs. Riley.

In dressing salad it should be thoroughly saturated with oil, and seasoned with salt and pepper *before* vinegar is added. The salt should not be dissolved in the vinegar but in the oil, by which means it is more equally distributed through the salad.

CUCUMBERS FOR PRESENT USE.

Mrs. Riley.

The best way of utilising cucumbers for *present use* is to parboil them in a solution of water, vinegar, and salt. They should be split in two before boiling, and, if done properly, will present a beautiful green colour.

TOMATO MUSTARD.

Mrs. Spaulding.

One peck of tomatoes, ripe, half-pound salt, six red peppers, three tablespoonsful of black pepper, one ounce ginger, one ounce allspice, half ounce mace, half ounce cloves, a few cloves of garlic, two onions, quarter pound mustard, a tablespoonful of red peppers, and a half pint vinegar. Peel the tomatoes, and boil an hour with six red peppers; then add the other spices (excepting the mustard and vinegar, which are added after the sauce is strained through a colander and cooled), and boil another hour.

WORCESTER SAUCE.

Mrs. T. B. Riley.

One ounce cayenne pepper, one quart vinegar, two tablespoonsful soy, three cloves garlic pounded, three cloves shalots pounded, five anchovies bruised fine. The whole to be well mixed and rubbed through a sieve. Keep for ten days corked up, and then bottle for use. Strain or not as preferred.

TOMATO CATSUP.

Mrs. T. B. Riley.

Take one bushel of ripe tomatoes, boil them until they are soft, squeeze them through a fine wire sieve, and add half a gallon of vinegar, one pint of salt, two ounces of cloves, a quarter of a pound of allspice, two ounces cayenne pepper, three tablespoonsful of ground peppers, five heads of garlic (skinned and separated). Mix together and boil three hours, or until reduced to about *one half*. Bottle without straining.

HORSE-RADISH SAUCE.

Grate very fine a stick of horse-radish; with two tablespoons of it mix a teaspoonful of salt and four tablespoons of cream; stir briskly and add by degrees a wineglass of vinegar.

TOMATO MUSTARD.

Mrs. Carson.

One peck of tomatoes, one teacupful of salt; boil in a preserving pan half an hour; pulp it through a colander and return to kettle with the following: one dessert spoon of cloves, (ground spices), one of allspice, one of black pepper, one of ginger, one of cayenne, a little garlic, some onions, and a little curry powder. Let it boil down considerably, then strain through a sieve and add flour of mustard, until the proper thickness is obtained, and simmer for a short time; then bottle for use.

TOMATO CATSUP.

Mrs. Carson.

One bushel of good ripe tomatoes, one-half gallon of good vinegar, also fresh ground spices, quarter pound allspice, two ounces cloves, three tablespoons black pepper, six large onions or two heads garlic, one pint and a half of salt, four large red peppers; boil for a length of time, and strain through a sieve, and add the vinegar last; boil until it is thick enough.

EAST INDIA PICKLES.

Mrs. Ellas.

One half peck sliced green tomatoes, one half peck sliced white onions, twenty-five small cucumbers, two cauliflowers cut in small branches; sprinkle salt over these plentifully and let stand twenty-four hours, and then drain well; mix half a cup of grated horse-radish root with half an ounce of turmeric, (get at drug store), half an ounce of each of ground cinnamon and cloves, one ounce of ground pepper, one pint of ground mustard seed, one pint of brown sugar, two bunches of chopped celery. Put this mixture into a porcelain kettle in layers with the vegetables. Cover with cold cider vinegar, and boil slowly for two hours. The turmeric gives the pickles the yellow colour peculiar to East India pickles, and in taste and appearance they cannot be distinguished from the genuine.

MRS. ELLAS' CHOW CHOW.

Two quarts tomatoes, two white onions, half dozen green peppers, one dozen cucumbers, two heads of cabbage, all chopped fine; let this stand over night; sprinkle a teacup of salt in it. In the morning drain off the brine, and season with one tablespoonful celery seed, one ounce turmeric, half teaspoon cayenne pepper, one cup brown sugar, one ounce cinnamon, one ounce allspice, one ounce black pepper, one quarter ounce cloves, vinegar enough to cover, and boil two hours.

DRAWN BUTTER, OR MELTED BUTTER.

Miss Beaty.

Rub in two teaspoonsful of flour into a quarter of a pound of butter; add five tablespoonsful of cold water; set it into boiling water and let it melt, and heat until it begins to simmer, and it is done. Never simmer it on coals, as it fries the oil and spoils it. Be careful not to have the flour in lumps. If it is to be used with fish, put in chopped eggs and nasturtium, or capers. If used with boiled fowl, put in oysters while it is simmering, and let them heat through.

BURNT BUTTER FOR FISH OR EGGS.

Miss Beaty.

Heat two ounces of butter in a frying-pan till a dark brown, then add a teaspoonful of vinegar, half a teaspoonful of salt, and half a dozen shakes from the pepper-box.

TOMATO CATSUP.

Miss Beaty.

Pour boiling water on the tomatoes; let them stand until you can rub off the skin, then cover them with salt and let them stand twenty-four hours. Then strain them, and to two quarts put three ounces of cloves, two ounces of pepper and two nutmegs. Boil half an hour, then add a pint of wine.

CURRIED DISHES.

Miss Beaty.

Chickens and veal are most suitable for curries. Boil the meat till tender, and separate the joints. Put a little butter in a stew-pan with the chickens, pour on a part of the liquor in which the meat was boiled, enough to cover it, and let it stew twenty minutes more. Prepare the curry thus: for four pounds of meat take a tablespoonful of curry powder, a teacup of boiled rice, and a tablespoonful of flour and another of melted butter, a teacup of the liquor and half a teaspoonful of salt; mix them, and pour them over the meat, and let stew ten minutes more. Rice should be boiled for an accompaniment.

RIPE TOMATO PICKLES.

Mrs. C. M. Dickerman.

To seven pounds of ripe tomatoes add three pounds sugar, one quart vinegar, boil them together fifteen minutes, skim out the tomatoes and boil the syrup a few minutes longer. Spice to suit the taste with cloves and cinnamon.

PICCALILLI.

Mrs. Lamkin.

One peck of green tomatoes; (if the flavour of onions is desired, take eight, but it is very nice without any), four green peppers; slice all, and put in layers, sprinkle on one cup of salt, and let them remain over night; in the morning press dry through a sieve, put it in a porcelain kettle and cover with vinegar; add one cup of sugar, a tablespoon of each kind of spice; put into a muslin bag; stew slowly about an hour, or until the tomatoes are as soft as you desire.

TO PICKLE MUSHROOMS BROWN.

Miss Brokovski.

Take the small buttons and rub them very clean with

a flannel, and some vinegar; then put them in a dish with a little salt over them to draw the liquor from them, then put them into a kettle to stew very gently in their own liquor; boil them in good vinegar, with mace, cloves, and black pepper.

TOMATOES WHOLE FOR WINTER USE.

Mrs. J. Saulter.

Fill a large stone jar with ripe tomatoes, then add a few whole cloves and a little sugar; cover them well with one half cold vinegar and half water; place a piece of flannel over the jar well down into the vinegar, then tie down with paper. I have kept tomatoes in this way the year round, and can cheerfully recommend them. Should mildew collect on the flannel it will not injure the tomatoes in the least.

CHOW-CHOW.

Mrs. John Corthell.

Two heads cabbage, two heads cauliflower, one dozen cucumbers, six roots of celery, six peppers, one quart of small white onions, two quarts green tomatoes; cut into small pieces, and boil each vegetable separately until tender, then strain them. Two gallons of vinegar, one-fourth pound of mustard, one-fourth pound of mustard seed, one pot of French mustard, one ounce of cloves, two ounces of turmeric; put the vinegar and spices into a kettle and let them come to a boil; mix the vegetables and pour over the dressing.

PICKLED OYSTERS.

Mrs. Carl Hammond.

Wash the oysters and scald them in strong salt and water; skim them out and throw into cold water; scald vinegar well and whole peppers; let it get cold. Put the oysters in a stone jar; make liquor to cover them of water they were scalded in, and vinegar. A cup of vinegar to one quart liquor, to be used cold.

BRINE THAT PRESERVES BUTTER A YEAR.

Mrs. D. McCraney.

To three gallons of brine strong enough to bear an egg, add one-quarter pound good loaf sugar, and one tablespoonful of saltpetre; boil the brine, and when it is cold strain carefully. Pack butter closely in small jars, and allow the brine to cover the butter to the depth of at least four inches. This completely excludes the air. If practicable make your butter into small roles, wrap each carefully in a clean muslin cloth, tying up with a string; place a weight over the butter to keep it all submerged in the brine. This mode is most recommended by those who have tried both.

BREAKFAST AND SUPPER.

*"Dinner may be pleasant;
So may social tea;
But yet, methinks the breakfast
Is best of all the three."*
—Anon.

RELISHES.

OYSTER STEW.

Mrs. A. S. Ewing.

Strain the juice from the oysters placed in the colander into a stew pan; let it come to a boil; remove the scum and a clear liquor will remain; turn cold water upon the oysters, and rinse thoroughly; add them to the liquor, with a cup of cream or milk, butter, salt, and cayenne pepper. Have ready buttered dice-shaped pieces of toast upon a meat dish; pour the oysters over, garnish with parsley, and serve hot.

TOAST.

Toast the bread very quickly, dip each slice in boiling water, (a little salt in the water), as soon as you have toasted it; then spread it with butter; cover and keep hot as you proceed. Make milk toast in the same way, keeping the milk at nearly boiling heat; it is better to spread the butter on the bread after it is dipped in hot milk, than to melt it in the milk; thicken what milk is left with a little corn starch, and pour over the toast when sent to the table.

SCRAMBLED EGGS.

Helena Smith.

Beat up six eggs with two ounces of butter, one tablespoonful of cream of new milk, a little chopped parsley, and salt; put all in a saucepan, and keep stirring over the fire until it begins to thicken, when it should be immediately dished on buttered toast.

FRENCH TOAST.

Mrs. M. J. Savage.

To one egg thoroughly beaten, put one cup of sweet milk and a little salt. Slice light bread, and dip into the mixture, allowing each slice to absorb some of the milk; then brown on a hot buttered griddle; spread with butter and serve hot.

TONGUE TOAST.

M. A. P.

Take cold boiled tongue, mince it fine; mix it with cream or milk, and to every half pint of the mixture, allow the well beaten yolks of two eggs; place over the fire and let it simmer a minute or two; have ready some nicely toasted bread; butter it; place it on a hot dish and pour the mixture over; send to the table hot.

LEMON TOAST.

E. A. Forsyth.

Take the yolks of six eggs, beat them well and add three cups of sweet milk; take baker's bread not too stale and cut into slices; dip them into the milk and eggs, and lay the slices into a spider, with sufficient melted butter hot to fry a nice delicate brown; take the whites of the six eggs, and beat them to a froth, adding a large cup of white sugar; add the juice of two lemons, heating well, and adding two cups boiling water; serve over the toast as a sauce, and you will find it a very delicious dish.

FRIED BREAD IN BATTER.

M. A. T.

Take one tablespoon sweet light dough; dissolve it in one cup sweet milk; add three or four eggs, one and a half cups flour, one teaspoon of salt; cut some thin slices of light bread, dip in this batter, and fry in hot lard; sprinkle with powdered sugar, and garnish with jelly.

CODFISH BALLS.

Mrs. Banks.

Take four cups of mashed potatoes, three cups of boiled codfish minced fine, add butter; mix well together; then add two well beaten eggs, beating it up again thoroughly; drop by spoonsful into hot lard and fry the same as doughnuts. Are nice fried in croquette baskets.

CODFISH PUFF.

Mrs. Banks.

Recipe the same as for codfish balls put in an earthen baking plate; smooth over the top, and put over some butter, and then in a hot oven to bake.

CODFISH HASH.

Mrs. N. P. Wilder.

One pint boiled picked codfish well freshened, one quart cold boiled chopped potatoes mixed well together, three slices salt pork freshened, cut in very small pieces and fried brown; remove half the pork, and add your fish and potatoes to the remainder; let it stand and steam five minutes without stirring; be careful not to let it burn; then add one-third cup milk and stir thoroughly; put the remainder of the pork around the edge of the spider, and a little butter over it; simmer it over a slow fire for half an hour, until a brown crust is formed, when turn it over on a platter and serve.

BEEF HASH.

Chop fine cold beef, either boiled or baked; have ready cold boiled potatoes; to one pint of meat put one pint and a little more of potatoes, chopped fine; have ready a spider, with a good piece of butter in it; put in the hash; season with pepper and salt, and then add rich milk or cream. Milk is a very great improvement.

CORNED BEEF HASH.

One and one-half pounds nice corned beef, boiled

tender and chopped fine; one-third more potatoes when chopped than meat; three large onions sliced fine and browned in butter, and when tender, add the meat and potatoes, well seasoned with salt and pepper; enough water to moisten. A small red pepper chopped fine is a great improvement. It is good without onions also.

BREAKFAST STEAK.

A nice steak of beef or veal; pound it with a steak mallet, if tough; lay in a baking tin, dredge it lightly with flour, season with salt and pepper, and, if you like, a little chopped parsley; then put in the oven and bake for twenty or thirty minutes, or until sufficiently well done; take it up, put it on the platter, spread with butter, and dredge into the juices of the meat in the baking pan a little flour, and season with butter; let this boil up and pour over the steak. This is very nice.

SIDE DISH.

R. A. Sibley.

Chopped cold meat well seasoned; wet with gravy, if convenient, put it on a platter; then take cold rice made moist with milk and one egg, season with pepper and salt; if not sufficient rice, add powdered bread crumbs; place this around the platter quite thick; set in oven to heat and brown.

ANOTHER SIDE DISH.

R. A. Sibley.

Cold turkey, chicken or any cold meat, chopped fine,

seasoned with salt, pepper, and gravy; lay pie crust round the edge of the platter, and cover the same; bake a nice brown in the oven. Very little meat makes a dish for several persons.

A NICE BREAKFAST DISH.

Harriet N. Jenks.

Mince cold beef or lamb; if beef put in a pinch of pulverized cloves; if lamb, a pinch of summer savoury to season it, very little pepper and some salt, and put it in a baking dish; mash potatoes and mix them with cream and butter and a little salt, and spread them over the meat; beat up an egg with cream or milk, a very little; spread it over the potatoes, and bake it a short time, sufficient to warm it through and brown the potatoes.

POTATO PUFFS.

S. S. Pierce.

Take cold roast meat (either beef, veal, or mutton); clear it from gristle; chop fine; season with pepper and salt; boil and mash some potatoes, and make them into a paste with one or two eggs; roll it out with a little flour; cut it round with a saucer; put your seasoned meat on one half; fold it over like a puff; turn it neatly round, and fry it a light brown; Nice for breakfast.

RICE CAKES.

Mrs. A. M. Gibbs.

One teacup of soft boiled rice, the yolk of one egg, a pinch of salt, two tablespoons of sifted flour, beaten well together; add sweet milk until it is about the consistency of sponge cake or thick cream, and just before baking stir in lightly the beaten white of the egg. The less flour used the better for invalids.

VEAL STEW.

Two pounds of veal steak cut in strips; put in cold water in a skillet or spider and over the fire. The water should be just sufficient to cover the meat. Pare, wash and slice one small potato and put in with the meat. Stew for twenty or thirty minutes gently, taking care that the water does not boil away. Have ready two or three eggs boiled in the shell. When the meat is tender add to the broth one cup of fresh milk and one heaping tablespoon of flour wet with milk; season all with butter, salt and pepper, and, if you like, a little parsley. Cut the hard boiled eggs in slices and put into the broth. Let all boil up once, and serve with or without toast on the platter. A very nice breakfast dish.

TO STEW MUSHROOMS.

Miss Brokovski.

Peel them and put them to stew in some milk till tender, when sufficiently done, put to them some butter and flour mixed together, a little cayenne, and some salt; part cream instead of milk will improve them.

BAKED EGGS.

Mrs. L. M. Angle.

Break six or seven eggs into a buttered dish, taking

care that each is whole, and does not encroach upon the others so much as to mix or disturb the yolks; sprinkle with pepper and salt, and put a bit of butter upon each. Put into an oven and bake until the whites are set. This is far superior to fried eggs, and very nice for breakfast, served on toast or alone.

POACHED EGGS.

Break as many eggs as you wish to use, one at a time, and drop carefully into a spider filled with boiling water. When the whites of the eggs are well set, slip a spoon carefully under and take out, laying each upon a small piece of buttered toast on the platter. Put a very small piece of butter on each egg, a slight dash of pepper, and serve immediately.

OMELET—(SPLENDID).

Six eggs, whites and yolks beaten separately; half pint milk, six teaspoons corn starch, one teaspoon of baking powder, and a little salt; add the whites, beaten to a stiff froth, last; cook in a little butter.

EGG-OMELET.

Mrs. Carson.

Six eggs beaten separately, half pint sweet milk, six teaspoons of corn starch made smooth in a little of the milk, one teaspoon baking powder, a little salt; add the whites last, cook in a hot pan with a little butter; when nicely browned, roll over on hot dish and serve at once.

OMELET.

Mrs. Midgley.

Six eggs, teacup of milk, pepper and salt; beat yolks and whites separately; add pepper and salt with yolks, then stir in the milk; lastly stir in the whites very lightly; have your pan very hot, put a good bit of butter in your pan, then the mixture. Cook ten minutes, put in the oven for three minutes, slip on a hot plate, and eat.

OMELET.

Miss E. C. Harris.

One cup of milk, one tablespoon flour stirred into the milk; four eggs, the yolks and whites beaten separately; one-half tablespoon melted butter stirred into the mixture; a little salt. Stir in the whites before putting into the spider. Cook on top of the stove about ten minutes, then set the spider in the oven to brown the top. To be eaten as soon as taken from the oven. Very nice.

FRIED OMELET.

Mrs. F. B. Orr.

Three eggs, two gills milk, two tablespoons flour, a ittle salt and pepper, fried on hot griddle.

FRIAR'S OMELET.

Mrs. DeForest.

Boil a dozen apples, as for sauce; stir in one-fourth

pound of butter, ditto white sugar; when cold, add four well beaten eggs and a few spoons of cream; put it into a baking dish, well buttered, and thickly strewn with bread crumbs on the bottom and sides; strew currants over the top. Bake forty-five minutes; turn on a platter, and sift sugar over it. Serve with sugar and cream, or a boiled custard; the latter is much the nicer.

FRENCH OMELET.

M.

One cup boiling milk with one tablespoon of butter melted in it; pour this on one cup of bread crumbs, (the bread must be light); add salt, pepper, and the yolks of six eggs well beaten; mix thoroughly; and lastly, add the six whites cut to a stiff froth; mix lightly and fry with hot butter; this will make two; when almost done, turn together in shape of half moon.

BAKED OMELET.

Mrs. Edward Ely.

Six eggs, two tablespoons of flour, a little salt, one cup of milk; take a little of the milk, and stir the flour into it; add the rest of the milk, and the yolks of the eggs; then beat the whites of the eggs to a stiff froth, and pour into the flour, milk, and yolks; put a piece of butter the size of a small egg into an iron spider, and let it get hot, but not so the butter will burn; then pour the mixture in and put in a moderate oven to bake in the spider. It takes about ten minutes to bake. Then slip a knife under and loosen, and slip off on a large plate or platter.

VEAL OMELET

Mrs. J. S. Gano.

Three pounds of lean veal, two eggs, six small butter crackers, one tablespoon of thyme, one of salt, one of pepper, two of milk; knead it like bread, and bake it two hours in a slow oven, basting it with butter often, then slice for tea.

CHEESE SCALLOP.

Soak one cup of dry bread crumbs in fresh milk. Beat into this three eggs; add one tablespoon of butter and one-half a pound of grated cheese; strew upon the top sifted bread crumbs, and bake in the oven a delicate brown. An excellent relish when eaten with thin slices of bread and butter.

FISH RELISH.

After Marion Harland.

One cup of drawn butter with an egg beaten in, two hard boiled eggs, mashed potato (a cup will do), one cup of cold fish (cod, halibut, or shad), roe of cod or shad, and one teaspoon of butter, one teaspoon of minced parsley, pepper and salt to taste. Method: Dry the roe previously well boiled; mince the fish fine and season; wash up the roe with the butter and the yolks of the boiled eggs; cut the white into thin rings; put a layer of mashed potatoes at the bottom of a deep buttered dish; then alternate layers of fish; drawn butter with the rings of the whites imbedded in this roe; more potato at top; cover and set in the oven until it smokes and bubbles; brown by removing the cover a few minutes Send to table in the baking dish, and pass pickles with it.

BREAKFAST GEMS.

Mrs. Brown.

One cup sweet milk, one and a half cups flour, one egg, one teaspoon salt, one teaspoon baking powder; beaten together five minutes; bake in *hot* gem pans in a hot oven about fifteen minutes.

POTATO CAKE.

Mrs. S. McMaster.

Crush cold boiled potatoes with butter and salt; mix in a small proportion of flour and a little yeast (the last may be omitted at pleasure), and with milk work the whole to the consistency of very firm dough; roll it out to the thickness of an inch and a half or two inches; cut it out the size of your frying pan, previously greased, and in it lay your cake after flouring it all over; bake covered with a plate, shake and shift it a little from time to time to prevent burning; when half done turn it, and cover with a plate again.

RICE FRITTERS.

Mrs. S. McMaster.

Boil three tablespoonsful of rice until it swells to the full size, then drain quite dry and mix with it four eggs well beaten, quarter pound of currants and a little grated lemon peel, nutmeg and sugar to the taste; stir in as much flour as will thicken it, and fry in lard.

BREAKFAST BUNS.

Mrs. J. W. Preston.

Two cups of flour, three-fourths cup of corn meal, three-fourths cup of butter, one-half cup of sugar, two eggs beaten, one cup of milk, three teaspoons baking powder; bake in hot oven twenty minutes.

QUICK SALLY LUNN.

One cup of sugar, one-half a cup of butter; stir well together, and then add one or two eggs; put in one good pint of sweet milk, and with sufficient flour to make a batter about as stiff as cake; put in three teaspoons of baking powder; bake and eat hot with butter, for tea or breakfast.

BREAKFAST CAKE.

Mrs. C. Bradley.

One pint of flour, three tablespoons of butter, three tablespoons of sugar, one egg, one cup sweet milk, one teaspoon cream tartar, one-half teaspoon soda; to be eaten with butter.

RYE CAKES FOR TEA.

Harriet N. Jenks.

Two teacups of rye flour, one of wheat flour, one of sour milk, one teaspoon of soda, put in the sour milk, and while foaming stir it in the flour and rye, with one-half teaspoon of salt, one-half teacup of molasses; make it stiff and turn it into a buttered pan; spread it smooth with a spoon dipped in hot water; bake one-half hour

JOLLY BOYS.

Jeannie Brayton.

One quart corn meal; scald and cool; one pint of flour, two eggs, one teaspoon soda, two of cream tartar, a little milk, salt; make as thick as pancakes, and fry in hot lard. Nice for breakfast.

GRAHAM BREAKFAST CAKES.

Mrs. Gibbs.

Two cups of Graham flour, one cup of wheat flour, two eggs well beaten; mix with sweet milk, to make a very thin batter; bake in gem irons; have the irons hot, then set them on the upper grate in the oven; will bake in fifteen minutes.

TEA CAKE.

Mrs. H. P. Stowell.

One egg, one cup sugar, one cup sweet milk, piece of butter size of an egg, one teaspoon cream-tartar, one-half teaspoon soda, one pint of flour. Eaten warm.

COTTAGE CHEESE.

Mrs. Gibbs.

Pour boiling water on the thick milk in the pan in which it has turned, stirring while you pour; as soon as the milk separates from the whey and begins to appear cooked, let it settle; in a minute or two most of the water and whey can be poured off; if not sufficiently cooked, more hot water may be used; set the pan on edge, and with your spoon or hand draw the curd to the upper side, pressing out as much water as possible; if desired, it can stand a few moments in cold water; when squeezed dry, work the curd fine, rolling it between the hands; add salt and cream to taste; in very warm weather when the milk has turned quickly, it is very palatable without the addition of cream.

WHITE CORN BREAD.

Mrs. E. S. Cheeseborough.

One pint of meal thoroughly scalded with hard-boiling water; butter the size of an egg, and one well-beaten egg; add milk to make it just thin enough to flow over the pan. Have the batter an inch thick, and then bake.

YPSILANTI EGG ROLLS.

Miss Norris.

Allow one egg for each person, two cups of milk for three eggs, four teaspoons of flour; beat whites and yolks separately, and add the eggs last. Put a very little of the mixture into a hot frying pan well greased with butter; roll as you would omelet, and put on a platter. Send in hot. For breakfast or tea. Can be eaten with sugar.

VEGETABLES.

> Witness, thou best *Anana*, thou the pride
> Of vegetable life, beyond whaet'er
> The poets imaged in the golden age.
> Quick, let me strip thee of thy tufty coat,
> Spread thy ambrosial stores, and feast with Jove."
> —THOMPSON.

BOILED POTATOES.

Old potatoes are better for being peeled and put in cold water an hour before being put over to boil. They should then be put into fresh cold water, when set over the fire. New potatoes should always be put into boiling water, and it is best to prepare them just in time for cooking. Are better steamed than boiled.

MASHED POTATOES.

Mrs. F. D. J.

Peel the potatoes, and let them stand in cold water for half an hour; then put in the steamer over boiling water and cook them until mealy and *quite tender*. Have ready an earthen basin, or a bright tin pan, into which you will put your potatoes, so that while mashing and preparing, they can be kept on the stove and hot. Now mash well and finely with the potato-masher, and then season with salt; allow a generous piece of butter, and lastly, add a teacup of rich milk; mix altogether well, and then take up on a deep dish.

There will now be three or four ways to finish this,

and which are, first by putting a little butter on the top, after smoothing nicely, and putting it a moment at the mouth of the oven, and then serving quite hot; or you may put it into the oven, which should be quick and hot, and bake the crust of a rich brown. Or, again, the top may be scored a golden brown with steel bars made for this purpose. Or, lastly, after mashing the potato, put it into a mould and shape it; then loosen it from the mould and turn it on to a flat piece of sheet iron, large enough to cover the bottom of the mould with handles at the sides. Then have ready hot lard in which you immerse the moulded potato and fry a rich golden brown. Take out and with a knife under, slide carefully on your platter. Garnish the dish around with curled parsley leaves. If the potato is put in the oven to brown, it should be put in a baking plate and may be sent to the table in the dish in which it is baked, with a knitted cover over.

FRENCH POTATOES.

Mrs. W. G. Davis.

Peel and cut some potatoes in slices lengthwise, wipe dry and drop them in boiling lard; serve very hot.

POTATOES AND CREAM.

Mince cold boiled potatoes fine; put them into a spider with melted butter in it; let them fry a little in the butter well covered; then put in a fresh piece of butter, season with salt and pepper, and pour over cream or rich milk; let it boil up once and serve.

POTATOES FRIED.

Mrs. A.

Pare potatoes; cut in pieces one-half inch wide, and as long as the potato; keep them in cold water till wanted; drop in boiling lard; when nearly done, take them out with a skimmer and drain them; boil up the lard again, and drop them back, and fry till done; this makes them puff up; sprinkle with salt and serve very hot.

POTATO CROQUETTES.

Take finely mashed potato and mix through it sufficient salt, pepper, and butter to season well, with sweet milk or cream to moisten; mix thoroughly with this one beaten egg, and then make up into small rolls, being careful to have the surface perfectly smooth. Have ready one plate with a beaten egg upon it, and another with cracker crumbs. Dip each roll into the egg and then into the crumbs, and fry of a rich golden brown in hot lard. Lay the croquettes on brown paper first, and serve on a napkin.

PARSNIPS.

Boil until tender in a little salted water; then take up; skim them, cut in strips, dip in beaten egg, and fry in melted butter or hot lard.

TURNIPS.

Boil until tender; mash and season with butter, pepper, salt, and a little rich milk or cream. Serve with mutton.

BEETS.

Clean these nicely, but do not pare them, leaving on a short piece of the stalk. Then put over to boil in hot water. Young beets will cook tender in an hour; old beets require several hours boiling. When done, skin quickly while hot; slice thin into your vegetable dish, put on salt, pepper and a little butter; put over a little vinegar and serve hot or cold.

BAKED SQUASH.

Cut in pieces, scrape well, bake from one to one and a half hours, according to the thickness of the squash; to be eaten with salt and butter as sweet potatoes.

FRIED SQUASHES.

Mrs. F. M. Cragin.

Cut the squash into thin slices, and sprinkle it with salt; let it stand a few moments; then beat two eggs, and dip the squash into the egg; then fry it brown in butter.

SUMMER SQUASHES.

Cook them whole; when tender, if large, skin and remove the seeds; if small, this will not be necessary; drain and press the water out with a plate; then put them in a stew-pan, and season well with butter, pepper, and salt, and a tablespoon of cream.

GREEN CORN—BOILED.

Throw the ears, when husked, into a kettle of boiling

water, slightly salted, and boil thirty minutes. Serve in a napkin.

GREEN CORN OYSTERS.

To a pint of grated corn add two well beaten eggs; one-half cup of cream, and a half cup of flour, with one-half spoon of baking powder stirred in it; season with pepper and salt and fry in butter, dropping the batter in spoonsful; serve a few at a time, very hot, as a relish with meats.

GREEN CORN PATTIES.

M.

Grate as much corn as will make one pint; one teacup flour, one teacup butter, one egg, pepper and salt to taste. If too thick, add a little milk, and fry in butter.

SOUTHERN WAY OF BOILING RICE.

Mrs. Stotesbury.

Pick over the rice; rinse it in cold water until perfectly clean, then put it in a pot of boiling water, allowing a quart of water to less than a teacup of rice; boil it hard seventeen minutes; drain off the water very close, and let it steam fifteen minutes with the lid off. When carefully done in this way, each kernel of rice stands out by itself, while it is perfectly tender. The water in which the rice has been boiled makes, it is said, good starch for muslin, if boiled a few minutes by itself.

CORN OYSTERS.

Mrs. Samuel McMaster.

One pint of green grated corn, two tablespoons of milk, three eggs, two tablespoons butter; flour to make a batter; and fry on griddle with butter.

SUCCOTASH.

One pint of green corn cut from the cob, and two-thirds of a pint of Lima beans; let them stew in just enough water to cover them until tender, then season with butter, pepper, salt, and a little milk; simmer together a few moments and serve.

CANADIAN BAKED BEANS.

Mrs. Higgins.

Boil the beans until they begin to crack, with a pound or two of salt fat pork; put the beans in the baking-pan; score the pork across the top, and settle in the middle; add two tablespoons of sugar or molasses, and bake in a moderate oven two hours; they should be very moist when first put into the oven, or they will grow too dry in baking. Do not forget the sweetening if you want Yankee baked beans.

GREEN PEAS.

Shell and put into boiling water, cook from thirty to thirty-five minutes; drain and season with rich milk or cream, butter, pepper, and salt; some cooks also add a little flour or corn starch to thicken the gravy, but which should be used very sparingly, not more than a teaspoon. Be sure the peas are young; old peas are fit for nothing but soup.

ASPARAGUS.

Cut off the green ends, and chop up the remainder of the stalks; boil until tender, and season with salt and pepper; have ready some toasted bread in a deep dish; mix together equal parts of flour and butter to a cream; add to this slowly enough of the asparagus water or clear hot water to make a sauce; boil this up once; put the asparagus on the toast and pour over all the sauce.

BAKED CABBAGE.

Boil a cabbage, then put in a colander, and drain it until perfectly dry; then chop fine; put in pepper, salt, and a little cream, and put in an earthen baking-pan and into the oven. Bake one hour.

DRESSED CABBAGE.

Mrs. B. J. Seward.

One small teacup of vinegar, one egg, two tablespoons of sugar, one teaspoon of salt, and butter half the size of an egg; beat the egg before mixing with the other ingredients, which should be previously put over the fire, then put in the egg; stir until it boils; cool and pour over chopped or shaved cabbage.

CAULIFLOWER.

Mrs. C. Belford.

Remove the leaves; cut the main stalk close to the flower; lay it in boiling milk and water slightly salted, with the stalk down; when done, take out carefully and drain in a colander, then place in the vegetable dish and pour over it a rich drawn butter dressing.

ESCALOPED TOMATOES.

Put into an earthen baking dish a layer of cracker crumbs and small bits of butter; then a layer of tomatoes with a very little sugar sprinkled over them; then another layer of cracker crumbs seasoned with butter, and a layer of tomatoes, until your dish is full, with the cracker crumbs at the top; pour over all this a little water to moisten, and bake half an hour.

STEWED TOMATOES.

Mrs. Saulter.

Put ripe tomatoes into hot water and skin them; then throw them into an *earthen* stew pan, (a new tin will do, but not so good); cut up and let the tomatoes cook gently a few minutes; season with butter, pepper, salt, and serve. Or you may add bread crumbs and sugar to the tomatoes if preferred. Some cooks stew tomatoes for a long time, but the flavour is finer if allowed to simmer but a few moments, just sufficient time to heat well through.

BAKED TOMATOES.

Wash, wipe and then cut in two; place them in a baking tin with the skin side down, and season with pepper and salt, and place in a hot oven; take up carefully when done, and put bits of butter on each piece of tomato.

FRIED TOMATOES.

Cut a large Feejee tomato in half, flour the cut side, heat very hot, and put the floured side down; when brown on one side, turn; when done, pour over a teacup of hot cream or rich milk.

TOMATO HASH.

Butter the dish well; put in a layer of sliced tomatoes, a layer of cold meat, sliced thin; then a layer of bread and butter, and so on until the dish is full, seasoning well with pepper and salt, and beaten eggs poured over the top. Bake brown.

MACARONI.

Mrs. M. C. Gridley.

Cook macaroni in water until soft; then put in a deep dish with alternate layers of grated crackers and cheese, a little salt; fill up the dish with milk and bake one hour.

MACARONI AU TOMATO.

Mrs. Bendelari.

Throw one pound of macaroni into a preserving kettl

half filled with boiling water, (be sure that the water is boiling), and a small teaspoon of salt. Let it boil for about twenty minutes, or until it is tender; then drain in a colander before putting on a dish. Have about two tablespoons of cheese grated and sprinkle over it, then pour over a tomato sauce which has been strained, and made as follows: Two hours before the macaroni is put on the fire, take a quart of canned or fresh tomatoes and put in a saucepan with a little salt and pepper, half a small onion, a teaspoon of parsley cut fine, a piece of lard the size of an egg. Let it boil slowly for two hours; if it gets too dry add a few spoonsful of water.

ONIONS—BOILED.

Select those of uniform size; remove the outer skin, then boil until tender in a large quantity of milk and water; the flavour will be more delicate. Drain them when tender, and season with butter, salt, and pepper

ONIONS—FRIED.

Peel and slice and fry in lard or butter; season with pepper and salt, and serve hot.

MUSHROOMS—FRIED.

When peeled put them into hot butter and let them heat thoroughly through—too much cooking toughens them. Season well with butter, pepper, and salt. Serve on buttered toast; a teaspoon of wine or vinegar on each mushroom is a choice method.

MUSHROOMS—STEWED.

If fresh, let them lie in salt and water about one hour, then put them in the stewpan, cover with water and let them cook two hours gently. Dress them with cream, butter and flour as oysters, and season to taste.

PUDDINGS.

"And solid pudding against empty praise."

EVE'S PUDDING.

If you want a good pudding, mind what you are taught;
Take eggs, six in number, when bought for a groat;
The fruit with which Eve her husband did cozen,
Well pared, and well chopped, at least half a dozen;
Six ounces of bread, let Moll eat the crust,
And crumble the rest as fine as the dust;
Six ounces of currants, from the stem you must sort,
Lest you break out your teeth, and spoil all the sport;
Six ounces of sugar won't make it too sweet,
Some salt and some nutmeg will make it complete;
Three hours let it boil without any flutter,
But Adam won't like it without wine and butter.

SUET PUDDING.

Mrs. E. R. Harmon.

One cup of suet chopped fine, one cup chopped raisins, one cup of molasses, one cup of sweet milk, three teaspoons baking powder; spice to your taste; four cups of flour; mix and steam three hours.

SUET PUDDING.

Mrs. J. H. Brown.

Two cups of chopped suet, two of raisins, two of molasses, four of flour, one of milk, three teaspoons of baking powder; boil three and one-half hours; eat while hot. Sauce for same: One cup of sugar, one-half of butter, one egg, one tablespoon of wine or vinegar; beat fifteen minutes and heat to a scald.

MADEIRA PUDDING.

Mrs. J. C. Smith.

One-half pound chopped suet, three-quarters of a pound bread crumbs, six ounces moist sugar, one-quarter pound flour, two eggs, two wineglasses of sherry; mix the suet, bread crumbs, sugar, and flour well together. When these ingredients are well mixed add the eggs and two glasses of sherry, to make a thick batter; boil three hours and a half; serve with wine sauce.

UNRIVALLED PLUM PUDDING.

Mrs. J. E. Smith.

Two pounds and a half of raisins, one or three quarters pound of currants, two pounds of the finest moist sugar, two pounds bread crumbs, sixteen eggs, two pounds finely chopped suet, six ounces of mixed candied peel, the rind of two lemons, one ounce of ground nutmeg, one ounce of ground cinnamon, half an ounce of pounded bitter almonds, one-quarter of a pint of brandy. Mode: stone and cut up the raisins, do not chop them; wash and dry the currants; cut the candied peel into thin slices; mix all the dry ingredients well together, and moisten with the eggs, which should be well beaten and strained; then stir in the brandy; and when all is thoroughly mixed, add butter and flour, and put the pudding into a stout new cloth; tie it down very tightly and closely; boil from six to eight hours, and serve with brandy sauce. This quantity may be divided and boiled in buttered moulds.

SUET PUDDING.

Mrs. Banks.

Three cups flour, one cup suet, one cup molasses, one cup sweet milk, one cup raisins, one and a half teaspoons soda; three hours hard boiling in a bag or pudding-dish.

PUDDING.

Mrs. Metcalf.

One teacup sugar, three tablespoons melted butter, one egg, one teacup of milk, two heaping cups of flour, one teaspoon soda, two cream tartar; if the milk be sour leave out the cream of tartar; bake in pan about half an hour. To put in a few currants improves it.

SUET PUDDING.

Mrs. W. Butterfield.

One cup of suet, one cup of molasses, one cup of milk, one cup of raisins, three and a half cups of flour, one egg, one tablespoon of cloves, one tablespoon of cinnamon, one nutmeg, a little salt, one teaspoon of soda, (dissolve in the milk); steam three hours.

STEAMED PLUM PUDDING.

Mrs. J. W. Farlin.

One and one-fourth cups beef suet, two cups raisins,

four cups flour, one cup milk, one cup molasses, one teaspoon soda, one teaspoon salt. Season with nutmeg, cloves, cinnamon, and allspice to taste; steam four hours. Do not uncover the steamer, but raise occasionally to fill the kettle with boiling water.

PLUM PUDDING.

Mrs. H. E. Houghton.

One cup suet, one cup sweet milk, one cup molasses, one cup sugar, one cup currants, two and a half cups raisins, four cups flour, one teaspoon cinnamon, one teaspoon cloves, one teaspoon spice, one teaspoon soda; boil three hours.

ENGLISH FRUIT PUDDING.

Mrs. H. S. Bristol.

One pound currants, one pound stoned raisins, one pound sugar, one pound suet, two pounds of grated or soaked bread, six eggs, one-half teaspoon saleratus, one teaspoon salt, and one grated nutmeg; crumb the soft part of the bread fine; soak the crust with boiling milk, or water will do; beat up the eggs and put all together, mixing thoroughly with the hands; take a square piece of cotton cloth and lay it in a tin pan, put the pudding into the cloth and tie down close; put into a pot of boiling water, and boil five hours; as the water boils away, keep adding more.

ENGLISH PLUM PUDDING.

M. Walker.

One pound raisins (stoned), one pound of currants, one pound suet very finely chopped, one pound flour, seven eggs, two wineglasses brandy, three of sweet wine, sugar and spice to taste, (it may require a little sweet milk); tie it tightly in a well floured cloth, which should be first dipped in hot water, and boil four hours, or it may be boiled in a pudding form.

SNOWDON PUDDING.

Madame E. Pernet.

Quarter pound bread crumbs, half pound suet, quarter pound sugar, two eggs well beaten, two tablespoonsful preserves, two ounces candied citron or orange peel. Butter a mould or basin, stick some of the citron over it, pour in your mixture, and steam for three or four hours; melt some of the preserves, and pour over the pudding for sauce.

FANNY L'S BATTER PUDDING.

Six eggs, eight tablespoons flour, one quart sweet milk, very little salt. Bake in a quiet oven.

PLUM PUDDING.

Mrs. E. Hempstead.

One pint raisins, one pint currants, one pint suet, one pint flour, one-half pint bread crumbs, one cup milk, five eggs, spices to taste, a little candied orange and lemon; mix all together and boil three hours. To be eaten with wine sauce.

BIRD'S NEST.

Mrs. F. M. Cragin.

Pare six or eight large apples (Spitzenbergs or Greenings are best), and remove the core by cutting from the end down into the middle, so as to leave the apple whole, except where the core has been removed; place them as near together as they can stand with the open part upward in a deep pie-dish; next make a thin batter, using one quart sweet milk, three eggs with sufficient flour, and pour it into the dish around the apples, also filling the cavities in them; bake them in a quick oven; eat them with butter and sugar.

CHOCOLATE PUDDING.

Miss Riley.

One quart milk, three tablespoons sugar, four tablespoons corn starch, two and a half tablespoons chocolate; scald the milk over boiling water; dissolve the corn starch in a little scalded milk, and before it thickens add the chocolate dissolved in boiling water; stir until sufficiently cooked. Use with cream, or sauce of butter and sugar stirred to a cream.

COCOANUT PUDDING.

C. A. Tinkham.

One quart sweet milk, ten tablespoons grated cocoanut, one cup powdered sugar, and whites of ten eggs; bake

ALMOND CUSTARD PUDDING.

Mrs. D.

Make a delicate sponge cake and stick it full of blanched almonds. Pour over a little wine, and then a rich vanilla custard.

POTATO PUDDING.

Boil until white, mealy, and very tender some potatoes; rub them finely washed through a colander; to a pint bowl of them while hot add one-quarter of a pound of butter, and mix well; beat the yolks of six eggs well with one pound of fine sugar; add the grated rind and juice of one lemon, and then the beaten whites; stir lightly in, and bake in pie plates lined with paste; eat cold.

QUEEN'S PUDDING.

Mrs. A. P. Wightman.

One quart of sweet milk, one pint of bread crumbs, five eggs, one teaspoon of corn starch, one large or two small lemons, one cup of common sugar, and one of pulverized sugar; bring the milk to a scald, pour it over the bread crumbs and let it cool; beat the yolks of the eggs and one cup of common sugar together, and mix in the corn starch also; just before putting in to bake, add the grated rind of the lemon, and bake twenty minutes. Beat the whites of the eggs and one cup of pulverized sugar together, and add the lemon juice; when the pudding is done, put this on the top and set it in the oven again for a few minutes; to be eaten cold.

ROLY—POLY.

M.

Take one quart of flour; make good biscuit crust; roll out one-half inch thick and spread with any kind of fruit, fresh or preserved; fold so that the fruit will not run out; dip cloth into boiling water, and flour it and lay around the pudding closely, leaving room to swell; steam one or one and one-half hours; serve with boiled sauce; or lay in steamer without a cloth, and steam for one hour.

STEAMED PUDDING.

Mrs. Arthurs.

One cup suet, half cup molasses, half cup sugar, two eggs, one cup sweet milk, two cups flour, one teaspoonful soda, two teaspoonsful cream tartar, dissolved in the milk, which you add the last thing. Butter a dish or bowl, strew raisins on the bottom; steam two hours.

PLUM PUDDING.

Mrs. Gale.

One and a half pounds of suet, one pound stoned raisins, one pound currants, eight eggs, half grated nutmeg, two ounces candied peel, one teaspoonful ground ginger, half pound bread crumbs, half pound flour, two pounds dark sugar, half pint milk. Boil ten hours and serve with brandy sauce. Excellent.

RICE PUDDING WITHOUT EGGS.

Mrs. C. H. Wheeler and others.

Two quarts of milk, half a teacup of rice, a little less than a teacup of sugar, the same quantity of raisins, a teaspoon of cinnamon or allspice; wash the rice, and put it with the rest of the ingredients into the milk; bake rather slowly from two to three hours; stir two or three times the first hour of baking. If properly done, this pudding is delicious.

COTTAGE PUDDING.

Mr. G. S. Whitaker.

One cup of sugar, one cup of sweet milk, one pint of flour, two tablespoons of melted butter, one teaspoon of soda, two teaspoons of cream tartar, one egg.

RICE AND APPLE PUDDING.

Mrs. R. Beaty.

One cup of rice boiled *very* soft; stir well to keep from burning; eight large apples, stewed; press the pulp through a sieve, mix it thoroughly with the rice; add half a teaspoonful of butter and yolks of two eggs well beaten; sweeten to taste. Bake. Beat the whites of the eggs and put on the top. It is nicer almost cold.

SUET PUDDING.

Mrs. J. Kent.

One cup of suet, one cup of sour milk, one-half spoon soda, one cup sugar, nutmeg and salt, and flour to stiffen.

A QUICK PUDDING.

Mrs. A. W. D.

One-half pint of milk, one-half pint of cream, three eggs beaten separately, little over one-half pint flour; season with lemon or vanilla.

BAKED INDIAN PUDDING.

Two quarts scalded milk with salt, one and one-half cups Indian meal (yellow); one tablespoon of ginger, letting this stand twenty minutes; one cup molasses, two eggs (saleratus if no eggs), a piece of butter the size of a common walnut. Bake two hours. Splendid.

CORN MEAL PUDDING.

Etta C. Springer.

One quart of sweet milk, boiled; stir in four tablespoons of corn meal; stand till cool; put in four beaten eggs, sweeten to taste; two tablespoons of butter. Bake two hours.

SAGO AND APPLE PUDDING.

Mrs. Arthurs.

Boil a cup of sago in boiling water with a little cinnamon, a cup of sugar, lemon flavouring; cut apples in thin slices, mix them with the sago; after it is well boiled add a small piece of butter; pour into pudding dish and bake half an hour.

YORKSHIRE PUDDING.

Mrs. S. McGee.

When roasting a piece of beef lay it on sticks in your bake pan, so that the juice of the meat will drop into the pan below; three-quarters of an hour before the beef is done, mix the following pudding and pour it into the pan under the meat, letting the drippings continue to fall upon it: one pint milk, four eggs well beaten, two cups flour, one teaspoon salt.

LEMON PIE.

Mrs. H. Baird.

The juice and grated rind of one lemon, one cup of water, one tablespoon corn starch, one cup sugar, one egg, and a piece of butter the size of a small egg; boil the water; wet the corn starch with a little cold water, and stir it in; when it boils up pour it on the sugar and butter; after it cools add the egg and lemon. Bake with upper and under crust.

AUNT LUCY'S APPLE CUSTARD PIE.

Peel some apples, stew until tender, (not too much water), put through the colander; for one pie take three eggs, one-third cup butter, one-third sugar, flavour with lemon (fresh or extract), and nutmeg; use only the yolks of the eggs in the pie, and cover with the whites, and brown the same as for lemon pies.

ORANGE PUDDING.

Mrs. Carson.

Peel and cut five good oranges into thin slices, taking out all seeds; put over them a coffee cup of fine white sugar. Let a pint of milk get boiling hot, by setting in hot water; add the yolks of three eggs well beaten, one tablespoon of corn starch made smooth in a little cold milk; stir all the time, and as soon as thickened pour it over the fruit. Beat the whites to a stiff froth, add a tablespoon of sugar, and spread it over the top for frosting; set in oven a minute to harden. Can be eaten hot, but is best cold.

SNOW PUDDING.

Mrs. Frisbie.

One-third of a box of gelatine, (the best you can find); soak ten minutes in cold water; put on the stove and stir until it is dissolved; let it cool, then beat to a froth; take the whites of two eggs beaten to a froth, one cup of sugar, flavour with lemon; mix all together and put in small cups first wet in water, and set away to cool and harden. Make a soft custard of the yolks, turn over the pudding when cold, and it is ready for the table.

COTTAGE PUDDING.

Mrs. Ira Metcalf.

One teacup of sugar, three tablespoons melted butter, one egg, one teacup of milk, two heaping cups of flour, one teaspoon of soda, two of cream tartar. If the milk be sour, leave out the cream tartar. Bake in a pan about half an hour; add fruit if you like, it is quite an improvement.

PUDDINGS.

Mrs. Upham.

APPLE DUMPLING.—One quart of flour, two tablespoonsful baking powder, two tablespoonfuls of lard or butter rubbed in flour, a little salt. Mix with water soft enough to roll. Slice your apples thin. Make either one large one or several small ones.

STEAM FRUIT PUDDING.—One cup sour milk, two eggs, butter size of half an egg, one teaspoonful of soda, a little salt. Stir flour to make a stiff batter.

SAUCE FOR PUDDING.—One half cup boiling water, one tablespoon corn starch, two tablespoonsful vinegar, one tablespoonful of butter, one cup sugar, one-half nutmeg.

FLOATING ISLAND.—Put a quart of milk over to boil, sugar, salt, and flavouring to taste; separate three eggs; beat the whites to a stiff froth; drop them in the boiling milk from a tablespoon, letting them remain half a second; then take two tablespoonsful and one-half of corn starch; put it into the boiling milk; let it remain five minutes, then add the yolks; let it then boil two minutes, and take it off to cool; then place it in a glass dish; drop the whites upon it with a spoonful of currant jelly on each.

PUDDINGS.

Mrs. Upham.

APPLE FLOAT.—A pint of stewed, well-mashed apples, the whites of three eggs beaten to a stiff froth, four large tablespoonsful of sugar; then add the apples and sugar alternately, a spoonful of each, and beat all together until it stands up perfectly stiff; it will swell immensely. Serve this in saucers on a custard made of the yolks of the eggs, one pint of milk, two tablespoonsful of sugar, and flavour with vanilla.

APPLE MERINGUE.—Prepare a pudding dish two-thirds full of nice sour apples, add one and one-half cups of water, and one cup of brown sugar, and some salt. Cover closely, and let them simmer in the oven until done to a mash. Beat the whites of five eggs, one cup of sugar, and the juice of a lemon, until they are a stiff froth; pour over the apples and set in the oven to brown. Peaches or other canned fruits are very nice. The yolks of the eggs make a rich custard if beaten and stirred into a quart of boiling milk. Sweeten, season, and pour over it.

SUET PUDDING.

Miss M.

Take three-quarters of a lb. of suet, three eggs, and half pint of milk, flour sufficient to make a thick batter; to be well mixed together, and the suet not chopped too small; boil two hours.

"OUR OWN LITTLE PUDDINGS."

Miss Brokovski.

Boil half a pint of milk, pour it over the crumbs of a "penny roll," or a "Sally Lunn" stale, two eggs, two ounces suet chopped fine, a little grated lemon peel, twelve bitter or sweet almonds; sweeten to your taste with fine sugar, and a little nutmeg; bake in teacup; sweet sauce put over them.

PRETTY PUDDING.

Mrs. Charles Bradbury.

One tablespoon flour wet with one-half cup of cold milk, the yolks of three eggs beaten, one small cup sugar; mix these together; put one quart of milk in a kettle and set it in boiling water; when the milk is at the boiling point, stir in the above mixture with vanilla or rose flavouring; stir till it begins to thicken, then take it off and let it cool a little; pour it into a pudding dish or cups; then beat the whites of the eggs to a stiff froth, add a teaspoon of fine white sugar, and drop it on the top of the custard in rounds about as large as an egg; put a small spoon of currant or other tart jelly on the middle of each round; serve cold.

POUND CAKE PUDDING.

Mrs. E. L. Nichols.

One cup sugar, one-half of butter, rub to a cream, add one cup of milk, three eggs, the yolks and whites beaten separately, one teaspoon of soda in the milk, two teaspoons of cream tartar in the flour; fruit; bake or steam an hour.

MADEIRA PUDDING.

Mrs. J. H. Mead.

Four eggs, four tablespoons butter, sugar and flour; beat all very light and then add flavouring; bake in small cups in a quick oven; serve immediately, with sauce.

MATRIMONY SAUCE.

Put a bit of butter into cold water in a saucepan, dust in a little flour, stirring one way till they are completely mixed; then add some brown sugar and a tablespoonful or so of vinegar; continue stirring till it boils; pour into a sauce dish and serve with your dumplings.

PUDDING—APPLE AND LEMON.

Mrs. R. Beaty.

Four eggs, whites of three to be kept for the top, six apples stewed or grated fine, four ounces of butter, six ounces of white sugar, juice and rind of one lemon. It is nicer cold.

PRESERVES PUDDING.

Mrs. R. Beaty.

One pint of bread crumbs, one quart of milk, eight tablespoons sugar, yolks of four eggs; beat yolks and sugar together, then stir in the crumbs with the *boiling* milk and the rind of one lemon. When the pudding is done, beat the whites to a stiff froth with two tablespoons white sugar. Spread the pudding with jam or jelly over the top, then put on the whites of egg and bake to a light brown.

TEN CENT PUDDING.

Mrs. Joseph Robinson.

One cup of molasses, one cup of suet, one cup of currants, one cup of raisins, one and a half cups of milk, quarter of a teaspoonful of soda, three cups flour, spices to taste, and a little brandy or whiskey. If mixed over night so much the better, adding the soda in the morning dissolved in a little warm water; tie in a cloth like plum pudding, and steam three hours. This size must not be boiled. If double quantity is made four hours' steaming is required. Sauce made as for plum pudding, or wine sauce. This pudding is very nice warmed up the second day.

BATTER PUDDING.

Mrs. H. L. Bristol.

One pint of milk, four eggs, the yolks and whites beaten separately, ten tablespoons of sifted flour, a little salt; beat in the whites of the eggs the last thing before baking; bake half an hour.

STEAMED BATTER PUDDING.

Mrs. M. G. Hubbell.

Two eggs to two teacups of sour milk, two teaspoons

saleratus and salt; stir very thick or it will be heavy; then add any fruit you wish; steam two hours; eaten with sweetened cream.

AMHERST PUDDING.

Mrs. F. M. Cragin.

Three cups of flour, one of suet, one of milk, one of molasses, two of raisins; salt and spice to your taste; one teaspoon saleratus; boil in a bag three hours. For sauce: One cup of sugar, one-half of butter, one egg.

CUP PUDDINGS.

Mrs. Midgley.

Three eggs, three-quarters of a cup of sugar, the same of flour, the same of milk, about half a cup of butter, and a teaspoonful and a half of baking powder; butter your cups, pour in a small quantity of preserves, then fill with batter half way, and steam twenty minutes.

MARMALADE PUDDINGS.

Mrs. J. H. Mead.

Half pound suet, half pound grated bread crumbs, half pound sugar, three ounces orange marmalade; mix these ingredients together with four eggs; boil four hours. Lay a few raisins open in the bottom of the mould. Sauce: Two ounces butter, and two ounces white sugar; beat to a cream and flavour with brandy or lemon.

SUET PUDDING.

Mrs. J. H. Mead.

Half pound stale bread crumbs, three-quarters of a pound of flour, ten or twelve ounces of beef suet, half a teaspoon of salt, two eggs well beaten, one cup milk; make into a smooth paste; add fruit if desired; boil three and a half hours.

POTATO PUDDING.

Mrs. P.

One pound of potatoes, half pound sugar, half pound butter, eight eggs, a nutmeg, sweet and bitter almonds to taste, one glass spirits, a small cup of cream; potatoes and butter to be beaten to a cream, then the other ingredients added and let stand for two hours before it is ovened. This quantity makes a large pudding.

APPLE AND BREAD-CRUMB PUDDING.

Mrs. S. McMaster.

Pare and chop fine half a dozen cooking apples, grease a pudding dish and put in a layer half an inch thick of grated bread, add bits of butter, put in a layer of chopped apples with sugar and nutmeg, and repeat till the dish is full; pour over the whole a teacup of cold water; bake thirty minutes. Requires no sauce.

COTTAGE PUDDING.

Two eggs, one cup sugar, one cup milk, three and a half cups flour, one teaspoon soda, two cream tartar, one tablespoon butter melted and put in the last thing; steam one and a half or two hours.

PARADISE PUDDING.

One pint bread crumbs, one pint suet, four eggs, four apples minced fine, one cup currants, half-cup raisins, one cup milk, spice to taste; thicken with flour, one and a half cups sugar; put in a mould and steam or boil three and a half hours.

SWEET MANCHESTER PUDDING.

One pint bread crumbs, three eggs, one cup sugar, one pint milk, piece of butter size of an egg, flavour with lemon; put a layer of bread crumbs in the dish, then one of jam, and so on till full; finish with crumbs; pour the custard on the top. To be eaten with cream.

SMALL AND CHEAP PLUM PUDDING.

One cup suet, one cup raisins, one cup currants, one cup molasses, one egg, four cups flour, one cup milk, one teaspoon soda, one teaspoon cloves, one teaspoon cinnamon; boil or steam three hours.

QUEEN OF PUDDINGS.

One pint of bread crumbs, one quart milk, four eggs, (the yolks), piece of butter size of an egg, sugar to sweeten, flavour with lemon. When baked, spread with jelly, then the whites of the eggs beaten to a stiff froth, with a little sugar and lemon spread on the top; brown slightly in a hot oven. To be eaten with sugar and cream.

SUET PUDDING.

One cup suet, one of bread crumbs, one of flour, half-cup of milk with half a teaspoonful of soda, one cup molasses, one spoonful cream tartar. If you wish to make it richer, add a cup of currants and a few raisins.

DELIGHTFUL PUDDING.

One quart boiled milk, put one half of a tumbler of mashed potatoes, one half tumbler of flour, and a small piece of butter; when cool add three beaten eggs; bake half an hour. To be eaten with sugar and cream or milk.

ANOTHER.

One cup sugar, one egg, one spoonful of butter, one cup sweet milk, one pint flour, two and a half teaspoons of baking powder; bake three quarters of an hour; serve with sauce.

COTTAGE PUDDING.

Mrs. D. McCraney.

Two cups of flour, one of sugar, one and a half cups of milk, two tablespoons butter, one or two eggs, one teaspoonful of cream of tartar and soda. Flavour with lemon; bake one hour in a moderate oven; serve with cream or sauce.

FRENCH RICE PUDDING.

Mrs. D. McCraney.

Steam or carefully cook one cup full of rice. Meanwhile take six grated tart apples, yolks of four eggs, one cup of sugar, nutmeg to taste, one glass best wine, and one lemon, part of juice of which you reserve for whites of eggs; bake these, well whipped together, in the oven. Then form a pyramid of layers of rice and the apple mixture, making the first and last of rice; then take the whites of the eggs whipped stiff and flavoured with the lemon juice; cover the whole evenly with a long bladed knife dipped in cold water; sift and put white sugar over the whole, and place in the oven until of a delicate brown colour. If the sugar be not sifted on top the surface is only glazed and pasty in appearance.

CHRISTMAS PLUM PUDDING.

Mrs. Snider.

One pound raisins chopped fine, one pound currants, three-quarters pound bread crumbs, half-pound flour, three-quarters pound of beef suet, three eggs, one-half pound citron and lemon peel, half a nutmeg, and one teaspoon ground ginger, two teaspoons cook's friend, sweet milk enough just to wet all; tie in a cloth and boil three hours.

STEAMED PUDDING.

Mrs. Snider.

One cup molasses, one cup suet, three cups flour, one cup sour milk, one teaspoon soda, two teaspoons cream tartar, one teaspoon ginger, one cup each of currants and raisins; steam two hours.

APPLE PUDDING.

Mrs. Snider.

Pare and slice half a dozen cooking-apples; grease a

pudding-dish, put a thick layer of grated bread crumbs, add bits of butter, then a layer of apples, with sugar and nutmeg, and repeat until the dish is full; pour over the whole a teacup of cold water, and bake thirty minutes.

PLUM PUDDING.

Miss M. R. Beard.

Half pound of raisins, quarter pound of currants, quarter pound of sugar, bread crumbs, quarter of a pound of flour, half pound suet, six eggs, half cup milk; nutmeg, cinnamon, and salt; half pound citron and lemon peel; to boil five hours.

CHARLOTTE PUDDING.

Miss L. Stagman.

Heat three pints of milk to a boiling point; stir into it the yolks of eight eggs well beaten, and one large tablespoonful of corn starch; let it then thicken a little, and sweeten and flavour to taste. Lay slices of sponge cake in a pudding dish; pour over the pudding; add to the top of it the whites of eight eggs well beaten, and flavour with lemon; then set it in the oven to brown lightly. To be eaten cold.

BREAD PUDDING.

Mrs. Freeman.

Soak a pint of bread crumbs in milk for an hour, then squeeze with the hands to a pulp, and mix well with a gill of milk; then add three tablespoons of sugar, one-quarter pound raisins, one-quarter pound of melted butter, and the yolks of four eggs; then beat the whites of the eggs to a froth and mix with the rest; turn the mixture into a dish and bake about forty minutes. Serve with wine sauce, hot or cold, according to taste.

BAKED CRACKER PUDDING.

Mrs. H. P. Stowell.

Two quarts of sweet milk, seven Boston butter crackers rolled, three eggs, a little nutmeg, a little salt, sweeten with sugar to taste. Bake two hours and a half in a moderate oven.

THE QUEEN OF PUDDINGS.

Mrs. John Morse.

One pint of bread crumbs, one pint of milk, the yolks of three eggs; bake in the oven a short time, until it becomes stiff; then place preserves over this, and beat the whites of the three eggs to a froth and lay all over this again; sprinkle white sugar on the top, and allow it to brown in the oven for a few minutes.

FIG PUDDING.

Mrs. John Morse.

Half pound suet, one pound figs, chopped; one pound bread crumbs, half pound sugar, one egg, one nutmeg, half teaspoonful of baking soda; grease the tin mould well; boil three hours tied in a cloth; it requires milk enough to moisten it, one cup of flour; to be eaten with *wine* sauce.

APPLE BREAD PUDDING.

Mrs. O. L. Wheelock.

Pare, core, and chop one-half dozen sour apples; dry bread in the oven until crisp, then roll; butter a deep dish and place in it a layer of crumbs and apples alternately, with spice, and one-half cup of beef suet chopped fine; pour in one-half pint of sweet milk, and bake till nicely browned; serve with hard sauce.

APPLE PUDDING.

Mrs. W. Guthrie.

Five eggs, one pint milk, four tablespoons flour, four apples grated; bake one hour and a quarter. Serve with sweetened cream or pudding sauce.

APPLE SAGO PUDDING.

Mrs. K.

One cup sago in a quart of tepid water, with a pinch of salt, soaked for one hour; six or eight apples, pared and cored, or quartered, and steamed tender, and put in the pudding dish; boil and stir the sago until clear, adding water to make it thin, and pour it over the apples; this is good hot with butter and sugar, or cold with cream and sugar.

HUCKLEBERRY PUDDING.

Mrs. Bartlett.

One brick loaf, wet it with boiling milk, say one pint, four eggs, little salt, and one quart of berries. Boil one and a half hours. Serve with wine sauce.

BLACKBERRY PUDDING OR OTHER BERRIES.

M.

One and one-half pints sifted flour; put a little of this into one and one-half pints of fresh berries. To the balance of the flour add salt sufficient to season, one even teaspoon soda dissolved in one-half teacup of sweet milk, then fill the cup three-fourths full of syrup or molasses; stir all into a smooth batter; lastly add the berries; mix lightly so as not to break. Put into a buttered mould and place in boiling water that does not quite reach the top of the mould. Do not let it stop boiling for an instant. It must boil *at least* two hours. Serve with boiled sauce.

FIG PUDDING.

E. M. Walker.

One-half pound figs, one-quarter pound grated bread, two and a half ounces powdered sugar, three ounces butter, two eggs, one teacup of milk. Chop the figs small and mix first with the butter, then all the other ingredients by degrees; butter a mould, sprinkle with bread crumbs, cover it tight and boil for three hours.

PLAIN FRUIT PUDDING.

Mrs. Hamilton.

One cup of suet, three cups flour, one cup currants, one cup of molasses, one cup of milk, one teaspoon of soda, one of salt, one of ginger, half teaspoon cloves, and one of cinnamon. Steam or boil three or four hours.

BATTER PUDDING.

Mrs. Hamilton.

Allow a pint of cold milk, four tablespoonsful of flour, two eggs, and a little salt; stir the flour smooth in a part and beat them well with the mixed flour; then add the remainder of the milk, and when well stirred together pour into a buttered dish and bake half an hour.

TAPIOCA PUDDING.

Mrs. J. D. Odell.

Soak one cup of tapioca over night, peel and core as many apples as needed, and fill the cores with sugar; place them in a dish and pour over the tapioca, and bake until transparent.

CURRANT PUDDING.

Mrs. Bartlett.

Slice a baker's loaf, add butter, stew and sweeten three pints of currants, turn over the bread, and set away until cold. Serve without sauce; slice the bread thin.

LEMON PUDDING.

Mrs. Wyllie.

Half pound of sugar, half pound of butter, five eggs, half gill brandy, rind and juice of one large lemon; beat well the butter and sugar; whisk the eggs; add them to the lemon, grate the peel; line a dish with puff paste and bake in a moderate oven.

BAKED BATTER PUDDING.

Mrs. Wyllie.

Beat separately the yolks and whites of three eggs, mix three tablespoons of flour with a pint of milk and a small piece of butter; add the eggs; bake in a quick oven. Serve with sauce.

STEAM PUDDING.

Mrs. Wyllie.

One and a-half cups flour, one and a-half cups suet, one cup of currants, one cup of golden syrup, spices to taste, two teaspoons cream of tartar. Steam four hours.

CHERRY PUDDING.

H. N. Jenks.

A pint of bread crusts or soft crackers, scalded in a quart of boiling milk, piece of butter the size of an egg, one teaspoon of salt, three eggs, one and a half teacups of sugar if eaten without sauce, and if with sauce a tablespoon of sugar; a pinch of pulverized cinnamon, and a quart of stoned cherries; bake quickly.

JELLY PUDDING.

Mrs. C. H. Wheeler.

One quart of milk, one pint of bread crumbs, yolks of four beaten eggs, one-half cup of sugar; bake about half an hour; when cool, spread jelly over the pudding, beat the whites with a little sugar, and spread on top for frosting; set back in the oven a few minutes after the whites have been spread on the pudding; excellent for Sunday dinners, as it may be eaten cold.

KISS PUDDING.

Mrs. C. Belford.

One quart of milk, three tablespoons of corn starch, yolks of four eggs, half cup sugar, and a little salt; put part of the milk, salt, and sugar on the stove and let it boil; dissolve the corn starch in the rest of the milk; stir into the milk, and while boiling add the yolks. Flavour with vanilla.

FROSTING.—Whites of four eggs beaten to a stiff froth, half a cup of sugar; flavour with lemon, spread it on the pudding, and put it into the oven to brown, saving a little of the frosting to moisten the top; then put on grated cocoanut to give it the appearance of snow flake.

CABINET PUDDING.

Mrs. Wyllie.

Take three or four penny sponge cakes, cut into squares; line a well buttered mould with raisins; place the cake in the mould, adding raisins; pour over a rich custard, and steam for one and a half hours.

TO MAKE A DANDY PUDDING.

Miss Brokovski.

One pound of flour, half a pound of currants, half a pound of suet, four ounces of treacle, a little nutmeg; mix it well together with milk, and boil it four hours.

MERINGUE PUDDING.

Mrs. O. A. Rogers.

One pint of stale bread crumbs, one quart of milk, the yolks of four eggs, butter the size of an egg, a small cup of sugar, salt, the grated rind of one lemon; bake three-quarters of an hour. When cool, spread the top with preserves or jelly; beat the whites of the eggs with five tablespoons of pulverized sugar; spread on the pudding, and brown in a quick oven; eat with cream.

ORANGE PUDDING.

Mrs. J. G. Hamilton.

Peel and cut five sweet oranges into thin slices, taking out the seeds; pour over them a coffee cup of white sugar; let a pint of milk get boiling hot, by setting it in a pot of boiling water; add the yolks of three eggs well beaten, one tablespoon of corn starch, made smooth with a little cold milk; stir all the time; as soon as thickened, pour over the fruit. Beat the whites to a stiff froth, adding a tablespoon of sugar, and spread over the top for frosting; set it in the oven for a few minutes to harden; eat cold or hot (better cold), for dinner or supper. Berries or peaches can be substituted for oranges.

LEMON PUDDING.

Mrs. White.

Put in a basin one-fourth pound of flour, the same of sugar, same of bread crumbs and chopped suet, the juice of one good-sized lemon, and the peel grated; two eggs, and enough milk to make it the consistency of porridge; boil in a basin for one hour; serve with or without sauce.

CRACKED WHEAT PUDDING.

Mrs. A. M. Lewis.

Cook cracked wheat enough for two meals; stir in a few minutes before taking up, raisins, dates, or any dried fruit; next day prepare a custard as usual, and stir thoroughly through the wheat, and bake just long enough to bake the custard; thus you have two desserts with but little trouble. Very palatable and nutritious.

GERMAN PUDDING.

A. S. Ewing.

Beat six eggs separately until very light; add one pint milk to the yolks, six tablespoons flour, one-half spoon butter, one-half nutmeg and saltspoon salt; stir in whites of eggs last. Bake half an hour.

SAUCE.—Six tablespoons sugar, one-half pound butter worked to a cream, one egg, one wineglass wine, one-half nutmeg; put on the fire and let it come to a boil.

CHOCOLATE PUDDING.

Mrs. E. Wood.

One and a half quarts milk, boiled, one-half cake of chocolate stirred in milk, small cup of corn starch dissolved in little water, add two eggs, with one cup of sugar, a little salt. Cream for sauce.

ORANGE PUDDING.

Mrs. S. F. McMaster.

Peel and cut five good sweet juicy oranges into thin slices, taking out all the seeds; pour over them a coffee cup of white sugar. Let a pint of milk get boiling hot by setting in boiling water; add the yolks of three eggs well beaten, one tablespoon corn starch made smooth in a little cold milk; stir all the time, and as soon as thickened pour over the fruit. Beat the whites to a stiff froth; add a tablespoon sugar and spread it on for frosting; set it in the oven a few minutes to harden. Substitute any fruit if you prefer; peaches are nice done this way.

STEAM PUDDING.

Mrs. B.

Two cups flour, half cup suet, one cup sugar, one cup milk, one egg, a teaspoonful of soda, fruit to suit your taste; steam two and a half hours.

CARROT PUDDING.

Mrs. McMaster.

One and a half cups flour, one cup sugar, one cup suet, one cup raisins, one cup currants, one cup potatoes grated, one cup carrots grated, one teaspoon soda; steam or boil three hours.

BOILED PLUM PUDDING.

Mrs. Hill.

One cup milk, one cup molasses, one cup suet chopped,

one cup raisins, one teaspoon soda, three cups flour, half a nutmeg; boil three hours and serve with wine sauce.

TAPIOCA PUDDING.

Mrs. Rice.

Cover three tablespoons tapioca with water; stand over night; add one quart milk, a small piece of butter, a little salt, and boil; beat the yolks of three eggs with a cup of sugar, and boil the whole to a very thick custard; flavour with vanilla; when cold cover with whites of eggs beaten.

CREAM TAPIOCA PUDDING.

Mrs. A. T. Hall.

Soak three tablespoons of tapioca in water over night; put the tapioca into a quart of boiling milk, and boil half an hour; beat the yolks of four eggs with a cup of sugar: add three tablespoons of prepared cocoanut; stir in and boil ten minutes longer; pour into a pudding dish; beat the whites of the four eggs to a stiff froth, stir in three tablespoons of sugar; put this over the top and sprinkle cocoanut over the top and brown for five minutes.

SNOW PUDDING.

Mrs. D.

One-half package Coxe's gelatine; pour over it a cup of cold water and add one and one-half cups of sugar; when soft, add one cup boiling water, juice of one lemon and the whites of four well beaten eggs; beat all together until very light; put in glass dish and pour over it custard made as follows : One pint milk, yolks of four eggs and grated rind of one lemon; boil. Splendid.

RICE SNOW BALLS.

Boil a pint of rice in two quarts of water, with a teaspoon of salt, until quite soft, then put it in small cups, having them quite full; when perfectly cold, turn them into a dish, take the yolks of three eggs, one pint of milk, one teaspoon corn starch; flavour with lemon, and cook as you do soft custard; turn over the rice half an hour previous to eating it. This is a nice dessert in hot weather. Sweet meats are a good accompaniment.

CHOCOLATE PUFFS.

Mrs. O. L. Parker.

One pound sugar sifted, one of chocolate chopped very fine; mix together; beat the white of an egg, and stir in your chocolate and sugar; continue to beat until stiff paste; sugar your paper, drop them on it, and bake in a slow oven.

CREAM PUFFS.

Mrs. Watson Thatcher.

One and one-half cups of flour, two-thirds of a cup of butter, one-half pint of boiling water; boil butter and water together, and stir in the flour while boiling; let it cool, and add five well-beaten eggs; drop on tins, and bake thirty minutes in a quick oven. Fill them with the following: One pint of milk, one cup of sugar, two-thirds of a cup of flour, two eggs; beat the eggs, flour, and sugar together, and stir them in the milk while it is boiling. When partially cool flavour with lemon. These are favourites in bake shops.

DESSERT PUFFS.

Mrs. N. C. Gridley.

One pint sweet milk, scant pint flour, three eggs, (whites and yolks beaten separately); bake in cups. To be eaten with liquid sauce.

PUFF PUDDING.

Mrs. C. A. Rogers.

Five tablespoons of flour, five tablespoons of milk, five eggs stirred smooth; turn on a pint of boiling milk, and bake twenty minutes. To be eaten with hard sauce

GERMAN PUFFS.

H. M. Brewer.

One pint sweet milk, five tablespoons flour, one tablespoon melted butter, six eggs, leaving out the whites of three; bake in buttered cups, half filled, twenty minutes in hot oven.

For Sauce.—Beat the whites of five eggs to a stiff froth, and one coffee cup powdered sugar, and the juice of two oranges; turn the pudding from the cups on to a platter, and cover with the sauce just before sending to the table.

GERMAN PUFFS.

Mrs. E. P. Thomas.

One pint sweet milk, four eggs, five tablespoons flour, and a little salt. Bake three quarters of an hour.

LEMON FRITTERS.

After Marion Harland.

Beat up the whipped and strained yolks of five eggs with one-half a cup of powdered sugar; add the grated peel of half a lemon, one teaspoon of mingled nutmeg and cinnamon, a little salt, and one-half a cup of cream; then the whites of the eggs, and then two heaping cups of prepared flour; work all together quickly and lightly into a soft paste, just stiff enough to roll out; pass the rolling-pin over it until it be about three-quarters of an inch thick; cut into small circular cakes with a tumbler or cake-cutter, and fry in hot lard. They ought to puff up like crullers. Drain on clean hot paper, and eat warm with a sauce made of the juice of two lemons and the grated peel of one, one cup of powdered sugar, one glass of wine, and the whites of two eggs beaten stiff.

PUDDING SAUCES.

*"I crack my brains to find out tempting sauces,
And raise fortifications in the pastry."*

PUDDING SAUCE.

Anonymous.

One cup of butter, one cup of milk, one cup of sugar, three eggs, flavour to taste.

PUDDING SAUCE.

Mrs. Dunham.

One-half cup of butter, one cup of sugar, two eggs well beaten, and pour on one cup of bo'ling water; flavour with nutmeg or other flavour.

PUDDING SAUCE.

Mrs. A. R. Scranton.

Four tablespoons of white sugar, two tablespoons of butter, one tablespoon of flour; beat all to a cream and add the white of one egg well beaten; then add one gill boiling water; stir well; flavour to taste.

FOAMING SAUCE.

Mrs. King.

One-half teacup of butter, the same of sugar; beat to a froth; put in a dish and set in a pan of hot water;

add a tablespoon of hot water, or if preferred a little vanilla; stir one way until it comes to a very light foam.

WINE PUDDING SAUCE.

One cup of sugar, one-half cup butter, one-half cup of wine, one egg; beat butter, sugar, and eggs together; set it on the stove and heat, pour in the wine, add a little nutmeg; pour from one dish to another a few times, and send to the table.

WINE SAUCE.

M. A. T.

Two teacups of sugar, one teacup of butter, ; stir to a cream; beat two eggs very light, and stir all together; add one teacup of wine; mix and set on top of tea kettle of boiling water. It must not be put on the stove, nor boil.

PUDDING SAUCE.

Mrs. R. Beaty.

One cup of milk, one teaspoonful butter, one egg, one-half cup pulverized sugar, one glass wine, nutmeg, one teaspoonful corn starch; beat sugar and butter together well; beat the egg well, and mix. Boil the milk and cornstarch, and mix all together before bringing to table.

EXTRA NICE PUDDING SAUCE.

Mrs. Hamilton.

One cup of butter, two of sugar, well beaten, then

add two eggs and beat some-time; when ready for cooking add a cup of sherry wine, and put it over a pot of boiling water, and let it cook ten minutes, stirring very often. It is then ready for the table.

PUDDING SAUCE.

Mrs. B. P. Hutchinson.

Two eggs well beaten, one cup pulverized sugar. When mixed pour over one cup boiling milk, and stir rapidly. Flavour as you please.

PUDDING SAUCE.

Mrs. Andrews.

One cup of sugar, one-half cup of butter, yolks of three eggs; one teaspoon of corn starch or arrow root; stir the whole until very light; add sufficient boiling water to make the consistency of thick cream; wine or brandy to suit the taste.

SAUCE FOR APPLE PUDDING.

M.

Boil good molasses with a little butter and serve hot.

HARD SAUCE FOR PUDDINGS, RICE, ETC.

M.

Take one teacup sugar, one-half teacup butter, stir together until light; flavour with wine or essence of lemon. Smooth the top with a knife and grate nutmeg over it.

WINE SAUCE.

Brown one cup of sugar and a piece of butter the size of a hen's egg, in a saucepan. Pour two-thirds of a teacup of boiling water slowly over the mixture; when ready to serve add one-half cup of currant wine.

WINE SAUCE.

Mrs. Pulsifer.

Two ounces of butter, two teaspoons of flour, one-quarter of a pound of sugar, one gill of wine, and half a nutmeg grated; mix the flour and butter together, add one-half pint boiling water and the sugar and wine, just before serving add the grated nutmeg. Serve hot.

GERMAN SAUCE.

M. D. Harris.

The whites of two eggs, the juice of one lemon, sugar enough to beat up to a proper consistenc for serving.

PIES.

PASTRY.

> Drink now the strong beer,
> Cut the white loaf here,
> The while the meat is ashredding
> For the rare mince pie,
> And the plums stand by
> To fill the paste that's a kneading.
> —Old Song.

FINE PUFF PASTRY.

One pound of flour, a little more for rolling pin and board, and half a pound of butter and half a pound of lard. Cut the butter and lard through the flour (which should be sifted) into small thin shells and mix with sufficient ice water to roll easily. Avoid kneading it and use the hands as little as possible in mixing.

PLAINER PASTRY.

One cup of butter, one cup of lard, a little salt, cut through the flour and mix lightly together. Some cooks mix the lard through the flour and mix with water and then roll out; when in a sheet cut the batter into thin sheets, fold over and lay aside, cutting off from the roll what is used for the bottom or top crust as wanted.

PASTRY OF GRAHAM FLOUR.

Half a pound of Graham flour, one cup of sweet cream, a little salt; mix and roll and bake in the usual way with fruit between the crusts.

RICE PIE.

Mrs. A. S. Ewing.

One quart of milk, boiled; one small teacup of rice flour mixed in a little cold milk; add to the boiling milk two tablespoons of butter; when cold, add five eggs well beaten; sweeten to taste; flavour with vanilla, and bake.

FRUIT PIE.

Mrs. L. P. Carr.

Must be baked in a two-quart tin basin; to give it the right shape the basin must be of nearly the same size top and bottom; first make a nice pie crust; put a layer of it in the bottom, but not around the side of the dish; then a layer of chopped sour apples, two inches thick; then a layer of chopped raisins; sprinkle sugar over this, pieces of butter, and any spice you like—cloves and nutmeg are nice; another layer of crust and fruit, etc., until your dish is full; put a crust on the top; bake slowly for two hours; when done, turn bottom upwards on a plate, and before putting it on the table sprinkle fine sugar over it. It is quite as good when warmed again as when first baked. It takes one pound of raisins, ten or twelve good sized apples, two large cups of sugar, more if you like.

CENTENNIAL APPLE PIE.

Miss L. Winstanley.

Peel one dozen and a half of good apples, take out the cores, cut them small, put into a stewpan that will just hold them with a little water, a little cinnamon, two cloves, the rind of a lemon; stew over a slow fire until quite soft, then sweeten them, pass it through a hair sieve, add the yolks of four eggs and one white, quarter of a pound of good butter, half a nutmeg, the peel of a lemon grated, and the juice of one lemon; beat all well together; line the inside of the pie dish with good puff paste; put in the pie and bake half an hour.

PUMPKIN PIE.

Mrs. Carson.

One quart of strained pumpkins, two quarts rich milk, one teaspoon of salt, and two of ginger cooked with the pumpkins; six well beaten eggs, and one and a half teacups of sugar.

MINCE PIE.

Mrs. Carson.

Three cups chopped cooked meat, six cups of apples chopped fine; make moist with boiled cider and sweeten with molasses or dark sugar; spice to your taste, using cloves, cinnamon, allspice, and a very little black pepper; put currants and raisins into the pies when ready to bake.

PIE PLANT PIE.

Mrs. Carson.

One cup of stewed pie plant, one cup of sugar, one tablespoon of flour, yolk of one egg; flavour with lemon; beat all together thoroughly. Don't use pie plant too hot for fear it will cook the egg. Bake with just an under crust, and use white of an egg for frosting.

LEMON PIE.

Mrs. Carson.

One lemon rind and juice, one cup of sugar, one cup of water, one tablespoon of corn starch cooked in water till thick, three eggs, two of whites saved for frosting, half cup of sugar.

COCOANUT PIE.

Mrs. C. Belford.

One-half pound grated cocoanut, three-quarters of a pound of white sugar, six ounces of butter, five eggs (the whites only), two tablespoonsful rose water, one teaspoonful nutmeg. Cream the butter and sugar, beat till very light, and add the rose water; then add the cocoanut with as little and light beating as possible; finally whip in the stiffened whites of the eggs with a few skilful strokes, and bake at once in open shells. Eat cold, with powdered sugar sifted over them. These are very pretty and delightful pies.

LEMON PIE.

Mrs. George Virtue.

The juice and rind of two lemons, two cups white sugar, one cup of milk, two tablespoonsful corn starch, yolks of ten eggs; bake in two pies; beat the whites of eggs to a froth; beat into it a teaspoonful powdered sugar; pour over the pies, and put in the oven to brown.

MINCE PIES.

Miss Prissie.

Three pounds of raisins, stone and chop them a little; three pounds of currants, three pounds of sugar, three pounds of suet chopped very fine, two ounces candied lemon peel, two ounces of candied orange peel, six large apples grated, one ounce of cinnamon, two nutmegs, the juice of three lemons and the rinds grated, and half a pint of brandy. Excellent.

LEMON PIE.

Miss Prissie.

The juice and rind of one lemon, one cup of sugar, the yolks of two eggs, two tablespoonsful of flour, a teacupful of milk; line the dish with paste; pour in the custard; bake until done; beat the whites of the eggs; add four tablespoonsful of powdered sugar, spread on the pie and brown lightly.

LEMON PIE.

Mrs. Joseph Saulter.

One lemon, one cup of sugar, half a cup water, two eggs, one teaspoonful butter; line your pie plate with a nice crust; pour in the above; bake in a quick oven.

ANOTHER.

One lemon, one tablespoonful corn starch, butter the size of an egg, one teacup of sugar, one teacup water; bake as above.

MOCK MINCE PIES.

Mrs. J. King.

Six tablespoons of rolled crackers, two cups of warm water, one cup of chopped raisins, one cup of whole raisins, half a cup of vinegar, half a cup of melted butter, one cup of yellow sugar, one cup of molasses, one tablespoon cinnamon, cloves, and nutmeg.

LEMON PIE.

Mrs. G. Wyllie.

Half a cup of butter, two cups of sugar, two cups of sweet milk, yolks of six eggs, one tablespoon of flour, one good lemon; use whites for frosting.

LEMON PIE.

Mrs. Carson.

One lemon, juice and rind grated, one cup of sugar, yolks of two eggs, one cup of water, one heaped tablespoonful of corn starch; put all in a small tin pail, stand the pail in a pot of boiling water, and boil thick; make a nice puff paste, line the plate and cook the paste alone; when done a very light brown pour in your mixture; put on the top the whites of the eggs beaten stiff with sugar.

LEMON RAISIN PIE.

Anonymous.

One cup of sugar, one lemon, one cup of raisins, one cup water; chop lemon and raisins fine, cook in the water three-quarters of an hour.

MINCE PIES.

Six pounds of lean fresh beef boiled tender, when cold, chopped fine, a pound of beef suet chopped fine, five pounds of apples chopped, two pounds of raisins, (seeded), two pounds currants, half a pound of citron, two tablespoons of cinnamon, one of grated nutmeg, one tablespoon of cloves, one tablespoon of allspice, one tablespoon of salt, three pounds of brown sugar, a quart of wine, pint of brandy, and the liquor the meat is boiled in. Keep in a stone jar tied over with a double paper. It should be made, at least, the day before it is used, and when you make pies add a little more wine to what you take out for the pies, and more chopped apples.

MINCE MEAT.

Mrs. Higgins.

Six pounds of beef and six pounds of apples, chopped

fine; four pounds of sugar, two of citron, three of raisins, three of currants, one of suet, two quarts of boiled cider, one-half cup of salt, two nutmegs, two tablespoons of ground cloves, two of allspice, two of cinnamon; when used, enough sweet cider should be added to make the mixture quite moist.

MINCE MEAT.
Mrs. J. M. Durand.

Two pounds of raisins, one of currants, one of suet, two and one-half of sugar, one-quarter of citron, one-eighth of cinnamon, two chopped pippins, three lemons, two nutmegs; wine, brandy, and cloves to taste.

MINCE PIE.
Mrs. James Morgan.

Boil beef until tender (three pounds after it is boiled); when cold, chop fine; add three pounds of fine chopped suet, and mix with the beef; add a tablespoon of salt, six pounds of apples, four pounds of currants, six pounds of raisins, two pounds of citron; season to taste with powdered cinnamon, mace, cloves, and nutmeg; add boiled cider, brandy, and wine until quite soft; mix well and pack in stone jars, pour brandy over the top and cover tightly. This will make about five gallons; add two pounds sugar.

MOCK MINCE PIE.
Mrs. G. F. DeForest.

One egg, three or four large crackers, or six or eight

small ones, one-half cup of molasses, one-half cup sugar, one-half cup vinegar, one-half cup strong tea, one cup chopped raisins, a small piece butter, spice and salt.

CREAM PIE.

Mrs. M. A. Green.

Boil nearly one pint of new milk; take two small tablespoons of corn starch beaten with a little milk; to this add two eggs; when the milk has boiled, stir this in slowly with one scant teacup of sugar and one-half cup of butter, two teaspoons of lemon. Cakes: Three eggs, one cup of white sugar, one and a half of flour, one teaspoon of baking powder, mix it in flour; three tablespoons of cold water; bake in two pie-pans in a quick oven; split the cake while hot, and spread in the cream.

ORANGE TART.

Mrs. P.

Squeeze two oranges and boil the rind tender, add half a teacupful of sugar and the juice and pulp of the fruit, an ounce of butter; beat to a paste; line a shallow dish with light puff paste, and lay the paste of orange in it.

MINCE PIE.

Mrs. Samuel Platt.

Two pounds of boiled tongue, four pounds of suet, six pounds of currants, three pounds of chopped apples, the peel and juice of two lemons, a pint of sweet wine, a nutmeg, a quarter of an ounce of cloves, a quarter of an ounce of mace, one pound of citron, one pound of orange and lemon peel.

CRANBERRY TART.

Mrs. P.

Take Cranberries, pick and wash them in several waters, and put them in a dish with the juice of half a lemon, quarter pound of moist sugar or pounded loaf sugar, to a quart of Cranberries; cover it with puff paste or short crust, and bake it three-quarters of an hour. If short crust is used, draw it from the oven five minutes before it is done, and ice it; return it to the oven, and send it to the table cold.

CREAM PIE.

Mrs. John Thomas.

One cup powdered sugar, one cup flour, one teaspoon cream tartar and one-half teaspoon soda, five eggs beaten separately, grated rind of lemon. Cream: Set in hot water one-half pint of milk; when scalding hot add one-half cup sugar, a little salt and one egg beaten together; stir until thick, and when cool add one tablespoon vanilla; put between crusts.

SQUASH PIE.

Mrs. P. B. Ayer.

One crust, one small cup of dry maple sugar dissolved in a little water, two cups of strained squash stirred in the sugar; add four eggs, two teaspoons of allspice, two cups of milk, one teaspoon of butter, and two of ginger, added last. This makes two pies.

SQUASH PIE.

Mrs. L. H. Davis.

Two teacups of boiled squash, three-fourths teacup of brown sugar, three eggs, two tablespoons of molasses, one tablespoon melted butter, one tablespoon ginger, one teaspoon of cinnamon, two teacups of milk, a little salt. Make two plate pies.

CUSTARD PIE.

Mrs. E. E. Marcy.

Make a custard of the yolks of three eggs with milk, season to the taste; bake it in ordinary crust; put it in a brick oven, that the crust may not be heavy, and as soon as that is heated remove it to a place in the oven of a more moderate heat, that the custard may bake slowly and not curdle; when done, beat the whites to a froth; add sugar and spread over the top, and return to the oven to brown slightly; small pinch of salt added to a custard heightens the flavour; a little soda in the crust prevents it from being heavy. Very nice.

TORONTO PIE.

Mrs. D.

One cup of sugar, three eggs, one and one half cups of flour, one teaspoon of baking powder; flavour to taste; bake as for jelly cake in layers, and spread between the layers raspberry jam.

COCOANUT PIE.

Mrs. Thomas.

Grate fresh cocoanut; to one cup of cocoanut add one and one-half cups of sweet milk, the yolks of four eggs, a little salt, and sweeten to taste; one tablespoon of melted butter; beat the whole five or six minutes; beat the whites of the eggs to a stiff froth, and put over the top just long enough to slightly brown before taking the pie from the oven. If you use dessicated cocoanut, soak it in the milk over night.

COCOANUT PIE.

Mrs. Saulter.

One and one-half pints of milk, six eggs, one cocoanut, three cups of sugar, one-half cup of butter; mix sugar and butter, then the eggs, then the cocoanut, and lastly the milk.

LEMON TARTS.

Mrs. Edward Thomas.

Mix well together the juice and grated rind of two lemons, two cups of sugar, two eggs, and the crumbs of sponge cake; beat it all together until smooth; put into twelve patty pans lined with puff paste, and bake until the crust is done.

CUSTARDS, CREAMS, ETC.

"They serve up salmon, venison, and wild boars,
By hundreds, dozens, and by scores,
Hogsheads of honey, kilderkins of mustard,
Plum puddings, pancakes, apple pies, and custard."

RICE CUSTARD.

Mrs. G. M. Dickerman.

To half a cup of rice, add one quart of milk, and a little salt; steam one hour, or until quite soft; beat the yolks of four eggs with four tablespoons of white sugar; add this just before taking off the rice; stir in thoroughly, but do not let it boil any more; flavour with vanilla. Beat the whites of the eggs to a stiff froth, with sugar; after putting the mixture into the pudding dish in which you serve it, put the whites over it, and let it slightly brown in the oven.

RICH CUSTARD.

Mrs. Morgan.

One quart of cream, the yolks of six eggs, six ounces of powdered white sugar, a small pinch of salt, two tablespoons of brandy, one tablespoon of peach water, half a tablespoon of lemon brandy, an ounce of blanched almonds pounded to a paste; mix the cream with the sugar, and the yolks of the eggs well beaten; scald them together in a tin pail in boiling water, stirring all the time until sufficiently thick; when cool, add the other ingredients, and pour into custard cups.

BOILED CUSTARD.

Mrs. T. Kingsford.

Two tablespoons of the corn starch to one quart of milk; mix the corn starch with a small quantity of the milk and flavour it; beat up two eggs. Heat the remainder of the milk to *near* boiling, then add the mixed corn starch, the eggs, four tablespoons of sugar, a little butter and salt. Boil it two minutes, stirring briskly.

BOILED CUSTARD.

Mrs. R. M. Pickering.

One quart milk, eight eggs, one-half pound of sugar; beat to a good froth the eggs and sugar. Put the milk in a tin pail and set it in boiling water; pour in the eggs and sugar and stir it until it thickens.

TAPIOCA CREAM.

Mrs. Bendelari.

One teacup of tapioca, soaked over night in a pint of milk; in the morning add one quart more, and when boiled till the tapioca is clear add the yolks of three eggs, well beaten, with one cup of sugar. Beat the whites to a foam. Sweeten and flavour the whole with vanilla. This pudding is better eaten cold.

CHOCOLATE CUSTARD.

Mrs. Higgins.

Three ounces Baker's chocolate, three pints milk, four tablespoons white sugar, two tablespoons brown sugar; prepare a soft custard of the milk and the yolks of five eggs and the white of one; dissolve the chocolate in a cup of warm milk and heat it to boiling point; when cool, sweeten it with brown sugar and flavour with the extract of vanilla; pour the whole into a dish and cover with the whites of the five eggs beaten stiff, with a little sugar; brown slightly and serve cold.

SAGO CUSTARD.

C. D. Adams.

Three tablespoons sago boiled in a little water till clear; add one quart of milk, let it come to a boil, then add five or six well-beaten eggs and sugar to taste. Put the vessel containing the custard in a kettle of boiling water; stir it briskly till it thickens a little; flavour with vanilla after it is partly cool.

APPLE CUSTARD.

Mrs. F. B. Orr.

Pare, core, and quarter one dozen tart apples, strew into it the grated rind of one lemon; stew until tender in very little water; then mash smooth with back of a spoon. To one and a half pints of strained apple, add one and a quarter pounds sugar; leave it until cold; beat six eggs light and stir alternately into one quart of milk with the apples; put into cups or deep dish, and bake twenty minutes; to be eaten cold.

APPLE CUSTARDS.

Mrs. O. M. Dickerman.

Take six tart apples, pare and quarter them, put into a baking dish with one cup water; cook until tender, but not to pieces, then turn them into a pudding dish and sprinkle sugar over to cover them; beat eight eggs with sugar, and mix with them three pints of milk, a little nutmeg; turn it over the apples, and bake twenty-five minutes.

CARAMEL CUSTARD.

Mrs. Perry Smith.

One quart of milk, one cup of white sugar, one cup of brown sugar, two tablespoons corn starch, four eggs and a pinch of salt and vanilla. Place the milk with the white sugar and salt in a farina kettle over the fire; if you have not such a kettle, a tin pail set in a pot of hot water will answer the purpose; beat the eggs without separating in a large bowl, and wet the corn starch with a little cold milk; put the brown sugar in a tin pan and set over the fire; stir until it is thoroughly scorched, but not burned; then turn the scalding milk on the eggs; put the mixture in the kettle again over the fire; stir in the corn starch until it thickens; lastly, stir in the scorched sugar and remove from the fire; then add a generous amount of vanilla. The scorched sugar falls into the custard in strings, but these will dissolve with vigourous stirring after removal from the fire. Turn into custard glasses and serve cold.

FLOATING ISLAND.

Mrs. E. E. Marcy.

One-half package gelatine, one pint of water; soak twenty minutes; add two cups of sugar; set it on the stove to come to a boil; when nearly cold, add the whites of four eggs beaten stiff, the juice and rind of two lemons, and pour into a mould; turn over the form. Make a custard of the yolks of four eggs, a quart of milk, and a small tablespoonful of corn starch; sweeten to taste.

FLOATING ISLAND.

Mrs. E. S. Miller.

One tumbler of currant jelly, one pint of powdered sugar, five eggs; beat the whites of the eggs very stiff before putting in the jelly; then beat well; add the sugar gradually and beat it perfectly stiff; chill it thoroughly on the ice and serve in a glass dish half filled with cold milk; cover it with the island in spoonsful standing in peaks. It is to be eaten with cream.

APPLE FLOAT.

Mrs. O. L. Parker.

To one quart of apples, partially stewed and well mashed, put the whites of three eggs well beaten, and four heaping tablespooons of loaf sugar; beat them together for fifteen minutes, and eat with rich milk and nutmeg.

WHIPPED CREAM.

Mix one pint of cream with nine tablespoons of fine sugar and one gill of wine in a large bowl; whip these with the cream dasher, and as the froth rises, skim into the dish in which it is to be served. Fill the dish full to the top, and ornament with kisses or macaroons.

SPANISH CREAM.

Mrs. J. H. Brown.

Boil one ounce of gelatine in one pint of new milk until dissolved; add four eggs well beaten and half a pound of sugar; stir it over the fire until the eggs thicken; take it off the fire and add a full wine-glass of peach water; and when cool pour it into moulds; serve with cream.

VELVET CREAM.

Mrs. R. Harris.

Nearly a box of gelatine, soaked over night in a cup of wine; melt it over the fire, with the sugar; when it is warm, put in a quart of cream or new milk and strain it into moulds. If the wine is too hot, it will curdle the milk.

CHOCOLATE CREAM.

Mrs. Spruance.

Soak one box of Coxe's English gelatine (in cold water sufficient to cover) one hour; one quart of milk boiled;

scrape two ounces of French chocolate, mix with eight spoons of white sugar; moisten this with three spoons of the boiling milk; then stir in the gelatine and the yolks of ten well-beaten eggs; stir three minutes briskly; take off, strain, and add two teaspoons of vanilla; strain and put in moulds to cool. Serve with sugar and cream.

CHOCOLATE CREAM.

Mrs. King.

Half a cake of chocolate dissolved in a little hot water; put in a cup of milk, and when it boils have five eggs well beaten and mixed with two cups of milk; pour the hot chocolate into the eggs and milk; stir well and boil all together for a few minutes; sweeten to your taste. To be eaten cold.

COCOANUT PUFFS.

The whites of three eggs, one cup of ground sugar, one teaspoonful of the extract of vanilla, one tablespoonful of corn starch, two cups of dessicated cocoanut. Beat the whites well, then add the sugar, and beat over steam, until a crust forms on the bottom and sides of the dish. Take it off the steam, add the other ingredients and drop in small pieces on buttered tins. Bake rather quickly to a light brown.

CHOCOLATE CARAMELS.

Miss E. Winstanley.

One cup of grated chocolate, three cups of sugar, one cup of molasses, one cup of milk, and a small piece of butter. Boil for about twenty minutes, stirring all the time; pour into a buttered pan; when nearly cold mark off in small squares.

COFFEE CREAM.

Soak half an ounce of Coxe's gelatine in a little cold water half an hour; then place it over boiling water and add one gill of strong coffee and one gill of sugar; when the gelatine is well dissolved, take from the fire; stir in three gills of cold cream and strain into your mould. Be sure that this has been previously wet with cold water.

ORANGE CREAM.

Make according to above rule, adding one gill of orange juice and the grated rind of one orange which has been previously soaked in the orange juice while the gelatine is dissolving over the boiling water, and the beaten yolks of two eggs when you take off, and quite hot.

APPLE CREAM.

Mrs. Mann.

One cup thick cream, one cup sugar, beat till very smooth; then beat the whites of two eggs, and add; stew apples in water till soft; take them from the water with a fork; steam them if you prefer. Pour the cream over the apples when cold.

FRUIT CREAMS.

These consist of a rich cream; blanc mange poured over fruit and set on ice to chill.

PISTACHIO AND ALMOND CREAMS.

Make a nice vanilla ice-cream; have ready pistachio nuts, which have been prepared by pouring boiling water over them and letting them stand in it a few moments; then strip off the skins and pound to a paste in a mortar, and mix with the cream. Freeze.

ITALIAN CREAM.

E. V. Case.

Take one quart of cream, one pint of milk sweetened very sweet, and highly seasoned with sherry wine and vanilla; beat it with a whip dasher, and remove the froth as it rises until it is all converted into froth. Have ready one box of Coxe's sparkling gelatine dissolved in a little warm water; set your frothed cream into a tub of ice; pour the gelatine into it, and stir constantly until it thickens, then pour into moulds, and set in a cool place.

TAPIOCA CREAM.

Two tablespoons of tapioca dissolved very soft, three yolks of eggs beaten and sweetened to the taste; boil one quart of milk, when cool stir in the tapioca and flavour; beat the whites very light and mix all together; let boil ten minutes, pour into moulds.

TAPIOCA MERINGUE.

Mrs. Spruance.

One teacup of tapioca soaked in one and a half pints of warm water three hours; peel and core eight tart apples; fill apples with sugar, grating a little nutmeg or moistening with wine. One hour before needed pour the tapioca over the apples and bake, serving in the dish baked in. The addition of the whites of four well-beaten eggs spread over the top and browned slightly improves it.

LEMON SPONGE.

Mrs. Lambkin.

Two ounces of gelatine; pour over one pint of cold water; let it stand fifteen minutes; add half a pint of boiling water, three-quarters of a pound of white sugar, and the juice of four lemons. When the gelatine is cold, before it begins to get firm, add the well beaten whites of three eggs; beat the whole fifteen minutes, until the mixture is quite white, and begins to thicken; then put in a mould first wet in cold water.

SNOW SOUFFLE.

Mrs. J. Louis Harris.

Beat the whites of two eggs to a stiff froth; dissolve one-half box of gelatine in a little more than a pint of hot water, two cups of sugar, and the juice of two lemons; when this is dissolved and cooled, stir into it the eggs you have beaten, beat the whole together until it is white and stiff; mould and pour around it soft custard.

CHARLOTTE RUSSE.

Mrs. A. M. Gibbs.

Whip one quart rich cream to a stiff froth, and drain well on a nice sieve. To one scant pint of milk add six eggs beaten very light; make very sweet; flavour high with vanilla. Cook over hot water till it is a thick custard. Soak one full ounce Coxe's gelatine in a very little water, and warm over hot water. When the custard is very cold, beat in lightly the gelatine and the whipped cream. Line the bottom of your mould with buttered paper, the sides with sponge cake or lady-fingers fastened together with the white of an egg. Fill with the cream, put in a cold place or in summer on ice. To turn out dip the mould for a moment in hot water. In draining the whipped cream, all that drips through can be rewhipped.

CHARLOTTE RUSSE.

Mrs. J. P. Holt.

Take one quart of thin cream, sweeten and flavour; whip the cream until all in froth; then take half box of gelatine, put in as little cold water as possible to soak, and set on the stove to melt; have the gelatine cool before putting into the cream; have a dish already lined with cake or lady-fingers, pour the cream into it and set on ice until ready for use.

CHARLOTTE.

Mrs. W. W. Kimball.

One quart rich cream, three tablespoons of Madeira wine, whites of two eggs beaten to a stiff froth, one teacup of powdered sugar, half a box of gelatine dissolved in half a cup of sweet milk; flavour with vanilla; beat the cream and wine together; add the eggs, then the sugar, and last, the gelatine.

RICE CHARLOTTE.

E. M. Walker.

Blanch one-fourth pound of rice, and boil in one quart of milk, with a little sugar and vanilla; when soft, let it cool, and then mix it with one pint of whipped cream; oil a mould and fill with a layer of rice and preserves, or marmalade, alternately; let it stand until stiff, and then turn it out.

BLANC MANGE—ARROWROOT.

Mrs. P. B. Ayer.

Boil one quart of milk, reserving one gill to wet up your arrowroot with; when it boils up, stir in two and a half tablespoons of arrowroot, and after a few minutes add one tablespoon crushed sugar, one tablespoon rosewater, and a little salt; pour into moulds.

CHOCOLATE MANGE.

S. D. F.

One box of Coxe's gelatine dissolved in a pint of cold

water, three pints of milk; put over to boil, with one cup of French chocolate; when the milk is just scalded, pour in the gelatine; sweeten to taste; boil five minutes, then take from the fire, flavour with vanilla, pour into moulds. When cold, serve with powdered sugar and cream.

MONT BLANC.

Mrs. F. B. Orr.

One-third box of gelatine, grated rind of two lemons, two cups of sugar, one pint of boiling water. Before the mixture gets stiff, stir in the whites of five eggs beaten to a stiff froth. Eat with custard, boiled, made with yolks of eggs and one pint of boiling milk. Sweeten to taste, flavour with vanilla. Excellent.

A SIMPLE DESSERT.

A. S. Ewing.

Put a teacup of tapioca into sufficient cold water; boil until the lumps become almost transparent; squeeze the juice of two lemons partially into the mixture, then slice them into it, sweeten or not, then eat when cold, with cream and sugar.

JELLIED GRAPES.

Mrs. A. M. Lewis.

A very delicate dish is made of one-third of a cup of rice, two cups of grapes, half a cup of water, and two spoons of sugar. Sprinkle the rice and sugar among the grapes, while placing them in a deep dish; pour on the water, cover close and simmer two hours slowly in the oven. Serve cream as sauce, or cold as pudding. If served warm as pudding, increase slightly the proportion of rice and sugar.

ICES.

> Glittering squares of coloured ice,
> Sweetened with syrups, tinctured with spice;
> Creams and cordials and sugared dates;
> Syrian apples, Othmanee quinces,
> Limes and citrons and apricots,
> And wines that are known to Eastern princes.
> .   .   .   .
> And all that the curious palate could wish,
> Pass in and out of the cedarn doors.
> —T. B. Aldrich.

Use one part of coarse table salt to two parts of ice broken the size of a walnut. This should be firmly packed around the cream pail to the height of the freezer. For three pints of cream, one and a half pints of water should be poured over the ice in the freezer, and for every additional quart of cream one pint of water should be added to the ice after packing. When there is no ice-cream freezer convenient, ices may be frozen by putting the cream to be frozen in a tin pail with a close cover. This ice and salt for packing may be put in a larger pail and packed firmly around the pail of cream to be frozen. Let this stand to chill for twenty or thirty minutes, then remove the cover and stir the freezing mixture within until stiff. Then re-pack, cover the whole closely with a woollen cloth or carpet and leave for an hour or two in a cool place.

CURRANT ICE.

One pint of currant juice, one pound of sugar, and one pint of water; put in freezer, and when partly frozen add the whites of three eggs well beaten.

ORANGE AND LEMON ICES.

The rind of three oranges grated and steeped a few moments in a little more than a pint of water; strain one pint of this on a pound of sugar and then add one pint of orange or lemon juice; pour in the freezer, and when half frozen add the whites of four eggs beaten to a stiff froth.

ORANGE ICE.

Juice of six oranges, grated peel of three, juice of two lemons, one pint of sugar, one pint of water, and freeze

STRAWBERRY ICE CREAM.

Mrs. Thomas.

Mash with a potato pounder in an earthen bowl one quart of strawberries with one pound of sugar, rub it through the colander and add one quart of sweet cream and freeze. Very ripe peaches or coddled apples may be used instead of strawberries.

LEMON ICE.

Mrs. Carson.

Six lemons, juice of all and grated rind of three, one large sweet orange, juice and rind, one pint of water, one pint of sugar; squeeze out every drop of juice, and steep in it the rind of orange and lemons one hour, strain, squeezing the bag dry; mix in the sugar, and then the water; stir until dissolved, and freeze by turning in a freezer, opening three times to beat all up together. Many prefer it to ice cream.

ORANGE ICE.

Mrs. Carson.

Six oranges, juice of all, and grated peel of three, two lemons, the juice only, one pint of sugar, dissolved in one pint of water; prepare and freeze as you would lemon ice.

ICE CREAM.

M.

One pint milk, yolks of two eggs, six ounces sugar, one tablespoon corn starch; scald until it thickens; when cool, add one pint whipped cream and the whites of two eggs, beaten stiff; sweeten, flavour, and freeze.

ICE CREAM.

Mrs. W. H. Ovington.

Scald one quart of milk with one sheet of isinglass (broken), and a vanilla bean; when cool, strain, mix with one pint of cream whipped to a froth; sweeten to taste and freeze.

A NICE DESSERT DISH.

Mrs. J. Thorney.

Fill a quart bowl with alternate layers of thinly sliced apples and sugar, and add half a cup of water, covered with a saucer, held in place by a weight; bake slowly three hours; let it stand until cold, and you will turn out a round mass of clear red slices, imbedded in firm jelly. For an accompaniment to a dessert of blanc mange, rennet custard, cold rice pudding, or similar dishes, or even with nice bread and butter, there is nothing better.

AN EXCELLENT DESSERT.

Mrs. J. Young Scammon.

One can or twelve large peaches, two coffeecups of sugar, one pint of water and the whites of three eggs; break the peaches with and stir all the ingredients together; freeze the whole into form; beat the eggs to a froth.

DISHES FOR DESSERT.

SNOW DRIFTS.

Mrs. S. McMaster.

Half a box of gelatine, one pint of boiling water, juice of two lemons, two cups of sugar, whites of five eggs; dissolve the gelatine in the water; add the lemon and sugar mixed together; put in mould to cool; when *cool, but not cold*, take the whites of the eggs beaten stiff, sweetened and flavoured, and float them on boiling milk for about one minute. Now take the gelatine from your mould (instantly place the mould in cold water), and with a fork beat up the gelatine that has become firm into *bits*, but not into liquid. Now take your mould and add spoon about of the broken up jelly and the whites of eggs, filling up the mould with the jelly that became soft in spite of you; place to cool. Serve on a dish surrounded by a custard made from the yolks of the eggs and one more; one pint of milk.

MACEDOINE OF FRUIT.

Wine jelly and fruit in alternate layers frozen together. The fruit may be of any and all sorts, and may be candied or preserved, or slices of pear, apple, etc.; may be boiled in syrup and then drained; the mould must be filled after the jelly has begun to form, but before it is stiff, and the first layer should be of jelly; when filled, place the mould in salt and ice prepared as for freezing ice cream; cover closely, and let it remain several hours.

FRUITS.

> "Fruit of all kinds, in coat
> Rough, or smooth rind, or bearded husk, or shell,
> She gathers tribute large, and on the board
> Heaps with unsparing hand."
> —Paradise Lost.

> Bring me berries or such cooling fruit
> As the kind, hospitable woods provide.
> —Cowper.

Fruits for preserving should be carefully selected, removing all that are imperfect. They are in the best condition when not fully ripe, and as soon as possible after they are picked. Small fruits should not be allowed to stand over night after they are picked when they are to be preserved. Use only the finest sugar for preserving. When fruit is sealed in glass cans, wrap paper of two or three thicknesses around the cans. The chemical action of light will affect the quality of the preserves when perfectly air-tight. With this precaution, glass cans are preferable to any other for preserving fruit. One-half a pound of sugar to a pound of fruit is a good rule for canned fruit, although many housekeepers use but one-quarter of a pound of sugar to a pound of fruit.

An excellent rule for canning the larger fruits, as peaches, pears, etc., is to place them in a steamer over a kettle of boiling water, laying first a cloth in the bottom of the steamer. Fill this with the fruit and cover tightly. Let them steam for fifteen minutes, or until they can be easily pierced with a fork, (some fruits will require a longer time). Make a syrup of sugar of the right consistency. As the fruit is steamed, drop each for a moment in the syrup, then place in the cans, having each one-half full of fruit, and then fill up with the hot syrup, then cover and seal.

A SUGGESTION.

For canning all large fruits, where no other method is given by contributors, the directions for canning large fruits are given in the recipe for Preserved Peaches. For canning all of the small fruit, follow the directions given in preserved Cherries. They are both excellent. If less sugar is preferred use one-quarter of a pound of sugar to a pound of fruit. The syrup should be prepared by adding a pint of water in your preserving kettle to each pound and a half of sugar; let it boil up gently and skim until perfectly clear, when it is ready for the fruit.

SUGARED FRUITS.

Beat the white of the egg just enough to break, then dip fine stems of cherries or currants into the egg and then into powdered sugar, and dry on a sieve.

BAKED APPLES.

Pare as many apples as you wish of some nice variety, neither sweet nor sour; core them by using an apple corer or a steel fork; set them in biscuit tins and fill the cavities with sugar, a little butter, and some ground cinnamon, if you like; set them in the oven and bake until done.

BAKED PEARS.

Place in a stone jar, first a layer of pears (without paring); then a layer of sugar, then pears, and so on until the jar is full. Then put in as much water as it will hold. Bake in oven three hours. Very nice.

QUINCE PRESERVE.

Mrs. Bendelari.

Pare, core, and quarter your fruit, then weigh it and allow an equal quantity of white sugar. Take the peelings and cores and put in a preserving kettle; cover them with water and boil for half an hour; then strain through a hair sieve and put the juice back into the kettle and boil the quinces in it a little at a time until they are tender; lift out as they are done with a drainer and lay on a dish; if the liquid seems scarce add more water. When all are done throw in the sugar and allow it to boil ten minutes before putting in the quinces; let them boil until they change colour, say one hour and a quarter, on a slow fire; while they are boiling occasionally slip a silver spoon under them to see that they do not burn, but on no account stir them. Have two fresh lemons cut in thin slices, and when the fruit is being put in jars lay a slice or two in each.

BAKED QUINCES.

One dozen nice quinces, cored and well rubbed. Put in baking pans, and fill the centre with pulverized sugar. Bake and serve cold, with or without cream.

PRESERVED PEACHES.

Select peaches of fine quality and firm. If too ripe they are not likely to keep perfectly. Pare them and place them in a steamer over boiling water and cover tightly; an earthen plate placed in the steamer under the fruit will preserve the juices which afterwards may be strained and added to the syrup. Let them steam for fifteen minutes or until they can be easily pierced with a fork; make a syrup of the first quality of sugar, and as the fruit is steamed drop each peach into the syrup for a few seconds, then take out and place in the cans; when the cans are full, pour over the fruit the hot syrup and seal immediately. Inexperienced house-wives will do well to remember that the syrup should be well skimmed before pouring over the fruit. We prefer the proportions of half a pound of sugar to a pound of fruit for canning, although many excellent house-keepers use less. This rule is excellent for all of the large fruits—as pears, quinces, apples, etc.

PRESERVED PLUMS.

Jennie June.

Allow to every pound of fruit three-quarters of a pound of sugar; put into stone jars alternate layers of fruit and sugar, and place the jars in a moderately warm oven. Let them remain there until the oven is cool. If prepared at tea time let them remain until morning; then strain the juice from the plums, boil and clarify it. Remove the fruit carefully to glass or china jars, pour over the hot syrup and carefully cover with egg, tissue paper, or thick white paper pasted, or bladder tied closely down.

PRESERVED PEARS.

Mrs. Midgley.

To six pounds of pears, four pounds of sugar, two coffee cups of water, the juice of two lemons, and the rind of one, a handful of whole ginger; boil all together for twenty minutes, then put in your pears and boil till soft, say about a quarter of an hour; take them out and boil your syrup a little longer; then put back your fruit and give it a boil; bottle whilst hot; add a little cochineal to give them a nice colour.

PRESERVED CHERRIES.

Jennie June.

Stone the fruit, weigh it, and for every pound take three-quarters of a pound of sugar. First dissolve the sugar in water in the proportion of a pint of water to a pound and a half of sugar; then add the fruit and let it boil as fast as possible for half an hour, till it begins to jelly. As soon as it thickens put in pots, cover with brandied paper, next the fruit, and then cover closely from the air.

CANNED CHERRIES.

Prepared in the same manner, allowing but half a pound of sugar to a pound of fruit; after putting the fruit into the syrup let it scald, (not boil hard), for ten or fifteen minutes and then can and seal. A few of the cherry stones put in a muslin bag and put into the syrup to scald with the fruit imparts a fine flavour; they should not be put in the jars with the fruit. This method is excellent for use with all the small fruits, as strawberries, raspberries, and also plums.

PRESERVED ORANGE PEEL.

Mrs. A. N. Arnold.

Peel the oranges and cut the rinds into narrow shreds, boil till tender, change the water three times, squeeze the juice of the orange over the sugar; put pound to pound of sugar and peel; boil twenty minutes all together.

CITRON PRESERVES.

Carter.

Cut the citron in thin slices, boil in water with a small piece of alum until clear and tender, then rinse in cold water. Make a syrup of three-fourths pound of sugar to a pound of citron; boil a piece of ginger in the syrup; then pour the citron in and let it boil for a few minutes. Put in one lemon to five of the fruit.

SPICED PEACHES OR PEARS.

Mrs. Henry M. Knickerbocker.

To ten pounds good mellow peaches, use five pounds sugar, one pint of good vinegar, and some whole cloves or cinnamon. Take the sugar, vinegar, and cloves, and let them come to a boil, and turn over the fruit. This do three days in succession, and the last day put the fruit into the syrup, a few at a time, and let them just boil up.

CANNED PINE APPLE.

Mrs. F. L. Bristol.

For six pounds of fruit when cut and ready to can make syrup with two and a half pounds of sugar and nearly three pints of water; boil syrup five minutes and skim or strain if necessary; then add the fruit, and let it boil up; have cans hot, fill and shut up as soon as possible. Use the best white sugar. As the cans cool keep tightening them up.

CANNED STRAWBERRIES.

Miss Blaikie.

After the berries are pulled, let as many as can be put carefully in the preserve kettle at once, be placed on a platter. To each pound of fruit add three-fourths of a pound of sugar; let them stand two or three hours, till the juice is drawn from them; pour it in the kettle and let it come to a boil, and remove the scum which rises; then put in the berries very carefully. As soon as they come thoroughly to a boil put them in warm jars, and seal while boiling hot. Be sure the cans are air tight.

CANNED CURRANTS.

Mrs Wicker.

Put sufficient sugar to prepare them for the table, then boil them ten minutes and seal hot as possible.

GELATINE JELLY.

Mrs. W. Arthurs.

Small packet gelatine, pint and a half boiling water poured on the gelatine, stir until dissolved; one teacup of white sugar, a little tartaric acid, the whites of three eggs beaten, flavour with lemon; pour into a shape and let stand till next day.

APPLE PRESERVE, GOOD.

E. Pernet.

Weigh equal quantities of good brown sugar and apples, peel, core, and cut the apples into small square pieces; make a syrup of one pint of water to three pounds of sugar, boil until pretty thick, then add the apples, the grated peel of a lemon or two, a little whole white ginger (if liked); boil until the apples are clear and begin to fall, then it will be done.

TO CAN TOMATOES.

Mrs. Edward Ely.

Wash your tomatoes and cut out any places that are

green or imperfect; then cut them up and put over to cook with a little salt; boil them till perfectly soft; then strain them through a colander; turn them back to cook, and when they have come to boiling heat, pour them into stone jugs (one or two gallon jugs, as you prefer). They will keep a day or two in winter if all are not used at a time; put the cork in, and have some canning cement hot and pour over the cork. The jug must, of course, be hot, when the tomatoes are poured in.

CRANBERRY SAUCE

Mrs. Bartlett.

One quart cranberries, one quart water, one quart sugar, stew slowly.

LEMON BUTTER.

Mrs. D. S. Munger.

Beat six eggs, one-fourth pound butter, one pound sugar, the rind and juice of three lemons; mix together and set in a pan of hot water to cook. Very nice for tarts, or to eat with bread.

PEACH BUTTER.

Mrs. M. L.

Take pound for pound of peaches and sugar; cook peaches alone until they become soft, then put in one-half the sugar, and stir for one-half hour; then the remainder of sugar, and stir an hour and a half. Season with cloves and cinnamon.

TOMATO BUTTER.

Mrs. Johnson.

Nine pounds peeled tomatoes, three pounds sugar, one pint vinegar, three tablespoons cinnamon, one tablespoon cloves, one and one-half tablespoons allspice: boil three or four hours until quite thick, and stir often, that it may not burn.

APPLE JELLY.

Mrs. J. H. Brown.

Take green apples that will cook nicely; quarter the apples without paring, put them in a pan or kettle and cover over with water, and keep them covered; let them boil slowly until entirely done; then put in a bag and drain (not squeeze) them. Put a pound of white sugar to a pint of juice. This is very easily made in the winter; is best made day before using.

APPLE JELLY FOR CAKE.

Mrs. P. B. Ayer.

Grate one large or two small apples, the rind and juice of one lemon; add one cup sugar; boil three minutes.

DAMSON CHEESE.

Mrs. J. H. Mead.

Twelve pounds of damsons; put them into the oven; when they are soft take out the stones, crack them, and then blanch the kernels, then add three and a half pounds of lump sugar; boil about three hours; wet the moulds before using them; weigh the damsons before they are put into the oven.

APPLE JELLY.

Miss Beaty.

Boil tart peeled apples in a little water till glutinous, strain out the juice, and put a pound of white sugar to a pint of juice. Flavour to taste; boil till a good jelly, then put into moulds.

APPLE JELLY.

Take seven pounds of ripe apples—such as are excellent boilers—and if the rind is red the colour of the jelly will be beautifully tinged; cut the fruit in pieces, without peeling or extracting the cores, and only removing the stalks and the eyes; add two quarts of water, and boil or bake till the whole is a pulp, which pour into a jelly bag, placed near the fire, (as the pulp thickens in cooling); add eight ounces of white or loaf sugar to each pint of the liquid, with the juice of a small lemon, and the peel cut very thin; boil to a tolerably thick jelly, which may be ascertained by trying a little on a plate; strain again through the bag or a piece of muslin, and run into moulds or pots. When cold lay a piece of tissue paper over, and put by in a dry place. This jelly will keep two or three years.

TO MAKE AN ORNAMENTAL PYRAMID FOR A TABLE.

Miss Beaty.

Boil loaf sugar as for candy, and rub it over a stiff

form, made for the purpose, of stiff paper, which must be well buttered; set it on a table, and begin at the bottom and stick on to this frame with the sugar a row of macaroons, kisses, or other ornamental articles, and continue till the whole is covered. When cold draw out the pasteboard form and set the pyramid in the centre f the table with a small bit of wax candle burning with it, and it looks very beautiful.

CUSTARD JELLY.

Make a boiled custard of one quart of fresh milk, three eggs, one teacup of sugar, two teaspoons of vanilla; dissolve a half box of gelatine in as little water as will cover it, and when well dissolved add the juice of one lemon and two glasses of sherry; stir the custard well while pouring in this mixture; strain through a sieve into a mould. Serve with whipped cream, flavoured with wine and vanilla, or with rich cream.

SNOW JELLY.

A package of gelatine soaked till quite soft in a cup of cold water, then add about a quart of boiling water; stir till quite dissolved; add juice and grated rind of three lemons; sugar to taste; strain through muslin, and set in a cold place. When quite stiff, beat in the whites of four well-beaten eggs, and then pour into moulds. It will make about a quart and a half. This is very suitable for invalids who cannot take wine, also an exceedingly ornamental jelly.

ORANGE MARMALADE.

Mrs. Midgley.

Nine Seville oranges, three sweet oranges, four lemons cut across the grain as finely as possible; place in a deep dish with four quarts of water; let it stand thirty-six hours; boil two hours, (water as well); then add eight pounds of crushed sugar; boil one hour longer, or until you think it will jelly; the addition of a wineglassful of spirits when nearly boiled has the effect of causing all impurities to rise to the surface, and clarifies the jelly.

APPLE JELLY.

Mrs N. P. Inglehart.

Take juicy apples, (Ramboes, if possible); take the stem and top off, and wash them nicely, then cut up into quarters and put cold water upon them, just enough to cover them: boil them soft, afterward strain them through a jelly bag; then take two pints at a time with two pounds of crushed sugar; boil twenty minutes, then do the same with the other juice; to be economical, pare and core the apples; don't strain so close, but that you can, by adding a little more water, use the apples for sauce or pies.

CRAB APPLE JELLY AND JAM.

Mrs. Ludlam.

Remove stems and blossoms from the apples; let them scald, and pour off the first water; next put them in plenty of water and let them cook slowly; as they begin to soften dip off the juice for jelly, straining it through flannel. One pound of juice to a pound of sugar for jelly. Next add more water; let apples stew very soft; strain through a sieve, which takes out cores and seeds; to this pulp add brown sugar, pound for pound; it needs careful cooking and stirring.

LEMON JELLY.

Mrs. W. Guthrie.

One paper of gelatine; let it stand one hour in warm water; then add one quart of boiling water, the juice of three or four lemons, and a pint and a half of sugar.

ORANGE JELLY.

Mrs. J. P. Hoit.

Soak one package of gelatine in one-half pint cold water for one hour; add the juice of three lemons, two pounds sugar and one quart boiling water; when all are dissolved add one pint of orange juice; strain carefully and set on ice till ready for use; eight oranges usually make it.

CURRANT JELLY.

Mrs. J. P. Hoit.

Jam and strain the currants; to each pint of juice add one pound sugar; boil the juice fifteen minutes without sugar, and the same time after it is in; strain into glasses.

When pouring hot fruit or jelly in cans or glasses, wring a towel out of cold water, lay it on a table, and set the cold cans upon it, pouring the boiling fruit into them.

Care should be taken not to set two cans on the same spot without first wetting the towel.

GELATINE.

Mrs. J. H. Mead.

Take a good packet of gelatine, the juice and rinds of three lemons, soak for one hour in a pint of cold water; then add three pints of *boiling* water, two pounds of white sugar, one pint of wine; strain into moulds, and set out to cool.

TO PRESERVE QUINCES.

Mrs. W. Arthurs.

Pare, core, and quarter a peck of quinces, then weigh them; put the parings, cores, and seeds into a preserving kettle, cover them with water, and boil slowly for twenty minutes; then strain them, put the water back, and put in the quinces, a few at a time, and simmer them gently until tender, say five to ten minutes; lay them on a dish; when all are done add the sugar and a little warm water. Let them boil for a few minutes until clear, then put in all the quinces and boil them without stirring until they become a clear garnet, which will be about one hour. Have ready two lemons sliced thin and seeds taken out; put them in a few minutes before taking off the fire.

CURRANT JELLY.

Mrs. C. Wheeler.

Take the currants when they first ripen; pick them

from the stems and put them on the stove in a stone jar, bruising them with a wooden spoon; then when warm, squeeze through a coarse cloth or flannel, and put the juice on in a new tin pan or porcelain kettle; one quart of juice requires two pounds of sugar, or a pound to a pint; boil fifteen minutes; to be a nice colour the currants should not come in contact with iron spoons or tin dishes, unless new and bright; should be made quickly. It never fails to jelly good if the currants are not too ripe. The same method for jam, only do not strain the currants, but mash them well. Currants should not be dead ripe for jelly or jam.

GOOSEBERRY JELLY.

E. M. Walker.

Boil six pounds of green unripe gooseberries in six pints of water, (they must be well boiled, but not burst too much); pour them into a basin, and let them stand covered with a cloth for twenty-four hours, then strain through a jelly bag, and to every pint of juice add one pound of sugar. Boil it for an hour, then skim it and boil for one half hour longer with a sprig of vanilla.

TO PRESERVE CITRON.

Mrs. W. Arthurs.

Pare the citrons and cut them into slices about an inch and a half thick, then into strips the same thickness, leaving them the full length of the fruit; take out all the seeds with a small knife, then weigh, and to each pound of citron put a pound of white sugar, make a syrup; to ten pounds put a pint of water, and simmer gently for twenty minutes; then put in the citron and boil for one hour, or until tender; before taking off the fire put in two lemons, sliced thin, seeds taken out, and two ounces of root ginger; do not let them boil long after the lemon and ginger are put in; do not stir them while boiling. The above is very fine if carefully attended to.

ARTIFICIAL HONEY.

Mrs. Oliphant.

Mix together ten pounds white sugar, two pounds clear bees' honey, one quart of hot water, half an ounce of cream tartar; when cool flavour with two or three drops otto roses and sprinkle in a handful of clear yellow honey comb broken up. This will deceive the best judges, and is perfectly healthy.

CORN STARCH JELLY.

One quart boiling water; wet five tablespoons corn starch, one teacup sugar, a pinch of salt, with cold water, and one teaspoon lemon or vanilla extract for flavouring; stir the mixture into the boiling water, boil five minutes, stir all the while; pour into cups previously dipped in cold water. This quantity will fill six or seven cups. If wished richer, milk may be used instead of water. Good for invalids.

GELATINE JELLY.

Dissolve one ounce package of sparkling gelatine in a pint of cold water for one hour; add the rind and juice of two or three large lemons, one and a half pounds of sugar, then pour on this mixture one quart of boiling water, add one pint of orange or raspberry juice, and pour into mould. This flavouring is very nice, and is to supersede the necessity of wine, which some consider indispensable in the same proportion.

RHUBARB JAM.

Mrs. T. W. Anderson.

Cut into pieces about an inch long, put a pound of sugar to every pound of rhubarb, and leave till morning; pour the syrup from it and boil till thickens; then add the rhubarb and boil gently fifteen minutes; put up as you do currant jelly in tumblers; it will keep good a year.

GOOSEBERRY JAM.

Take what quantity you please of red rough ripe gooseberries, take half the quantity of lump sugar, break them well, and boil them together for half an hour, or more, if necessary. Put into pots and cover with papers.

LEMON PRESERVE FOR TARTS.

Mrs. W. G. Davis.

One pound of sugar, four ounces of butter, six eggs, leaving out the whites of two, the juice and grated rind of three lemons; put into a saucepan and stir over a slow fire until it becomes as thick as honey.

GRAPE JAM.

Mrs. S. W. Cheever.

Take your grapes, separate the skin from the pulp, keeping them in separate dishes, put the pulps in your preserving kettle with a teacup of water; when thoroughly heated, run them through a colander to separate the seeds; then put your skins with them and weigh; to each pound of fruit, put three-fourths of a pound of sugar; add merely water enough to keep from burning; cook slowly three-fourths of an hour. This is a delicious jam, and worth the trouble.

BLACKBERRY JAM.

M. A. T.

To each pound of fruit add three-fourths of a pound of sugar; mash each separately; then put together and boil from one-half to three-fourths of an hour.

RASPBERRY JAM.

To five or six pounds of fine red raspberries (not too ripe) add an equal quantity of the finest quality of white sugar. Mash the whole well in a preserving kettle; add about one quart of currant juice, (a little less will do), and boil gently until it jellies upon a cold plate; then put into small jars; cover with brandied paper, and tie a thick white paper over them. Keep in a dark, dry, and cool place.

QUINCE JAM.

Mrs. P. B. Ayer.

Boil your fruit in as little water as possible, until soft enough to break easily; pour off all the water and rub with a spoon until entirely smooth. To one pound of the quince add ten ounces of brown sugar, and boil twenty minutes, stirring often.

PINE-APPLE JAM.

Mrs. P. B. Ayer.

Grate your pine-apple; to one pound of the apple add three-fourths of a pound of loaf sugar; boil ten minutes.

ORANGE MARMALADE.

Mrs. J. Young Scammon.

One dozen Seville oranges, one dozen common oranges, one dozen lemons; boil the oranges and lemons whole in water for five hours; scoop out the inside, removing the seeds; cut the peel into thin slices with a knife, and add to every pound of pulp and peel a pint of water and two pounds of sugar. Boil twenty minutes.

ORANGE MARMALADE.

Mrs. Wm. Bracket.

Take seven oranges and five lemons; boil in water two or three hours; throw away the water, and open the oranges and lemons, taking out the seeds and preserving all the pulp and juice possible; cut the rinds in small strips or chop them, but cutting in strips is better;

weigh it all when this is done; then put three pounds of sugar to two of the pulp, and boil slowly till clear.

SIBERIAN CRAB JELLY.

Mrs. W. Arthurs.

Boil a peck of crabs for two hours in as much water as will cover them, then put them into a jelly bag and allow to drain, (do not squeeze them); to each pint of syrup, put one pound of loaf sugar, and boil for half an hour. Select the reddest crabs you can find and the jelly will be a beautiful colour.

APPLES FOR PRESENT USE.

Mrs. Joseph Saulter.

Take about twenty nice snow or other good cooking apples, and wipe them clean, and place them in a preserving kettle with water enough to about half cover them; then add two cups of sugar, half a cup of vinegar, and a dessertspoonful of ground cinnamon; cover them down tightly, and let them simmer over a slow fire until the apples become soft; use them cold.

CANDY.

Sweets to the Sweet."

In order to understand the secret of candy making, it will be necessary to understand the action of heat upon sugar. The first step in this process is the reduction of sugar to a syrup, which is done by adding water to sugar in the proportion of a pint and a half of water to three and a half pounds of sugar. When this boils up in the kettle we have simple syrup. A few more minutes of boiling, reduces the water which holds the sugar in a perfect solution. At this stage, if the syrup is allowed to cool, the candy crystallizes on the sides of the dish, and we have rock candy. If, instead of allowing it to cool at this point, we allow it to reach a higher degree of heat, we shall find, in putting a spoon into the syrup, when drawing it out a long thread of sugar will follow the spoon. It is to this point that confectioners bring the syrup for the greater number of candies produced. The greatest skill is required on the part of the operator to push the boiling sugar to this point without allowing it to reach the caramel state, when it becomes bitter and dark and is no longer fit to use as a confection. The proportion of sugar and water for candy making will be three and one-half pounds of sugar to one and one-half pints of water. To this add one teaspoon of cream of tartar, which will prevent the tendency of the sugar to assume the granular condition. To test the candy, drop into cold water. When this becomes at once hard and brittle the vessel should be at once removed from the fire. Flat sticks are formed by pouring the candy into long flat pans, and when cooling crease the mass, which will readily break into sticks when cold. To make round stick candy, when cool enough to handle and while warm enough to mould, roll into sticks with the hands. To colour candies, take small portions of the candy while cooling, and colour, then put together in strips and twist slightly.

LEMON CANDY.

Put into a kettle three and one-half pounds of sugar, one and one-half pints of water, and one teaspoon of cream of tartar. Let it boil until it becomes brittle when dropped in cold water; when sufficiently done take off the fire and pour in a shallow dish which has been greased with a little butter. When this has cooled so that it can be handled, add a teaspoon of tartaric acid and the same quantity of extract of lemon, and work them into the mass. The acid must be fine and free from lumps. Work this in until evenly distributed, and no more, as it will tend to destroy the transparency of the candy. This method may be used for preparing all other candies, as pine-apple, etc., using different flavours.

CREAM CANDIES.

Three and one-half pounds of sugar to one and one-half pints of water; dissolve in the water before putting with the sugar one-quarter of an ounce of fine white gum arabic, and when added to the sugar put in one teaspoon of cream of tartar. The candy should not be boiled quite to the brittle stage. The proper degree can be ascertained if, when a small skimmer is put in and taken out, when blowing through the holes of the skimmer, the melted sugar is forced through in feathery filaments; remove from the fire at this point and rub the syrup against the sides of the dish with an iron spoon. If it is to be a chocolate candy, add two ounces of chocolate finely sifted and such flavouring as you prefer, vanilla, rose, or orange. If you wish to make cocoanut candy, add this while soft and stir until cold.

EVERTON TOFFEE.

Miss Wyllie.

Take one pound of treacle, the same quantity of moist sugar, half a pound of butter; put them in a saucepan large enough to allow of fast boiling over a clear fire; put in the butter first, and rub it well over the bottom of the saucepan, and add the treacle and sugar, stirring together gently with a knife; after it has boiled for about ten minutes ascertain if it is done by having ready a basin of cold water, and drop a 'little of the mixture into it from the point of a knife; if it is sufficiently done, when you take it from the water it will be quite crisp. Now prepare a large, shallow tin pan or dish rubbed all over with butter to prevent its adhering, and into this pour the toffee from the saucepan to get it cold, when it can be easily removed

CANDY.

One pound sugar, one and a half cups water, three tablespoons rose water; boil twenty minutes; then pull.

CANDY.

Carrie A.

One-half pound sugar, one-half cup syrup, butter the size of a walnut; add little water to the syrup, and have the sugar thoroughly dissolved; to try it, drop a spoonful in a glass of ice water, if brittle, it is done.

CANDY CARAMELS.

Mary H.

One pint cream, one pound sugar, one cup butter, one-fourth cup chocolate, one cup of molasses.

CHOCOLATE CARAMELS.

One cup of fine granulated sugar, one cup of New Orleans molasses, one-fourth cup of milk, a piece of butter the size of an egg, one cup of chocolate after it is cut up, if made single quantity; if doubled, it is as well not to put the chocolate in till about done, and then the same quantity of the recipe will suffice, as it retains the flavour if not cooked as much. Boil till it will stiffen in water; pour into flat buttered pans to the thickness of half an inch. Use Baker's chocolate.

CHOCOLATE CARAMELS.

Mrs. P. B. Ayer.

Two cups of brown sugar, one cup molasses, one cup

chocolate grated fine, one cup boiled milk, one tablespoon flour; butter the size of a large English walnut; let it boil slowly and pour on flat tins to cool; mark off while warm.

CREAM CANDY.

One pound white sugar, one wineglass vinegar, one tumbler water, vanilla; boil one-half hour, and pull, if you choose.

COCOANUT DROPS.

Mrs. P. B. Ayer.

To one grated cocoanut, add half its weight of sugar and the white of one egg, cut to a stiff froth; mix thoroughly and drop on buttered white paper or tin sheets. Bake fifteen minutes.

KISSES.

E. S. P.

One egg, one cup sugar, one-half cup of butter, one half cup milk, one teaspoon cream of tartar, one-half of soda, flour enough to make a stiff dough; drop on tins and sprinkle over with powdered sugar. Bake in a quick oven.

MOLASSES CANDY.

Mrs. Benham.

One cup molasses, two cups of sugar, one tablespoon vinegar, a little butter and vanilla; boil ten minutes, then cool it enough to pull.

MOLASSES CANDY.

Julia French.

One cup molasses, one cup sugar, one tablespoon vinegar, piece of butter size of an egg; boil (but do not stir) until it hardens when dropped in cold water; then stir in a teaspoon of soda, and pour on buttered tins; when cool, pull and cut in sticks.

Or, two cups sugar, two tablespoons vinegar, boil; when done add a teaspoon soda, cool and pull, or cut in squares without pulling; do not stir while it is boiling.

BUTTER SCOTCH CANDY.

Four cups brown sugar, two of butter, vinegar to taste, two tablespoons water, and a little soda; boil half an hour; drop a little in hot water, and if crisp, it is done.

BUTTER SCOTCH.

Fanny Waggoner.

Three tablespoons of molasses, two of sugar, two of water, one of butter; add a pinch of soda before taking up.

SUGAR TOFFEE.

Mrs. Joseph B. Leake.

Three pounds best brown sugar, one pound butter, enough water to moisten the sugar; boil until crisp when dropped into cold water, then pour into pans, or upon platters, as thin as possible. It usually requires to boil fast, without stirring, three-quarters of an hour.

BREAD AND YEAST.

"There is scent of Syrian myrrh,
There is incense, there is spice,
There are delicate cakes and loaves,
Cakes of meal and polypi."
—Grecian Ode

"But I ate naught
Till I that lovely child of Ceres saw,
A large sweet round and yellow cake; how then
Could I from such a dish, my friends, abstain?"

GENERAL DIRECTIONS FOR MAKING BREAD.

In the composition of good bread, there are three important requisites: Good flour, good yeast and strength to knead it well. Flour should be white and dry, crumbling easily again after it is pressed in the hand.

A very good method of ascertaining the quality of yeast will be to add a little flour to a very small quantity, setting it in a warm place. If in the course of ten or fifteen minutes it rises, it will do to use.

When you make bread, first set the sponge with warm milk or water, keeping it in a warm place until quite light. Then mould this sponge, by adding flour into one large loaf, kneading it well. Set this to rise again, and then when sufficiently light mould it into smaller loaves, let it rise again, then bake. Care should be taken not to get the dough too stiff with flour; it should be as soft as it can be to knead well. To make bread or biscuits a nice colour, wet the dough over top with water just before putting into the oven. Flour should always be sifted.

YEAST.

Mrs. E. S. Chesebrough.

Put two tablespoons of hops in a muslin bag and boil them in three quarts of water for a few minutes; have ready a quart of hot mashed potatoes, put in one cup of flour, one tablespoon of sugar, one of salt; pour over the mixture the boiling hop water, strain through a colander, put a pint or less of fresh baker's yeast, or two cakes of yeast in while it is warm, and set it in a warm place to rise. This yeast will keep three or four weeks, if set in a cool place. In making it from time to time, use a bowl of the same to raise the fresh with.

YEAST.

Mrs. Mary Ludlam.

Six good potatoes grated raw, a little hop tea, one quart of boiling water, three-fourths cup of brown sugar, one-half teaspoon salt; when cool, add yeast to rise; keep covered and in a cool place.

BEST BAKING POWDER.

Mrs. Oliphant.

Tartaric acid, four parts, by weight; bicarbonate soda, five parts, by weight; baked flour, nine parts, by weight. The flour should be absolutely dry. The tartaric acid and the soda must also be dry, and pulverized as fine as possible *separately* in a clean porcelain mortar. When thus prepared sift all together repeatedly till perfectly mixed; then put into well-corked bottles, and use two teaspoonsful to each pint of flour.

BOSTON BROWN BREAD.

Mrs. Oliphant.

To make one loaf :—Rye meal unsifted, half a pint; Indian meal sifted, one pint; sour milk, one pint; molasses, half a gill. Add a teaspoonful of salt, one teaspoonful of soda dissolved in a little hot water; stir well, put in a greased pan, let it rise one hour, and steam four hours.

SALT RISING BREAD.

Mrs. Upham.

At supper time take one-fourth teaspoonful of salt, same of soda, and one teaspoonful of white sugar; over this pour one teacupful of boiling water, and add one cupful of cold water; stir in three desertspoonsful of Indian meal and flour enough to make a thick batter, and cover tightly. In cold weather place it where it will be warm all night. In the morning place your bowl in a dish of water as hot as *you* can *hold your finger in*. Stir it often and thoroughly for an hour. Sift in a ten quart pan two-thirds full of flour, into it stir enough warm water, one tablespoonful of salt, and one-half teaspoonful soda, to make a thin batter; then stir your yeast in thoroughly and place in a warm place, where no draughts of cold air will reach it. Let it rise to the top of pan

YEAST.

Mrs. W. C. Harris.

Boil in separate pans one-half cup of hops and two potatoes; strain both liquids boiling hot on a large cup of flour, one spoon of salt, half cup of sugar, and a cup of yeast. Pour it into a jug and set it in a cool place.

GOOD YEAST.

Mrs. Packard.

Grate six good sized potatoes (raw); have ready a gallon of water in which has been well boiled three handfuls of hops; strain through a cloth or sieve, while boiling hot, over the potatoes, stirring until well cooked, or the mixture thickens like starch; add one teacup of sugar, one-half cup of salt; when sufficiently cool, one cup of good yeast. Let it stand until a thick foam rises upon the top. Care must be taken not to bottle too soon, or the bottles may burst. Use one coffee cup of yeast to six loaves of bread. If kept in a cool place this yeast will last a long time, and housekeepers need not fear having *sour* bread.

YEAST FOR BREAD.

Miss L. Stagman.

Grate ten or twelve good sized raw potatoes in a colander and let the water drip off them, and then add three parts of a saucerful of flour to the potatoes, and three parts of a cup of sugar; then boil a good pinch of hops twenty minutes and throw over all; when lukewarm add a cup of yeast, and when it rises add a tablespoonful of salt. This will keep three weeks.

YEAST THAT WILL NOT SOUR.

Mrs. J. B. Adams.

Boil two ounces of hops in two quarts of water; put one cup of brown sugar in a jar; boil and strain the hops and pour into the jar. Add one cup of flour stirred smooth; let it stand in a warm kitchen till it ferments. Add six potatoes boiled and mashed, and one cup of salt.

YEAST.

Mrs. Anna Marble.

Two quarts of wheat bran, one of Indian bran, two gallons of boiling water; simmer an hour or so; put in a handful of hops. As soon as the water boils, add one teacup of molasses and one tablespoon of ground ginger. When cold put in a teacup of yeast and cork tightly. Keep cool.

BREAD.

Mrs. E. S. Chesebrough.

Take four quarts of sifted flour and a teacup of yeast, a pinch of salt, and wet with warm milk and water stiff enough to knead. Work it on the board until it requires no more flour. If made at night the bread will be light enough to work over and put in pans early in the morning. This quantity will make two large loaves. One-third of the lump may be taken for rolls, which can be made by working in butter the size of an egg, and setting aside to rise again: when light the second time make out in oblong shapes; cover them with a cloth and let them rise again. As soon as they break apart bake in a quick oven. They will not fail to be nice if they are baked as soon as they seam. This is the great secret of white, flaky rolls. Two or three potatoes will improve the bread. Good housekeepers always have flour sifted in readiness for use, and never use it in any other way.

BREAD.

M. E. B. Lynde.

The sponge is made over night in the centre of a pan of flour, with milk and warm water and a cup of home-made hop and potato yeast to about four loaves. The yeast is put in when about half the flour and water are mixed, and then the remainder of the water is added and the sponge beaten with a wooden spoon for fifteen minutes and left to rise over night in a moderately warm place. In the morning, the bread-dough mixed and kneaded for half an hour, adding flour to make a stiff dough, and left to rise in a mass. It is then made into small loaves, being kneaded with as little flour as possible, and put in pans to rise the second time, all the while kept moderately warm, and when light bake in a moderately hot oven. The important part of said recipe is the beating of the sponge fifteen minutes, as given.

EXCELLENT BREAD.

Mrs. Geo. W. Pitkin.

Four potatoes mashed fine, four teaspoons of salt, two quarts of lukewarm milk, one-half cake compressed yeast dissolved in one-half cup of warm water, flour enough to make a pliable dough; mould with hands well greased with lard; place in pans, and when sufficiently light, it is ready for baking.

YEAST.

Mrs. John A. Fraser.

Monday—boil two ounces of hops in four quarts of water for half an hour, strain it, and let it stand till cold, then put in a small handful of salt and half a pound of sugar, beat up one pound of flour, with some of the liquor, mix all together. On Wednesday boil and mash three pounds of potatoes and add to it, let it stand till Thursday, then bottle and it is ready for use; shake well before using. To be kept warm while making, and in a cool place after.

SUPERIOR BREAD.

Mrs. D. C. Norton.

Scald one quart of sour milk; when cool enough, set your sponge with the whey; take about three quarts of flour, make a hole in the centre, put in the whey about a good teaspoon of salt, one teacup of good hop yeast (home made is best), and stir quite stiff with a spoon; wrap in a thick cloth so as to keep as warm as possible in cold weather, in summer it is not necessary. In the morning knead well, adding flour until stiff enough, and keep warm until light; then set it in pans to rise; no saleratus is needed. Bread made in this way will never fail to be good if good flour and yeast are used.

WHEAT BREAD.

Mrs. D. W. Thatcher.

Take a pan of flour, and put in a small handful of salt and a bowl of soft yeast and one pint of lukewarm milk, mix stiff with flour and let it rise. Then knead it into pans, and let it rise, and if wanted very white, knead it down two or three times; this makes it whiter, but losen its sweet taste; bake forty-five minutes.

RICE BREAD.

Mrs. E. S. Chesebrough.

Boil a teacup of rice quite soft; while hot, add butter the size of an egg, one and a half pints of milk, rather more than one-half pint of bolted corn meal, two tablespoons of flour, two eggs and a little salt. Bake just one hour. The bread should be about two inches thick.

SPLENDID BROWN BREAD.

One quart sour milk, half cup of molasses, one cup of lard, one tablespoon even of soda, one tablespoon salt, Graham flour enough to make a stiff batter; put it in a two quart tin pail and cover with the lid; suspend the pail by a stick through the handle in a pot of boiling water and keep boiling three hours, take it off and after removing the lid bake in the same pail in a slow oven.

STEAMED BROWN BREAD.

Mrs. O. G. Smith.

One pint of sweet milk, four tablespoons of molasses, one cup of Indian meal, two cups of rye or Graham flour, one teaspoon of salt, one of saleratus; mix with a spoon, and steam three hours, and bake half an hour or more.

BOSTON BROWN BREAD.

Mrs. F. E. Stearns.

One and one-half cups of Graham flour, two cups of corn meal, one-half cup of molasses, one pint of sweet milk, and one-half a teaspoon of soda; steam three hours.

BROWN BREAD TOAST.

Cut the bread in slices and toast. Put it in the dish for the table, take a bowl of thick cream, add a little salt, then pour over the toast; put it in the oven until it heats through.

TRAVELLER'S BREAD.

Take Graham flour (unsifted); and currants, figs, dates or raisins may be used by chopping them; stir quite stiffly with the coldest water as briskly as possible, so as to incorporate air with it; then knead in all the unbolted wheat flour you can; cut in cakes or rolls one-half inch thick, and bake in a quick oven.

STEAMED CORN BREAD.
Mrs. Jane Conger.

Take three cups of meal, and one of flour, scald two cups of the meal with boiling water, add the other cup of meal and flour, two cups of sour milk, one cup molasses, one teaspoon of soda, a little salt. Steam three hours.

OLD FASHIONED GRAHAM BREAD.
Mrs. Pulsifer.

One tea cup of good yeast, one quart of warm water, one teaspoon of salt, two cups sugar, or less, one small teaspoon soda, stir in enough white winter wheat Graham flour to make it stiff enough to drop off the spoon readily, grease your bread pans, put in, and set to rise, let it get quite light, then bake in a moderate oven for three-quarters of an hour.

BROWN BREAD.
Mrs. Wm. Blair.

Take part of the sponge that has been prepared for your white bread, warm water can be added, mix it with Graham flour (not too stiff).

FOR BROWN BISCUIT.—Take this Graham dough, as prepared for bread, working in a little butter. Butter the size of an egg is sufficient for two dozen biscuits.

CORN BREAD.
Mrs. Juliet L. Strayer.

One-half pint of buttermilk, one-half pint of sweet milk; sweeten the sour milk with one-half teaspoon of soda; beat two eggs, whites and yolks together; pour the milk into the eggs, then thicken with about nine tablespoons of sifted corn meal. Put the pan on the stove with a piece of lard the size of an egg; when melted pour it in the batter; this lard by stirring it will grease the pan to bake in; add a teaspoon of salt.

CORN BREAD.

Mrs. Wm. H. Low.

Two tablespoons of sugar, one tablespoon butter, two eggs; stir all together, add one cup of sweet milk, three teaspoons of baking powder, and three-fourths of a cup corn meal; flour to make it quite stiff.

INDIAN BREAD.

Mrs. A. T. Hall.

One pint of meal, one pint of flour, one pint of milk, one teacup of molasses, one teaspoon of soda, one-half of cream tartar; steam two hours and bake half an hour.

GRAHAM BREAD.

Mrs. J. B. Hobbs.

For one loaf, take two cups of white bread sponge, to which add two tablespoons of brown sugar, and Graham flour to make a stiff batter; let it rise, after which add Graham flour sufficient to knead, but not very stiff; then put in the pan to rise and bake.

GRAHAM BREAD.

Mrs. H. P. Stowell.

Set sponge of fine flour, same as for wheat bread; when sufficiently raised, instead of mixing with fine flour, mix with Graham to the usual consistency; mould with fine flour a little, raise once, then it is ready for the oven. Sweeten with syrup or sugar, if desired. though I think it better without either.

ROLLS.

Mrs. H. F. Waite.

To the quantity of light bread dough that you would take for twelve persons, add the white of one egg well beaten, two tablespoons of white sugar, and two tablespoons of butter; work these thoroughly together; roll out about half an inch thick; cut the size desired, and spread one with melted butter and lay another upon the top of it. Bake delicately, when they have risen.

FRENCH ROLLS.

Mrs. Thos. Orton.

Take one-half cup of yeast, rub a small one-half cup of butter in the flour (you will have to guess the quantity), then add the yeast, and water enough to wet; mix as for soda biscuit. Let it rise till morning. Roll in thin sheets, and cut into squares, spread a very little butter on each, and sprinkle a little flour on to roll up. Put in the pan when light, bake twenty minutes. Nice.

FRENCH ROLLS.

Etta C. Springer.

One quart flour, add two eggs, one-half pint milk, tablespoon of yeast, knead it well; rise till morning. Work in one ounce of butter and mould in small rolls; bake immediately.

BROWN ROLLS.

Mrs. Malancthon Starr.

One quart Graham flour, milk enough to make a stiff batter, one-third cup of yeast, and mix over night; in the morning add two eggs, one large tablespoon of sugar, one-fourth teaspoon of soda, piece of butter half the size of an egg, and a little salt; put in cups, and let stand twenty minutes before baking.

FRENCH BISCUITS.

Mrs. Lind.

Two cups of butter, two cups of sugar, one egg, (or the whites of two), half a cup of sour milk, half a teaspoon of soda, flour to roll; sprinkle with sugar.

TEA BISCUITS.

Mrs. Norcross.

One cup of hot water, two of milk, three tablespoons of yeast; mix thoroughly; after it is risen, take two-thirds of a cup of butter and a little sugar and mould it; then let it rise, and mould it into small cakes.

TO MAKE STALE BREAD OR CAKE FRESH.

Mrs. M. G. Adams.

Plunge the loaf one instant in cold water; lay it upon a tin in the oven ten or fifteen minutes. Cake and rolls may be thus made almost as nice as if just baked, but must be eaten immediately.

GRAHAM BISCUIT.

Mrs. Brodie.

One quart of Graham flour, three and one-half heaping teaspoons of baking powder, one teaspoon of salt, one of butter. Make into soft dough with milk.

RYE BISCUIT.

Mrs. Lamkin.

Two cups rye meal, one and a half cups flour, one-third cup molasses, one egg, a little salt, two cups sour milk, two even teaspoons saleratus.

BUNS.

Two coffee-cups bread dough, two eggs, one cup sugar, spices, a few currants. Mould like rusk and let them rise before baking.

BUNS.

M.

Take one large coffee-cup of warm milk, one-quarter cake of yeast and salt; make sponge; let rise; when light work into a dough, adding one-half teacup of sugar, one egg, butter twice the size of an egg; let rise; roll into a sheet; butter it; cut into strips three inches wide and six inches long; fold, not quite in the middle; let rise again and bake; when in a dough, if it rises before you are ready, push it down. Excellent.

RUSKS.

Mrs. P. B. Ayer.

To one tumbler of warm milk add a half gill of yeast, three eggs and a coffeecup of sugar beaten together, two ounces of butter rubbed into flour, of which use only enough to enable you to mould it; let it rise over night; when very light, roll and put on tins to raise again, after which bake in a quick oven twenty minutes.

RUSKS.

Milk enough with one-half cup of yeast to make a pint; make a sponge and rise; then add one and a half cups of white sugar, three eggs, one-half cup of butter; spice to your taste; mould, then put in pan to rise. When baked, cover the tops with sugar dissolved in milk.

SODA BISCUITS.

M.

To each quart of flour add one tablespoon of shortening, one-half teaspoon of salt, and three and a half heaping teaspoons of Price's Cream Baking Powder; mix baking powder thoroughly through the flour, then add other ingredients. Do not knead, and bake quick. To use cream tartar and soda, take the same proportions without the baking powder, using instead two heaping teaspoons cream tartar and one of soda. If good they will bake in five minutes.

CREAM BISCUITS.
Mrs. A. M. Gibbs.

Three heaping tablespoons of sour cream; put in a bowl or vessel containing a quart and fill two-thirds full of sweet milk, two teaspoons cream tartar, one teaspoon of soda, a little salt; pour the cream in the flour, mix soft and bake in a quick oven.

STRAWBERRY SHORTCAKE.

Make good biscuit crust; bake in two tins of same shape and size; mix berries with plenty of sugar; open the shortcake, butter well and place berries in layers, alternated with the crust; have the top layer of berries and over all put charlotte russe or whipped cream.

ORANGE SHORTCAKE.
M.

Make a nice shortcake; spread in layers of sliced oranges with sugar and a little cream. To be eaten with sweetened cream.

APPLE SHORTCAKE.
M.

Season apple sauce with butter, sugar, etc.; make a nice shortcake, open and butter it and put the apple sauce in layers. Serve with sweetened cream.

SALLY LUNN.

Mrs. J. H. Brown.

One quart of warm milk, one-half cup of butter, one of sugar, five eggs and one cup of yeast; flour enough for stiff batter. Bake one hour.

CREAM CAKES.

Six eggs, beaten separately, a half pint of sour cream, one pint of sweet milk, one and one-half teaspoons of baking powder, flour enough to make a thin batter; bake in cups.

BREAKFAST CAKES.

Mrs. Rice.

One cup milk, one pint flour, three eggs, piece butter size of an egg, two teaspoons cream tartar, one teaspoon soda, one tablespoon butter.

TEA CAKES.

Mrs. E. S. Chesebrough.

One quart of sifted flour, one pint sweet milk, butter size of egg, two eggs, two teaspoons sugar, one of soda, two of cream tartar; bake in small patty-pans.

WHEAT GEMS.

Mrs. W. H. Ovington.

One pink milk, two eggs, flour enough to make a batter not very stiff, two large spoons melted butter, yeast to raise them, a little soda and salt. Bake in gem irons.

GRAHAM GEMS.

Mrs. E. R. Harmon.

One quart of sweet milk, one cup syrup, one teaspoon soda, two teaspoons cream tartar, little salt; mix cream tartar in Graham flour, soda in milk, and make it as stiff with the flour as will make it drop easily from the spoon into muffin rings.

POP OVERS.

Mrs. Andrews.

One cup milk, one cup flour, one egg, beaten separately. Bake in cups, a tablespoon to each cup.

POP OVERS.

S. S. Pierce.

One cup flour, one cup milk, one egg, piece butter size of a walnut, a little salt; to be baked in scallops in a very quick oven. This rule makes twelve.

POP OVERS.

Mrs. King.

Three cups of milk, three cups flour, three eggs, a little salt, one tablespoon melted butter put in the last thing; two tablespoons to a puff.

PUFFS.

Mrs. Wren.

Two eggs beaten separately, two cups milk, two cups of flour, butter the size of a walnut; drop into hot irons and bake quickly.

GRAHAM PUFFS.

Mrs. O. S. Wheelock.

One pint of Graham flour, one egg, teaspoon salt, one tablespoons baking powder; wet with milk or water.

FRITTERS.

Mrs. Brown.

One pint-sweet milk, four eggs, one quart flour and three teaspoons baking powder sifted together. Serve warm with maple syrup.

APPLE FRITTERS.

M.

One teacup of sweet milk, one tablespoon of sweet light dough dissolved in milk, three eggs beaten separately, one teaspoon of salt, one and one-half teacups of flour, one tablespoon of sugar, and the grated peel of a lemon, peeled apples sliced without the core; drop into hot lard with a piece of apple in each one; sprinkle with powdered or spiced sugar. Let them stand after making and they will be lighter. Good.

MUFFINS.

Mrs. W. H. Low.

One tablespoon of butter, two tablespoons sugar, two eggs—stir all together; add one cup of sweet milk, three teaspoons of baking powder, flour to make a stiff batter. Bake twenty minutes in a quick oven.

MUFFINS.

Beat four eggs into a full tablespoon of lard, mix into them one and one-half pints sour milk, effervescing with a teaspoon of soda; add enough flour to make the consistency of pound cake. Bake in heated rings.

RYE MUFFINS.

Mrs. Bartlett.

Two cups of rye, one of flour, one of sugar, one egg, one teaspoon of soda, and a little salt; mix quite stiff with sour milk.

INDIAN MEAL MUFFINS.

Two cups of Indian meal scalded with as little water as possible, one coffeecup of flour, one teacup of sweet milk, one tablespoon of shortening, one-half cup of brown sugar, a small cup of yeast; mixed over night.

WAFFLES.

M.

Yolks of three eggs, one quart milk, half cup melted butter, one heaping teaspoon baking powder. Afterwards add the whites of the eggs and flour enough to make a thin batter.

WAFFLES.

M.

One pint sour milk, three tablespoons melted butter,

three eggs, beaten separately, one teaspoon soda, a little salt, flour enough to make a thick batter.

RICE CROQUETTES.

O. T. C.

Boil one cup of rice in one quart of milk or water, till tender; while warm add a piece of butter the size of an egg, two eggs; make into rolls, dip them in crumbs and fry them in lard or butter.

RICE CROQUETTES.

One teacup rice, one pint milk, one pint water, a little salt; butter a tin, put in the mixture and swell on the stove, where it will not quite simmer. When dry, add two eggs, beaten light, with two tablespoons of sugar and one of butter. Have ready cracker crumbs spread on a board thickly. Make a roll of the rice in the crumbs; drop in hot lard and brown.

GOOD BREAKFAST CAKES.

Mrs. J. H. Brown.

Three eggs well beaten, two and a half teacups of flour, one pint of sweet milk, a little salt. Make a batter of these, put in cups or rings and bake in a quick oven.

BANNOCKS.

M.

One pint corn meal, pour on it boiling water to thoroughly wet it. Let it stand a few minutes; add salt and one egg and a little sweet cream, or a tablespoon melted butter. Make into balls and fry in hot lard.

ENGLISH PANCAKES.

Mr. Joseph Robinson.

Make a batter of two teacups of flour, four eggs, and one quart of milk. Add, as a great improvement, one tablespoonful of brandy with a little nutmeg scraped in. Make the size of frying pan. Sprinkle a little granulated sugar over the pancake, roll it up, and send to the table hot.

WAFFLES.

Mrs. S. McMaster.

One quart of sweet or sour milk, four eggs, two-thirds of a cup of butter, half a teaspoonful of salt, three teaspoons of baking powder; flour enough to make a nice batter. If you use sour milk leave out the baking powder and use two teaspoons soda. Splendid.

MUFFINS, FOR BREAKFAST.

Mrs. S. McM.

Three eggs, one cup milk; one tablespoon of good butter melted, one tablespoon sugar, a little salt, two heaping teaspoons good baking powder, flour enough to make a batter; bake in muffin rings; when almost done moisten over the top with a feather dipped in sweetened milk.

TEA BISCUITS.

Mrs. Arthurs.

One quart flour, four teaspoonsful baking powder, about the size of an egg of butter, one tablespoonful of brown sugar, a teaspoonful of salt, and half cup of currants; grate in a little nutmeg; bake twenty minutes in a quick oven.

MRS. CURTIS' MUFFINS.

Mrs. Upham.

One quart flour, two and one-half teaspoonsful baking powder. Mix all dry in flour. Add cold water enough to make a stiff batter, and then a tablespoonful of melted lard.

MUFFINS.

Mrs. J. D. Odell.

One quart of milk, four eggs, one tablespoon sugar, two tablespoons of butter, one teaspoon salt, two teaspoons baking powder, two tablespoons yeast; flour to make a stiff batter; bake in rings when light.

BREAD CAKE.

Mrs. J. D. Odell.

Two cups dough, one and one-half cups sugar, one-half cup butter, one cup raisins, one cup currants, one teaspoon soda, two eggs, one teaspoon each of cinnamon, cloves, and allspice.

GEMS.

Mrs. Munshaw.

One piece butter size of a walnut, three teaspoons sugar, three eggs, one-half cup sweet milk, flour enough to make a nice thick batter; have your gem-pans burning hot; bake in a very hot oven.

PORT HOPE BISCUITS

Mrs. Crawford.

Two eggs, two cups sugar, one of butter, one-half cup of milk, one teaspoonful of cream tartar, one teaspoonful of carbonate soda, flour sufficient to roll very thin; flavour with nutmeg.

COFFEE CAKE.

Mrs. Carson.

One cup of molasses, one cup of brown sugar, one cold coffee, four cups sifted flour, half cup of butter, small teaspoon of allspice, two teaspoons of baking powder.

STEAMED BROWN BREAD.

Mrs. Carson.

Three cups of yellow corn meal, one cup of flour, two cups of sweet milk, one cup of sour milk, half cup of molasses, one teaspoon of soda; dissolve soda in hot water, pour half in the sour milk and half in molasses; steam three hours and bake half an hour in a quick oven; just brown the top.

SALLY LUNN FOR BREAKFAST.

Mrs. Carson.

Four teacups of flour, two tablespoons of sugar, one of lard, four eggs, four teaspoonsful of baking powder use half milk and half water to a thin batter, and bake in a quick oven.

WAFFLES.

Mrs. Carson.

One quart of milk, four eggs, two-thirds cup of butter, half teaspoon of salt, three teaspoons of baking powder; flour enough for a batter, and bake in waffle irons and eat hot.

CORN BREAKFAST CAKES.

Mrs. Parmelee.

One-half cup of sweet milk, two cups of flour, one corn meal, two eggs, butter size of an egg, tablespoon of baking powder mixed with flour; bake in small gem tins and cook quarter of an hour in a quick oven.

MUFFINS.

Mrs. Spense.

One quart of flour; mix five teaspoonsful of Cook's Friend in the flour, a piece of butter the size of two eggs, five teaspoons of sugar, and as much milk as will make a stiff batter. Bake twenty minutes in rings.

GRAHAM CAKES.

Mrs. Spence.

One pint Graham flour, one pint white flour, one tablespoonful of butter or shortening, two tablespoonsful of molasses, two teaspoonsful of cream tartar, one teaspoonful of soda; sift cream tartar and soda in with the white flour; do not sift the Graham flour; rub well together; then rub your shortening in thoroughly; wet with milk or water not too stiff; roll out and cut in cakes; bake in a quiet oven. Baking powder may be used instead of cream of tartar and soda.

BUNS.

Miss Miller.

Set in the evening, a pint of milk, butter the size of an egg, three tablespoons of yeast, and flour enough to make a thick batter. Warm the milk and butter together; add the yeast and flour. In the morning add two eggs, four tablespoons of sugar, and enough flour to roll in the hand, *not* on the board. After mixing let it stand till quite light; then make into buns, and let them stand four hours in the pans before baking. Bake about a quarter of an hour.

SALLY LUNN.

Mrs. Carson.

Four teacups flour, two tablespoons sugar, one tablespoon of lard, four eggs, four tablespoons of baking powder; mix with half milk and water to a thin batter; bake in a quick oven.

GEMS FOR BREAKFAST.

Mrs. Carson.

One and a half cups of sweet milk, two cups of flour, one cup of corn meal, two eggs, butter the size of an egg, one tablespoon of baking powder mixed dry in the flour; bake in small tins, and cook quarter of an hour in a quick oven.

JOHNNIE CAKE.

Mrs. H. Baird.

One pint of corn meal, one teacup of flour, two eggs, one pint of sweet milk, one tablespoon of molasses, one tablespoon of melted butter, a little salt, one teaspoon of soda, one teaspoon of cream of tartar; bake in square tins.

GRIDDLE CAKES.

Mrs. Orson Smith.

Two quarts warm water, one teaspoon salt, one cup flour, one cup corn meal, one-half teacup yeast, two eggs well beaten and added the last; raise over night.

CORN BREAKFAST CAKES.

Mrs. W. A. Carson.

One and one-half cups sweet milk, two of flour, one of corn meal, two eggs beaten light, butter size of an egg, tablespoon of baking powder mixed in flour; bake in gem pans, and have them hot before putting in the mixture; cook quarter of an hour in a quick oven.

SPLENDID CORN CAKE.

Mrs. W. A. Carson.

One pint of corn meal scalded with hot water; make as thin as mush, let it stand until quite cool; then add one teaspoon of salt, one tablespoon of melted butter, three eggs beaten light; make about as thick as pound cake, and bake one hour in a slow oven.

JOHNNIE CAKE.

Edith.

Scald the meal at night; let it stand where it will keep slightly warm until morning; then, for any ordinary four quart panful, add sufficient sour milk to render the right consistency—generally a large teacupful is enough; saleratus, one tablespoonful; salt, at time of scalding the meal; if the meal is very fine, do not use boiling water.

QUICK BUCKWHEAT CAKES.

One quart of buckwheat flour, one-half a teacup of corn meal or wheat flour, a little salt, and two tablespoons of syrup. Wet these with cold or warm water to a thin batter, and add, lastly, four good tablespoons of baking powder.

BUCKWHEAT CAKES.

Lake Forest.

One quart buckwheat flour, four tablespoons yeast, one tablespoon salt, one handful Indian meal, two tablespoons molasses, not syrup. Warm water enough to make a thin batter; beat very well and set in a warm place. If the batter is the least sour in the morning, add a little soda.

OATMEAL GRIDDLE CAKES.

Mrs. J. M. Wetherell.

One cup oatmeal, one cup flour, one teaspoon sugar, one teaspoon baking powder, one-half teaspoon salt; sift the baking powder in with the flour; add cold water to make a batter of the consistency of buckwheat cakes; beat very well together and bake immediately. This receipt is sufficient for a family of three.

MUSH.

Indian or oatmeal mush is best made in the following manner: Put fresh water in a kettle over the fire to boil, and put in some salt; when the water boils, stir in handful by handful corn or oatmeal until thick enough for use. In order to have excellent mush, the meal should be allowed to cook well, and long as possible while thin, and before the final handful is added. When desired to be fried for breakfast, turn into an earthen dish and set away to cool. Then cut in slices when you wish to fry; dip each piece in beaten eggs and fry on a hot griddle.

OATMEAL GRUEL.

Take two tablespoons of oatmeal, pour on it a pint of cold water; let it stand half a day, then pour it through a sieve and boil well one-quarter of an hour, stirring all the time; season according to taste. The coarse meal to be rejected. Good for invalids or children.

WEIGHTS AND MEASURES.

Ten eggs are equal to one pound.

One pound of brown sugar, one pound of white sugar, powdered or loaf sugar broken, is equal to one quart.

One pound of butter, when soft, is equal to one quart.

One pound and two ounces Indian meal is equal to one quart.

One pound and two ounces of wheat flour is equal to one quart.

Four large tablespoons are equal to one-half gill.

Eight large tablespoons are equal to one gill.

Sixteen large tablespoons are equal to one-half pint.

A common sized wine glass holds half a gill.

A common sized tumbler holds half a pint.

Four ordinary teacups of liquid are equal to one quart.

CAKES.

> But then my fare was all so light and delicate;
> The Fruit, the Cakes, the Meats so dainty frail,
> They would not bear a bite—no, not a munch—
> But melted away like ice.
> —Hood.

SUGGESTIONS.

In making Cake, it is very desirable that the materials be of the finest quality. Sweet, fresh butter, eggs and good flour are the first essentials. The process of putting together is also quite an important feature, and where other methods are not given in this work by contributors, it would be well for the young housekeeper to observe the following directions: Never allow the butter to oil, but soften it by putting it in a moderately warm place before you commence other preparations for your cake; then put it into an earthen dish (tin, if not new, will discolor your cake as you stir it), and add your sugar; beat the butter and sugar to a cream; add the yolks of the eggs, then the milk, and lastly the beaten whites of the eggs and flour. Spices and liquors may be added after the yolks of the eggs are put in, and fruit should be put in with the flour.

The oven should be pretty hot for small cakes, and moderate for larger. To ascertain if a large cake is sufficiently baked, pierce it with a broom-straw through the centre; if done the straw will come out free from dough; if not done, dough will adhere to the straw. Take it out of the tin about fifteen minutes after it is taken from the oven (not sooner), and do not turn it over on the top to cool.

ICING.

The following rules should be observed where boiled icing is not used:

Put the whites of your eggs in a shallow earthen dish, and allow, at least, a quarter of a pound or sixteen tablespoons of the finest white sugar for each egg. Take part of the sugar at first and sprinkle over the eggs; beat them for about half an hour, stirring in gradually the rest of the sugar; then add the flavour. If you use the juice of a lemon, allow more sugar. Tartaric acid and lemon juice whitens icing. It may be shaded a pretty pink with strawberry juice or cranberry syrup, or coloured yellow by putting the juice and rind of a lemon in a thick muslin bag and squeezing it hard into the egg and sugar.

If cake is well dredged with flour after baking, and then carefully wiped before the icing is put on, it will not run and can be spread more smoothly. Put frosting on to the cake in large spoonsful, commencing over the centre; then spread it over the cake, using a large knife, dipping it occasionally in cold water. Dry the frosting on the cake in a cool, dry place.

FROSTING.

Mrs. Louise Dewey.

One pint granulated sugar, moisten thoroughly with

water sufficient to dissolve it when heated; let it boil until it threads from the spoon, stirring often; while the sugar is boiling, beat the whites of two eggs till they are firm; then when thoroughly beaten, turn them into a deep dish, and when the sugar is boiled, turn it over the whites, beating all together rapidly until of the right consistency to spread over the cake. Flavour with lemon if preferred. This is sufficient for two loaves.

FROSTING FOR CAKE.

Ella Guild.

One cup frosting sugar, two tablespoons of water boiled together; take it off the stove and stir in the white of one egg beaten to a stiff froth; stir all together well; then frost your cake with it, and you will never want a nicer frosting than this.

ICE CREAM ICING FOR WHITE CAKE.

Mrs. P. R. Ayer.

Two cups pulverized sugar boiled to a thick syrup; add three teaspoons vanilla; when cold, add the whites of two eggs well beaten, and flavoured with two teaspoons of citric acid.

ICING.

Mrs. H. P. Stowell.

One pound pulverized sugar, pour over one tablespoon cold water, beat whites of three eggs a little, not to a stiff froth; add to the sugar and water; put in a deep bowl; place in a vessel of boiling water and heat. It will become thin and clear, afterward begin to thicken. When it becomes quite thick remove from the fire and stir while it becomes cool till thick enough to spread with a knife. This will frost several ordinary sized cakes.

CHOCOLATE FROSTING.

Mrs. C. H. Wheeler.

Whites of two eggs, one and one-half cups of fine sugar, six great spoons of grated chocolate, two teaspoons of vanilla; spread rather thickly between layers and on the top of cake. Best when freshly made. It should be made like any frosting.

BLACK FRUIT CAKE.

Mrs. C. H. Wheeler.

Three-fourths pound of butter, one pound sugar (brown), one pound flour, two pounds currants, three pounds raisins (seeded), one-half pound citron, one-fourth pound almonds, eight eggs, one nutmeg, cloves and cinnamon, one wineglass of brandy. The raisins are better if soaked in brandy over night.

BLACK CAKE.

Mrs. G. F. DeForrest

Two pounds of flour, two pounds sugar, two pounds butter, eight pounds raisins, four pounds currants, one pint brandy, two pounds citron, twenty-four eggs, two ounces nutmeg, two teaspoons of cloves; add a little molasses to make it more moist and black. This makes two very large loaves, baked in tin pans or hoops. For weddings. Splendid.

COOKIES.

Mrs. G. Wyllie.

One cup of butter, one cup of brown sugar, one teaspoon of soda, three eggs, flour enough to roll out thin.

MOLASSES COOKIES.

Mrs. G. Wyllie.

One cup of molasses, one tablespoon of soda; dissolve in half a cup of boiling water; one tablespoon ginger, two tablespoons butter, and flour enough to roll out thin; cut with cake cutter, and cook in quick oven.

SUGAR COOKIES.

Mrs. W. A. C.

One and a half cups of sugar, one of butter, two eggs, half a cup of sour cream, one teaspoon of soda; mix just so that you can roll out; then sprinkle with sugar just before putting in oven; bake quick.

COOKIES.

One tablespoon of butter, one cup of sugar, one egg, half a cup of milk, half a teaspoon of soda, one tablespoonful of ginger, flour to roll; cut in round cakes and bake in a rather quick oven.

COOKIES.

Mrs. W. Baird.

One cup of sugar, one of butter, two eggs, spices to taste, two tablespoons of milk, one teaspoon of soda and half of cream of tartar; beat all together with flour enough to roll out thin.

COOKIES.
Mrs. Stotesbury.

Two eggs, one cup of butter, one of sugar, half teaspoonful of soda, and flour enough to make a dough; roll thin and bake quickly.

DROP COOKIES.
Mrs. J. D. Odell.

Two cups of sugar, one cup of milk, half cup of butter, three-quarters cup of flour, two teaspoonsful baking powder, two eggs.

WHITE COOKIES.
Mrs. J. R. Silliman.

One cup of butter, two cups of sugar, one cup of milk, four eggs, two tablespoonsful caraway seeds; add flour enough to roll, and cut out.

COOKIES.
Mrs. W. A. Carson.

One cup of butter, two of sugar, one-half of sour milk, one teaspoon of soda, flour enough to roll out thin; cut with a sharp tin cake cutter; bake in a quick oven.

POOR MAN'S DOUGHNUTS.
Mrs. George Virtue.

One quart of flour, two saltspoons of salt, four teaspoonsful of yeast powder, one and one-half cups of sugar, one cup of milk, nutmeg.

DOUGHNUTS.

Ada King.

One cup of sugar, two eggs, two tablespoons of melted butter, two-thirds cup of milk, two even teaspoons of cream tartar, one even teaspoon of soda, flour enough to roll, salt and nutmeg.

NELL'S GINGER CAKE.

Mrs. S. McMaster.

Two cups molasses, one large tablespoon of lard, one of ginger, one of salt, one cup of sweet milk, one teaspoon of soda, four cups and one-half of sifted flour.

FRIED CAKES.

Mrs. S. McMaster.

Three eggs, two and one-half cups sweet milk, two cups sugar, two teaspoons of cream of tartar, one of soda; spices to taste; roll out and cut in shapes, and fry in boiling lard; while hot dip in fine sugar.

CREAM CAKE.

Mamie Nevett.

Two eggs, one cup of sugar, one cup of cream, two cups of flour, one teaspoonful of cream of tartar, and one teaspoonful of soda.

GINGER CAKES.

Mrs. Joseph Saulter.

Two cups of syrup and one cup of lard, scalded together; add one dessertspoonful of baking soda; when cool add flour enough to make a dough; ginger to taste; roll out and cut into shapes with cutter; bake in a medium oven; rub a little syrup over the tops before baking.

GINGERBREAD.

Miss L. Stagman.

One cup of butter, one cup of sugar, two cups of molasses, two and one-half cups of flour, six eggs, one cup of buttermilk, ginger and cinnamon essences to taste, and one dessertspoonful of soda.

WHITE GINGERBREAD.

Ettie.

Rub half a pound of butter into one pound of flour, add half a pound of loaf sugar, which should be finely pounded and sifted, and the rind of one lemon very finely minced, one ounce of ground ginger and a nutmeg grated. Mix these well together; make one gill of milk just warm, stir in half a teaspoonful of carbonate of soda, and work the whole into a smooth paste; roll it out into cakes, and bake in a moderate oven from fifteen to twenty minutes.

GINGER SPICE CAKE.

Mrs. J. D. Odell.

One cup of molasses, half a cup of butter, half a cup of milk, two eggs, one teaspoon of cloves, one teaspoon of cinnamon, one teaspoon of baking powder, salt; bake in a quick oven.

GINGER CAKE.

Mrs. Howe.

Three eggs, three-quarters of a cup of sugar, one cup of molasses, one cup of milk, three quarters of a cup of butter, one teaspoon of soda, one teaspoon of cream of tartar, one tablespoonful of ginger, one of cinnamon, allspice, three cups of flour.

WALNUT HILL'S DOUGHNUTS.

Mrs. Howe.

One teacup sour cream or milk, two teacups of sugar, one teacup of butter, four eggs; spice with nutmeg and cinnamon; one teaspoonful of soda; beat all well together with some of the flour; then mix with the hands till stiff enough to roll; cut in diamond cakes and fry in hot lard.

DOUGHNUTS.

Mrs. Howe.

One teacup of sugar, half a cup of sweet milk, two eggs, three tablespoons melted butter, half a teaspoonful of soda; spice with cinnamon and nutmeg.

RICE FLOUR CAKE.

Mrs. Howe.

Ten eggs, one pound of sugar, one pound of rice flour; flavour with lemon; beat the eggs and sugar half an hour, then add the flour.

SOFT GINGER CAKE.

Mrs. W. A. Carson.

Two eggs, one and one-half cups of molasses, three tablespoons of butter, one teacup of milk, one teaspoon of soda and two of cream of tartar.

GINGER COOKIES.

Mrs. W. A. Carson.

Two cups of molasses, two-thirds of a cup of butter, two teaspoons ginger, three teaspoons soda dissolved in a little boiling water in a cup; now fill the cup with butter milk; do not mix too thick.

SPICE CAKE.

Mrs. Cook.

One and one-half cups of sugar, half cup butter, half of sour milk, two cups of raisins chopped, three eggs, half a nutmeg, one teaspoon cinnamon, one of cloves, one saleratus; mix rather stiff; bake in loaf tins in moderate oven.

SPONGE JELLY CAKE.

Mrs. R. J. Belford.

Three eggs, one cup sugar, one cup flour, two teaspoonsful baking powder, five tablespoons boiling water. This is quickly made, and you may use any filling you choose.

FRITTERS.

Mrs. Isaac Shannon.

Two eggs, two cups sour milk, one teaspoon soda, four tablespoons butter, flour to thicken, fry in boiling lard.

SOFT GINGERBREAD.

Mrs. Ted Thomas.

One pint molasses, five eggs, one coffee-cup sour milk, one butter, one tablespoon ginger, one tablespoon soda, flour to thicken; bake in a long tin.

CREAM SPONGE CAKE.

Mrs. John Thomas.

One cup sugar, one-half cup cream, two eggs, one cup flour, one-half teaspoon cream tartar, one-fourth soda, flavour with a few drops of lemon essence.

JELLY CAKE.

Mrs. John Thomas.

One cup sugar, two tablespoons butter, two eggs, three tablespoons milk, one cup flour, essence, one teaspoon Cook's Friend, or one-half teaspoon cream tartar and one-fourth soda; bake in two jelly tins in a moderately warm oven; beat the sugar and butter well together.

LOAF CAKE.

Mrs. John Thomas.

One cup sugar, one-half cup butter, one egg, one cup sweet milk, one pint flour, one cup raisins, one-half teaspoon soda, one teaspoon cream tartar, essence.

LIGHT TEA CAKES.

Mrs. John Thomas.

One and one-half cups sugar, two-thirds cup butter, three eggs, three tablespoons sour milk, in which dissolve one-half teaspoon soda, flour; mix as soft as possible and roll white sugar on top before cutting into rings.

FEATHER CAKE.

Miss Knapp.

White sugar one cup, butter one-half cup, flour two cups, eggs three, two teaspoonsful of baking powder, nutmeg or other flavouring to suit the taste. Very good.

COCOANUT CAKE.

Augusta Simmers.

One cup of butter, three eggs, one of milk, four and one-half cups of flour, four teaspoonsful Cook's Friend, two teacups of desicated cocoanut.

GERMAN RINGS.

Augusta Simmers.

One-half pound of flour, one-half pound butter, one tablespoon sugar, one tablespoon brandy, two eggs;

beat all together; make them in rings and put cinnamon and sugar on the top.

POUND CAKE.

Augusta Simmers.

One pound of flour, three-fourths of a pound butter, three-fourths of a pound sugar, eight eggs; flavour to taste.

1, 2, 3, 4 CAKE.

Augusta Simmers.

One cup of butter, two of sugar, three cups of flour, four eggs add; a little more flour, roll out very thin on sugar, cut any shape, and bake quickly.

RICE CAKE.

Mrs. Bendelari.

Half a pound of sugar, half a pound of flour, six eggs, one teaspoon vanilla; break in the eggs on the flour and sugar, whip for half an hour with the back of a dinner knife; bake twenty minutes in a moderate oven.

RICE CAKE.

Mrs. Arthurs.

Break six eggs on half a pound of rice flour and half a pound of crushed white and sifted sugar, then beat all together for fifteen minutes, and flavour with a few drops of essence of lemon; line a dish with buttered paper and bake half an hour.

CUP CAKE.

S. T. M.

One and one-half cups sugar, one cup butter, three eggs well beaten, a little nutmeg, and two teaspoonsful of Cook's Friend or baking powder, and sufficient flour to make a rather thick batter.

CUP CAKE.

Mrs. Arthurs.

One cup of butter, one of sifted sugar, one of milk, three cups of flour, three eggs, three teaspoonsful of baking powder, flavour with essence of lemon; line a dish with buttered paper and bake one hour.

PLAIN FRUIT CAKE.

Mrs. Arthurs.

One-half pound of well washed currants, and one-half pound of raisins, one cup of butter beaten to a cream, one cup of white sugar, one cup of milk, three cups of flour, three eggs, and three teaspoonsful of baking powder; paper a dish and bake one hour.

DROP CAKES.

Mrs. Arthurs.

One pint of flour, one-half pound of butter, one-fourth pound of sifted sugar, half a nutmeg grated, a handful of currants, two eggs, and one teaspoonful of baking powder; to be baked in a slack oven for ten minutes. The above quantity will make about thirty cakes.

SPONGE CAKE.

Mrs. W. Arthurs.

Four eggs, two cups sugar, two cups flour, one-half cup cold water, three teaspoonsful Cook's Friend; beat the eggs separately.

CUP CAKE.

Mrs. Arthurs.

One cup butter, two cups sugar, three cups flour, four eggs, cup milk, three teaspoonsful Cook's Friend.

GERMAN LADIES' FINGERS.

Helena Smith.

Beat the yolks of five eggs with half a pound of sugar for fifteen minutes; add half a pound of blanched almonds cut fine, the grated rind of one lemon; mix well; add half a pound of flour very gradually; roll out the paste and cut into strips the length and size of the forefinger; bake in a moderate oven.

RICE CAKE.

Helena Smith.

One cup of white sugar, one of rice flour, five eggs, one teaspoonful of any essence preferred; beat all together for twenty minutes; bake half an hour in a moderate oven.

WHITE CAKE.

Mrs. George Virtue.

Beat one-half pound fresh butter to a cream, equal weight sifted sugar and dried sugar, the yolks and whites of eight eggs separately whisked, two ounces candied orange peel, one-half teaspoonful of mace, a glass of brandy, one pound flour stirred in by degrees, one and one-quarter pounds of currants, four ounces of powdered almonds; bake two hours.

SWEET SANDWICHES.

Clara Smith.

Five eggs, one-half pound white sugar, one-fourth pound butter, all beaten together until very light; add one-fourth pound flour mixed with a teaspoonful of Cook's Friend.

SHREWSBURY CAKE.

Clara Smith.

One cup butter, two of brown sugar, five eggs (not divided,) one cup milk, four of flour, one of raisins, spice to taste; use Cook's Friend in the flour; bake three hours.

COCOANUT CAKE.

Mrs. W. T. Eyre.

Two eggs, cup of sugar, cup of flour, two tablespoonsful of water; white of one egg and teaspoonful of sugar mixed together to make the cocoa stick.

CENTENNIAL CAKE.

Mrs. George Virtue.

Five eggs, three cups of powdered sugar, one cup of cream or milk, one cup of butter, four cups of flour, the rind and part of juice of one lemon, and a little baking powder, or use prepared flour.

LUNCHEON CAKE.

M. G.

One-half pound butter, one pound flour, one-half ounce caraway seeds, one-fourth pound currants, six ounces moist sugar, one ounce candied peel, three eggs, one-half pint milk, one small teaspoonful of carbonate of soda; bake in a moderate oven from one to one and one-half hours. Proved to be very good.

PLAIN SPONGE FOR JELLY OR COCOANUT CAKE.

Mrs. R. Beaty.

One cup flour, one cup sugar, three eggs, yolks and whites beaten separately, one teaspoonful cream tartar, one-half teaspoonful soda, four tablespoons cold water. Flavour to taste.

MOUNTAIN CAKE.

Fannie.

One cup of sugar, two eggs, one-half cup butter, one-half cup milk or water, two cups of flour, one teaspoonful of cream of tartar, one-half teaspoonful of soda, and a little nutmeg.

JOE'S CAKE.

Fannie S.

Two cups of sugar, one-half cup butter, two eggs, half a cup of raisins chopped fine, half a cup of currants, a little lemon-peel, one teaspoonful of essence of lemon, one-half cup of milk, two teaspoonsful of baking powder and three cups of flour.

CHOCOLATE DRESSING FOR CAKE.

Mrs. S. McMaster.

One bar and a half chocolate, five tablespoons sweet milk, four of powdered sugar; boil soft and thick; when cool add whites of two eggs and sugar to thicken.

PUFF CAKE.

Mrs. Sam. McMaster.

One cup of sugar, one of flour, three eggs, three teaspoons cold water, two of baking powder, a pinch of salt; bake in sponge cake pans.

THE PASTE FOR ABOVE.—One cup of milk, one tablespoon of corn starch, one egg, a pinch of salt; cook like boiled custard; split each cake open with a knife and fill the space with the paste, taking care not to let any appear outside the cakes. These may be made extra nice by iceing with chocolate dressing.

CHOCOLATE CAKE.

Mrs. J. D. Odell.

One and one-half cups sugar, one cup of milk, two cups of flour, piece of butter the size of a small egg, one egg, two teaspoonsful baking powder. Iceing. Whites of two eggs, one cup of sugar, one-half cup chocolate;

beat all together and cook in a dish set in boiling water until smooth like iceing; spread between the cakes.

CHOCOLATE CAKE.

M. R. Beard.

One cup of butter, one cup milk, three of sugar, four cups of flour, six eggs, one teaspoon of soda, two teaspoons of cream of tartar; bake in layers like jelly cake. Iceing for cake to place between: One cup of sugar, one cake of chocolate, the whites of two eggs whipped together.

COCOANUT CAKE.

M. R. Beard.

One cup of butter, three of sugar, one of milk, four of flour or one pint, one teaspoonful of soda, two of cream of tartar, five eggs; bake in layers like jelly cake. Iceing to place between the layers: Half a pound of white sugar to the whites of two eggs, whip the eggs and add the grated cocoanut in, and place between the layers.

MOUNTAIN CAKE.

M. R. Beard.

One-half cup of sugar, one-half cup of butter, one cup of milk, two and one-fourth cups of flour, one teaspoonful soda, two teaspoonsful of cream of tartar, two eggs, a little nutmeg.

COTTAGE PUDDING.

M. R. Beard.

One-half cup of sugar, one cup of milk, one pint of flour, three tablespoonsful of melted butter, one teaspoonful soda, two of cream of tartar, two eggs, a little salt; bake one-quarter of an hour in small pans.

FRUIT CAKE.

Mrs. Snider.

Half a pound of butter, half a pound of sugar; rub well together; four eggs well beaten, half a teaspoon of soda, one wine glass of whiskey, half a nutmeg, fruit to suit the taste, flour to stiffen; bake in a slow oven; this cake will keep for weeks.

CRULLIES.

Mrs. Snider.

Three eggs, two cups of sugar, one cup of butter, two cups of sour milk, two teaspoons Cook's Friend, spice, flour to stiffen; cut in rings and fry in hot lard.

MOLASSES CAKE.

Mrs. Snider.

One cup of butter, one cup of brown sugar, one cup of molasses, one cup of sweet milk, three cups of flour, four eggs, one and a half teaspoons of cream tartar, one teaspoon of soda, two pounds of raisins chopped fine, nutmeg; bake in a slow oven.

SOFT GINGERBREAD.

Mrs. Snider.

Five cups of flour, three cups of molasses, one cup of butter, one cup of milk or water, two tablespoons ginger, two eggs, one teaspoon soda; bake slowly.

SPONGE CAKE.

Mrs. Upham.

The weight of eight eggs in sugar, half the weight in flour, and the juice and rind of one lemon; beat two eggs separately.

GINGER SNAPS.

Mrs. Upham.

One pint of molasses, one cup of butter, a teaspoonful each of ginger, cloves, and soda; put all over the fire together and let it come to a boil, using a large vessel, as it is likely to foam over; when nearly cool add flour enough to make a stiff dough; roll out and cut into small cakes.

WINTER SPONGE CAKE.

Mrs. Upham.

Take four eggs, two cups of sugar, two coffee-cups of flour, two teaspoonsful cream tartar, two-thirds of a cup boiling water, and lemon to flavour; add the water last; pour into a pan and place into a well-heated oven. This, though apparently very thin, will come from the oven a most delightful cake.

WEDDING CAKE.

Mrs. Upham.

Five pounds of seeded raisins, two pounds of currants, one pound of citron, twelve eggs, one pound of butter, one pound sugar (brown), one coffee-cup of molasses, a little brandy, one tea-cup of spices.

ICEING FOR ANY CAKE.

Mrs. Upham.

Instead of beating the eggs to a stiff froth, as is generally the case, take four tablespoons of sugar to the egg, and stir thoroughly; then spread on cake; will make a much harder iceing than beating it.

CAKE.

Mr. Upham.

Cream filled cakes: These delicious cakes are very easily made if care is taken to have the water boiling. Measure out one-half pint and put in a small kettle; immediately after it comes to a boil again put in two-thirds of a cup of butter and one and a half cups of flour; stir briskly for a moment, leaving it over the fire; remove this mixture and place in a dish where it will get entirely cold; beat five large fresh eggs very thoroughly, then stir in your cold mixture a spoonful at a time; stir it all until smooth and free from lumps; drop them upon a greased dripping pan in small pear-shaped cakes; bake half an hour in a real hot oven; don't be afraid they will burn unless you see them doing so. When done they will be hollow inside, of a bright brown colour; if not well done they will flatten. The oven must be hot when you put them in, and if kept so success is sure.

Filling or Cream: Put a little more than one pint of milk in a pail and set in boiling water; beat two eggs, two-thirds cup of corn starch, one full cup sugar, one-half teaspoonful salt, and some vanilla, thoroughly together; add a full half cup of milk, and stir all into your boiling milk; it should be very thick; cut open your cakes near the bottom and fill very full of cream; be sure the cream is cold.

DRIED APPLE CAKE.

Mrs. Brodie.

Soak three cupsful of dried apples over night in warm water, chop slightly, then let them simmer for one hour and a half in two cups of syrup or molasses; add two eggs, one cup of sugar, one cup of sweet milk, half cup of butter, one teaspoonful of soda, flour enough to make a stiff batter; bake in a quick oven.

CHEAP AND GOOD CAKE.

Ada King.

One cup of sugar, one-fourth cup of butter, three-fourths cup water cold, one and three-fourths cup of flour, whites of two eggs, one teaspoon of lemon, baking powder used.

SPICE CAKE.

Ada King.

One cup of sugar, three-fourths cup of butter, fill up with milk, one egg, one and three-fourths cup of flour, one small teaspoon soda, one dessert spoon of cinnamon, cloves, and allspice.

FRUIT CAKE.

Mrs. J. D. Odell.

One cup butter, two cups of sugar, one cup molasses, six cups flour, one cup sour cream or milk, three eggs, one teaspoon soda, one pound raisins, one pound currants, one-fourth pound citron, three nutmegs, cloves and mace one tablespoon each. This will make one large cake or two small ones.

CORN STARCH CAKE.

Two cups pulverized sugar, two-thirds cup melted butter, one-half cup milk, two teaspoons baking powder, one teaspoon vanilla, one paper corn starch, six eggs.

CREAM PUFFS.

Mrs. J. D. Odell.

One and one-half cups flour, two-thirds cup butter, one-half pint water; boil butter and water together, stir in flour while boiling, let it cool, and add five well beaten eggs; drop on tins and bake in a quick oven. When cool fill with the following: One pint of milk, one cup sugar, two-thirds cup corn starch, two eggs; beat sugar, eggs, and flour together; stir in the milk while boiling; flavour with lemon or vanilla.

PLAIN FRUIT CAKE

Mrs. Hamilton.

Three cups of sugar, one and a half of butter, one and a half of molasses, one of milk, four eggs, one teaspoonful soda, two teaspoonsful cinnamon, two teaspoonsful cloves, two teaspoonsful nutmeg, two pounds currants, one-half pound citron, one glass of wine, flour to make a stiff batter.

MRS. J. R. SILLIMAN'S SPICE CAKE.

Take one cup of butter, two cups of molasses, four eggs, two tablespoonsful of allspice, two teaspoonsful of baking powder, one cup of milk, three cups of flour.

MRS. J. R SILLIMAN'S WHITE SPONGE CAKE.

Take two tumblers of white pulverized sugar, one and a half tumblers sifted flour, one teaspoonful cream tartar, white of ten eggs beaten very stiff; then add the flour and sugar, and beat as little as possible; bake in a slow oven.

LOVELY SPONGE CAKE.

Mrs. J. D. King.

One pound of sugar, one-half pound of flour, ten eggs, one grated lemon; beat sugar and yolks to a cream, whites to a stiff froth; add lemon to the sugar and eggs when beaten. Takes two persons to make it.

VANITY CAKE.

Mrs. Hamilton.

Two eggs, one cup flour rolled thin as a wafer; cut in patterns; boiled in lard.

SODA CAKE.

Mrs. Hamilton.

Two cups sugar, one-half cup butter, one cup of milk, three and a half of flour, two eggs, one teaspoonful Cook's Friend; flavour with lemon.

NICE LITTLE CAKES—CHEAP.

Madame E. Pernet.

One-half cup butter, one-half cup sugar, one-half cup milk, three cups flour, two eggs, two spoonsful baking powder. Mode—Beat the eggs, add the sugar, the batter well beaten, and half a nutmeg if the flavour be approved of, if not any other spice, or a few drops of essence of any kind; mix the baking powder well with the flour, and add by degrees to the mixture; bake in small patty pans half an hour in a quick oven. They will be found very good if properly made.

SANDWICH CAKE.

Miss Rrokovski.

One coffee cup of sugar, one large tablespoonful of butter beaten to a cream with the sugar, three eggs beaten separately, one heaping coffee-cup of flour, three teaspoonsful of baking powder mixed well through the flour, and one tablespoonful of milk; if cream of tartar, two teaspoonsful and one of soda, mixing the cream tartar in the flour, and putting soda in the milk. Mix all together, seasoning with extract of lemon; beat well for a few minutes; bake on four flat tins in a quick oven. This may be put together with jelly or custard or cocoanut, using the desicated cocoanut, moistened with the whites of three eggs beaten to a froth, and iced over.

LEMON CHEESE CAKE.

Mrs. Joseph Saulter.

Break one pound of loaf sugar into small lumps, put to it one-quarter pound of butter, the yolks of six eggs with the whites of four, the juice of three lemons, and the peel of two grated; put these into a pan, let them simmer over a slow fire until the sugar is dissolved; continue to stir it gently one way while it is on the fire, or it will curdle; keep it in a jar like mince meat; let it simmer till it begins to thicken, or looks like honey.

SHREWSBURY CAKE.

Miss Isaac Shannon.

One-half pound of flour, and butter and sugar firmly pounded, one egg, and a teaspoonful of mace; roll them out the size you like; bake them in a slow oven. Excellent.

EXCELLENT CAKE.

Mrs. Joseph Robinson.

One pound flour, one-half pound butter, three-fourths pound sugar, one-half pint of milk, five eggs, two tablespoonsful of brandy, one teaspoonful of soda and two of cream of tartar. Put half this quantity into a cake tin for a plain cake, then add one cup of currants to the remainder, which will make a nice variety of cake.

FRUIT CAKE.

Mrs. Ira Metcalf.

One pound butter, one pound brown sugar, one cup molasses, nine eggs, half a pint brandy, one pound flour, one-half pound mace, three pounds raisins, three pounds currants, one pound citron, nutmeg and cloves to taste; rub one-half pound flour with fruit; steam two hours in a dish, then bake one hour.

SPONGE CAKE.

Mrs. Ira Metcalf.

Three eggs, one cup white sugar, one teaspoon of cream of tartar, one-half of soda, three tablespoons of boiling water, flour to thicken.

FIG CAKE.

Mrs. Trusbie.

For the white part: Take two cups of sugar, two of flour, two-thirds of sweet milk, one-half of butter, whites of five eggs, two teaspoons baking powder; bake this in two round tins like you would jelly cake. For fig or dark part: Take one cup of brown sugar, butter size of walnut, one cup flour, one cup chopped figs, one-half cup sweet milk, one egg, one teaspoon baking powder; when done place the fig cake between the light cake, with a little frosting.

SPONGE JELLY CAKE.

Mrs. Carson.

Three eggs beaten separate, one cup sugar, one cup flour, two teaspoons baking powder put into the flour, and three tablespoons boiling water. Mix all together and cook in jelly tins in a quick oven; place either jelly or chocolate frosting between the cakes.

CHOCOLATE FROSTING.

Mrs. Carson.

One-half cup chocolate grated, one cup sugar, yolk of one egg, small cup half full of sweet milk; put on stove and stir while cooking till it will candy when dropped in cold water.

WASHINGTON CREAM CAKE.

Mrs. Carson.

Two cups sugar, one-half cup sweet milk, four eggs, three cups flour, three even teaspoons baking powder, butter size of an egg.

CREAM FOR WASHINGTON CAKE.—One pint of sweet milk, three eggs, one cup flour, one sugar, flavour with anything; after it is cooked add half cup butter, and place between the cakes as you would jelly.

COFFEE CAKE.

Mrs. Carson.

One cup molasses, one cup brown sugar, one cup cold coffee, four cups sifted flour, one-half cup butter, two teaspoons baking powder and a small teaspoon allspice.

DELICATE CAKE.

Mrs. Charles Rogers.

One-half cup butter, one cup sugar, one cup sifted flour, one-half cup corn starch, one-half cup milk, one teaspoon of baking powder, four eggs, using the whites only.

POUND CAKE.

Mrs. Charles Rogers.

One cup of butter, one cup of sugar, four eggs beaten separately, one and one-half cups sifted flour; mix butter and sugar to a cream, then put in yolks beaten light, the flour and whites last.

COCOANUT CAKE.

Mrs. Carson.

One cup butter, two cups white sugar, one cup milk, three coffee-cups sifted flour, whites of six eggs beaten light, three even teaspoons of baking powder, one cocoanut grated; do not use the milk of nut; mix and bake in oven.

GOLD CAKE.

Mrs. Ira Metcalf.

One half cup butter, two cups sugar, half cup milk, three of flour, three teaspoons baking powder, and yolks of four eggs.

For the silver cake use the same receipt, only in place of the yolks of eggs use the whites of four eggs.

For marble cake same receipt, using brown sugar one cup, and one cup molasses, and some spices, and drop in dish on the white cake or silver receipt.

CALIFORNIA CAKE.

Mrs. Charles Rogers.

Two cups sugar, one cup butter, one cup milk, two eggs, three teaspoons baking powder, put in three cups sifted flour, flavour and add fruit. This receipt makes two cakes.

LEMON CHEESE CAKE.

Mrs. Carson.

Two cups sugar, half cup butter, three-quarters cup sweet milk, whites of six eggs, three cups flour, three teaspoons baking powder.

Sauce for Lemon Cheese Cake.—Grated rind and juice of two lemons, yolks of three eggs, half cup butter, one cup sugar; mix all together, and set on stove, and cook till thick as sponge, stirring all the time; then use like jelly between the cakes.

GINGER DROP CAKES.

Mrs. Carson.

Two cups of molasses, two cups of sugar, two cups of butter or lard, two cups of sour milk, two tablespoons of soda, two spoons of cinnamon, one of cloves, nine cups of flour, and ginger to suit taste; drop from spoon into a pan, and cook in oven, taking care not to burn.

WHITE MOUNTAIN JELLY CAKE.

Mrs. Carson.

One cup of butter, two cups of sugar, three and a half cups of flour, one cup of milk, two eggs, two teaspoons cream of tartar, one teaspoon soda; stir all together without separating eggs; put soda in milk, and stir the cream of tartar in flour; bake the same as jelly cake, and use frosting between made of whites of three eggs and fine white sugar.

DELICATE CAKE.

Mrs. Taylor.

Half cup of butter, one of sugar, one of flour, one-half of corn starch, one-half cup of milk, one teaspoon of baking powder, four eggs, whites alone.

CALIFORNIA CAKE.

Mrs. Taylor

Two cups of sugar, half a cup of butter, one cup of milk, two eggs, three teaspoons of baking powder, three cups of sifted flour, flavour, or add fruit. This makes two cakes. Bake in bread tins.

PAN DADDLINGS.
Mrs. Rogers.

Four cups rye meal, two cups of Indian meal, one cup of molasses, plenty of suet, a little allspice, one egg, milk to thin it to a batter that will drop from the spoon, one teaspoon of soda, three chopped apples; fry in hot lard like fried cakes; dip the spoon in the lard and dip up your batter and drop into hot lard; fry a light brown.

FRIED CAKES.
Mrs. Carson.

One cup of sugar, two eggs, half a cup of shortening, one teaspoon of soda, one cup of sour milk, cut in rings; have your lard very hot, in which place a peeled potato to keep lard from burning, and drop in your cakes; they will come to the top of lard when light; fry a dark brown; when taken out sprinkle sugar over them.

FRENCH CAKES.

Five cups of flour, two cups of sugar, half a cup of butter, one cup of milk, one wineglass of wine, three eggs, spice to taste, one teaspoon of soda; rub the butter and sugar together, then add the milk; part of the flour, soda in the wine next; then the rest of the flour, and eggs beaten separately, the whites last; bake in square tins.

ORANGE CAKE.
Mrs. Smith.

One cup of sugar, half a cup of butter, half a cup of sweet milk, two cups of flour, three eggs, one and a-half teaspoonsful of baking powder; bake in jelly tins.

Orange Frosting for Same.—One orange, grate off the outside, and mix with juice, and add sugar until quite stiff, and make like jelly cake; make four layers of the cake.

MRS. ROGER'S CAKE.

Two cups of sugar, one cup water cold, whites of eleven eggs, three teaspoons of baking powder, one and one-half cups flour, two-thirds cup butter; stir butter and sugar up together till it is light; put whites into sugar and butter, flour and powder in last.

MRS. ROGER'S POUND CAKE.

One cup of butter, one of sugar, four eggs beaten separately, one and one-half cups of sifted flour; mix butter and sugar to a cream, then put in yolks beaten light, then flour and whites last.

CORN STARCH CAKE.

Mrs. Ira Metcalf.

One cup butter, three cups sugar, beaten to a cream, then add in the following order: two scant cups flour, whites of eight eggs, three teaspoons of baking powder mixed with flour, and lastly, one and one-half cups of corn starch mixed smooth in one cup of milk; flavour as you please; bake in an ordinary flat tin pan, and cut in diamonds when cold.

WHITE SPONGE CAKE.

Mrs. Ira Metcalf.

Whites of eight eggs, one and a half tumblers white sugar, one of flour, one teaspoon of cream of tartar, flavour to taste, bake in flat tins, and if you choose, ice with "chocolate icing" No. 1; cut in diamond shapes.

COCOANUT CAKE.

Mrs. Ira Metcalf.

One cup of butter, three cups of sugar, one cup of milk, three eggs, four teaspoons of baking powder, one large cocoanut grated.

COCOANUT CAKE.

Mrs. Rogers.

One cup of butter, two cups of white sugar, one cup of milk, three coffee cups of flour, whites of six eggs, well beaten, three teaspoons baking powder, one cocoanut grated ; do not use the milk of nut.

COCOANUT CAKE MADE AS JELLY CAKE.

Mrs. Ira Metcalf.

One cup of butter, three cups of sugar, one cup of milk, five cups of flour, six teaspoons of baking powder, whites of eight eggs ; bake in jelly cake pans ; for dressing to put between take the whites of six eggs beaten stiff, half a pound of dessicated cocoanut, and one cup of powdered sugar.

LEMON CHEESE CAKE.

Mrs. Ira Metcalf.

For the cake take part of two cups of sugar, ½ a cup of butter, three-quarters of a cup of sweet milk, whites of six eggs, three cups of flour, three teaspoons of baking powder.

JELLY FOR LEMON CHEESE CAKE.—Grated rind and juice of two lemons, yolks of three eggs, half a cup of butter, one cup of sugar, mix all together, and set on the stove and cook till thick as sponge, taking care not to burn; use like jelly between the cakes, or bake one square cake and put the dressing on top and cut in shape of diamonds.

CHOCOLATE CAKE.

Mrs. W. A. Carson.

One cup of butter, two cups of sugar, five eggs, leaving out two of the whites; one scant cup of milk, two full teaspoons of baking powder; mix well in three cups of sifted flour; bake in two long tins.

FOR FROSTING.—Beat whites of two eggs to a stiff froth, add a scant cup and a half of sugar; flavour with vanilla, six tablespoons grated chocolate; the cake must be cold.

GOLD CAKE.

Mrs. W. A. Carson.

Three-quarters of a cup of butter beaten to a cream, one cup of sugar; the yolks of eight eggs, two cups of sifted flour, one teaspoon of cream of tartar, half a teaspoon of soda dissolved in half a cup of sweet milk.

MARBLE CAKE.

Mrs. D. McCraney.

WHITE PART.—One cup of butter, two cups of white sugar, half a cup of sour cream or buttermilk, three and a half cups of flour, whites of seven eggs, one teaspoonful of soda.

BLACK PART.—Two cups of brown sugar, one cup of butter, one cup of molasses, five cups of flour, half a cup of sour cream or buttermilk, yolks of seven eggs, one grated nutmeg, two tablespoonsful of cinnamon, one tablespoonful of cloves, one tablespoonful of allspice, one teaspoonful of black pepper, one teaspoonful of soda.

JELLY CAKE.

Mrs. D. McCraney.

One cupful of white sugar, three eggs, yolks and whites beaten separately; one cup of flour, from which a tablespoon of flour is taken and its place supplied by corn starch; half a teaspoonful of soda, and one teaspoonful of cream of tartar. If for sponge cake use four eggs.

VELVET CAKE.

Mrs. D. McCraney.

Half pound of butter, one pound of pulverized sugar, one pound of flour, four eggs, one teacup of cold water, half teaspoonful of soda, one of cream of tartar, flavour to taste; bake an hour, add fruit and spice if desired, or make into chocolate cake by being baked as jelly cake.

LINCOLN FRUIT CAKE.

Mrs. D. McCraney.

One pound of butter, one pound of brown sugar, one pound of flour, six eggs, two cups of sour cream or buttermilk, one grated nutmeg, one teaspoonful of powdered cinnamon, one tablespoonful of rose water, lemon peel and fruit to taste, one teaspoonful of soda dissolved in hot water and stirred into the milk just before adding it to the cake.

CREAM CAKE.

Mrs. Ira Metcalf.

One pint of good cream, two tablespoons flour, one-half cup white sugar, whites of two eggs well beaten; bake in flat tins and frost with soft frosting.

CREAM CAKE NO. 2.

Mrs. Ira Metcalf.

One cup of cream, one cup of sugar, two cups of flour, two eggs, one teaspoon of soda.

SILVER CAKE.

Mrs. Ira Metcalf.

Two cups of fine white sugar, two and one-half cups of sifted flour, one-half cup of butter, one-quarter cup of sweet milk, one-half teaspoon of soda dissolved in the milk, one teaspoon of cream of tartar, the whites of eight eggs. Flavour to taste.

SPONGE CAKE.

Mrs. H. Baird.

Five eggs, one and one-half cups of flour, one and

one-half cups sugar, one-third cup of water, one-quarter teaspoon soda, one-half cream of tartar; flavour with lemon.

JELLY CAKE.

Mrs. H. Baird.

Three eggs, a small teacup of sugar, one cup of flour, whites and yolks of the eggs beaten together; flavour, and bake in two layers, in a quick oven.

COCOANUT CAKE.

Mrs. H. Baird.

Three eggs, one cup of sugar, one cup of milk, two cups and one-half of flour, one tablespoon of butter, one teaspoon of soda, two teaspoons of cream of tartar. Beat with a fork. Add milk and whites of the eggs together; only half of the whites; keep the rest for icing with cocoanut.

LUCY'S TEA CAKE.

Mrs. H. Baird.

Two eggs, one cup of sugar, one-half cup of butter, one teacup of milk, two cups of flour, and a few currants.

CORN STARCH CAKE.

Mrs. Baird.

Whites of six eggs, one cup of butter, two cups of flour, one cup of corn starch, two cups of sugar, one cup of sweet milk, one-half teaspoon of soda, one of cream of tartar.

CAKE—WASHINGTON.

Mrs. J. H. Mead.

One and three-quarters pounds of flour, one and one quarter of a pound of sugar, three-quarters of a pound of butter, four eggs, a wine glass of brandy and one of wine, one pint of milk, a teaspoon of soda, one nutmeg, two pounds of raisins, currants, and candied fruit.

SPONGE CAKE.

Mrs. J. H. Mead.

One dozen eggs, ten ounces of flour, one pound fine white sugar; break the eggs into the sugar, place on the stove and heat till milk warm, then take them off and beat till quite cold; flavour with essence of lemon, stir in the flour very lightly; butter your baking tins and sift sugar all over the bottom and sides; put in the mixture, sift sugar on the top and bake in a very moderate oven.

LEMON CAKE.

Mrs. J. H. Mead

Half a cup of milk, half a cup of butter, two small cups of sugar, three small cups of flour, whites of four eggs, two teaspoons of cream of tartar, one teaspoon of soda; flavour with lemon; beat the butter to a cream, add eggs well whipped, then sugar; mix cream of tartar in the flour, and soda in milk.

JELLY CAKE.

Mrs. J. H. Mead.

Two eggs, one cup of sugar, one tablespoon of butter, one and a half cups of flour, one tablespoon of baking powder, two-thirds of a cup of milk; beat the butter to a cream, and add the yolks of the eggs well beaten; beat the whites to a froth and add them to the sugar; mix all together; then put in the flour with the baking powder well mixed in; last of all add the milk; flavour with essence.

DELICATE CAKE.

Mrs. J. H. Mead.

The whites of twelve eggs, three-quarters of a pound of butter, three-quarters of a pound of sugar, one pound of flour, two tablespoonsful of milk, two tablespoonsful Cook's Friend. Beat the eggs to a froth, beat butter and sugar to a cream; mix the baking powder well with the flour, and add milk. If half corn starch is used in place of flour it will be an improvement, and if for jelly cakes bake in square tins, and when cold cut into slices; they are delicious filled with lemon honey in place of jelly.

RICE CAKE.

Mrs. Mickle.

Six eggs, one cup of white sugar, two cups of ground rice; beaten thoroughly.

CORN STARCH CAKES.

Mrs. Mackie.

One cup of flour, one cup of cornstarch, one cup of sugar, half cup of butter, whites of four eggs, half cup of sweet milk, one teaspoonful of cream of tartar, half of soda.

CLOVE CAKE.

Two eggs, one and one-half cups of sugar, one cup of butter, one cup of chopped raisins, one-half cup of sweet milk, two cups of flour, one tablespoon of cloves, one-half teaspoon of soda.

FRUIT CAKE.

Two pounds of raisins, stoned, two pounds of currants, one pound of butter, one pound of sugar, one and one-quarter pounds of flour, ten eggs, one wine glass of brandy, one wine glass of wine, one tablespoon of cloves, one tablespoon of allspice, two tablespoons of cinnamon, one nutmeg, one teaspoon of sweet almond-meats blanched and cut in slices, two ounces candied lemon, two ounces citron; a little molasses improves it, nearly a teacup; flour the fruit, using it out of that weighed out for the cake; put a half teaspoonful of soda or one teaspoonful of baking powder with it on the fruit; bake three hours, slowly.

POUND CAKE.

Ten eggs, one pound of sugar, one pound of butter, one pound of flour; flavour with lemon; beat the butter and sugar together, then add the yolks well beaten, after them the whites; beat to a stiff froth, then add flour Half a pound of figs and same of almonds sliced makes it very nice.

MARBLE CAKE.

WHITE PART.—Whites of seven eggs, two cups of white sugar, one cup of butter, one cup of sweet milk, four cups of flour, two teaspoonsful of cream of tartar, one teaspoon of soda.

BROWN PART.—Yolks of seven eggs, two cups of brown sugar, one cup of molasses, one cup of sour milk, one cup of butter, five cups of flour, two tablespoonsful of cloves, one nutmeg, one teaspoon and a half of soda.

PLAIN SPONGE CAKE.

One egg, one teacup of sugar, one cup of sweet milk, two cups and a half of flour, one dessert spoon of butter, two teaspoons cream of tartar, one teaspoon of soda, and a little salt. Bake fifteen minutes in pans size of a breakfast plate.

COFFEE CAKE.

One cup of butter, one cup of sugar, one cup of molasses, one cup of coffee cold, one cup of currants, one teaspoonful of soda, one teaspoonful of mixed spices, two or four eggs, flour to thicken.

CAKES WITHOUT BUTTER.

Five eggs well beaten, yolks and whites separately, one pound of powdered sugar; when well mixed let it stand an hour, then add one pound of flour, chop the mixture in very small cakes on tin plates; any flavouring may be used.

COMPOSITION CAKE.

Mrs. H. Baird.

Five cups of flour, two cups of butter, three of sugar, one of milk, five eggs, one teaspoon of soda, two of cream of tartar, fruit as you please, cinnamon, nutmeg and clove to taste.

FRUIT LOAF.

Mrs. H. Baird.

One pint of bread sponge, one cup of brown sugar, one cup of molasses, one of butter, half cup of sweet milk, one cup of raisins, one of currants, a little lemon and citron peel, one tablespoonful of cinnamon, one teaspoon of cloves, one of allspice, two or three eggs. Beat eggs, butter and sugar, add all together with flour enough to stiffen as an ordinary fruit cake.

ORANGE CAKE AS JELLY CAKE.

Mrs. H. Baird.

Cake part.—Five eggs, two cups of sugar, two cups of flour, half a cup of cold water, one teaspoon of cream of tartar, half a teaspoon of soda. Dressing—Use the grated rind of one large orange, and the juice; stiffen with the white of one egg and sugar.

GINGER NUTS.

Mrs. H. Baird.

One and three-quarter pounds of syrup, one pound of moist sugar, one pound of butter, two and three-quarter pounds of flour, one and a half ounces of ground ginger, one and a half ounces of allspice, one and a half ounces of coriander seed, salvolatile size of a bean, a little cayenne, flour enough to roll out but not thin, cut with a wineglass or roll between your hands into small balls and pinch.

GINGER CAKE.

Mrs. H. Baird.

One cup of molasses, half a cup of butter, two-thirds of a cup of water, one teaspoon almost full of ginger, two teaspoons of soda; mix in flour enough to let it drop off the spoon; bake in a tin about two inches deep.

CUP CAKE.

One cup of butter, two cups of sugar, three cups of flour, four eggs, a teaspoonful of soda dissolved in a cup of milk, two teaspoonsful of cream of tartar mixed into the flour; flavour with essence of any kind.

ALMOND CAKE.

Stir two eggs with half a pound of white sugar till very light; half a pound of unpeeled split almonds, as much soda as will lie on the point of a knife, half a pound of flour; roll it out and then put into a flat tin; brush it over with the yolk of an egg; bake till a light brown; then cut into long slices; set them on edge and roast them.

LEMON HONEY.

Four ounces of butter, one pound of sugar, six eggs, leaving out two whites; **grate the rinds of three lemons** and add the juice. Let all simmer over the fire till it becomes of the consistency of honey. Great care must be taken that it does not burn.

FRUIT CAKE.

One pound of flour, one pound of sugar, three-quarters of a pound of butter, two pounds raisins, two pounds currants, one pound mixed peel, one-quarter pound almonds, two ounces mace, ten eggs, rose water and brandy.

BIRTHDAY CAKE.

One pound and a half of fine sugar, one pound and a half of butter, theee pounds and one-half of currants, two pounds of flour, one-half pound candied peel, one-half pound almonds, two ounces spices, the grated rind of three lemons, eighteen eggs, one gill of brandy. Paper the hoops, and bake three hours. Ice when cold.

NELL'S CHOCOLATE CAKE.

One cup of butter, two of sugar, five eggs, leaving out two of the whites, one scant cup of milk, two full teaspoons of baking powder; mix well in three cups flour; bake in two long shallow tins. Dressing: Beat the whites of the two eggs to a stiff froth, add a scant cup and a half of sugar; flavour with vanilla, add six tablespoons of grated chocolate; add the dressing when the cake is cold, and cut in diamond slices.

ORANGE CAKE.

Mrs. S. McMaster.

Two cups of flour, two cups of sugar, one-half cup of water, two teaspoons of baking powder, yolks of five eggs, whites of three; bake like jelly cake. Dressing—Whites of the two eggs, grate the rind of two oranges, add the juice, sugar to thicken; put this between the cakes and set back in the oven for a minute.

DRINKS.

The bubbling and loud hissing urn,
Throws up a steaming column; and the cups
That cheer, but not inebriate, wait on each;
So let us welcome peaceful evening in.
—COWPER.

TEA.

When the water in the tea-kettle begins to boil, have ready a tin tea-steeper; pour into the tea-steeper just a very little of the boiling water, and then put in tea, allowing one teaspoon of tea to each person. Pour over this boiling water until the steeper is little more than half full; cover tightly and let it stand where it will keep hot, but not to boil. Let the tea infuse for ten or fifteen minutes, and then pour into the tea urn, adding more boiling water, in the proportion of one cup of water for every teaspoon of dry tea which has been infused. Have boiling water in a water pot, and weaken each cup of tea as desired. Do not use water for tea that has boiled long. Spring water is best for tea, and filtered water next best.

TEA A LA RUSSE.

Pare and slice fresh, juicy lemons; lay a piece in the bottom of each cup, sprinkle with white sugar, and pour hot, strong tea over. Or the lemon may be sent around in slices with the peel on. No cream is used.

ICED TEA A LA RUSSE.

To each glass of tea add the juice of half a lemon, fill up the glass with pounded ice, and sweeten.

CHOCOLATE.

Scrape Baker's chocolate fine, mix with a little cold water and the yolks of eggs well beaten; add this to equal parts of milk and water, and boil well, being careful that it does not burn. Sweeten to taste and serve hot.

COFFEE.

Miss Riley.

The following is a delicious dish either for summer breakfast or dessert: Make a strong infusion of mocha coffee; put it in a porcelain bowl, sugar it properly and add to it an equal portion of boiled milk, or one-third the quantity of a rich cream. Surround the bowl with pounded ice.

ROASTING COFFEE.—This process should be carefully watched and superintended. When the berry crackles and becomes crisp it is sufficiently roasted. Once taken off the roaster, it should be placed in several thick folds of flannel, to preserve the oil and aroma. When cool, place it in an air-tight cannister.

CURRANT WINE.

Mrs. J. D. Odell.

One quart currant juice, three pounds of sugar, sufficient water to make a gallon.

CREAM NECTAR.

Mrs. John Morse.

Four pounds of white sugar, six quarts of water, put over a slow fire, milk warm, add whites of two eggs well beaten; bring the whole to nearly boiling point; let boil and strain immediately; when cold add six ounces of tartaric acid; flavour with lemon; a wineglass to be used in a tumbler of water; add half a teaspoonful of baking soda.

SODA CREAM.

M. G. Rand.

Two and one-half pounds white sugar, one-eighth pound tartaric acid, both dissolved in one quart of hot water; when cold, add the beaten whites of three eggs, stirring well; bottle for use. Put two large spoons of this syrup in a glass of cold water, and stir in it one-fourth of a spoon of bicarbonate of soda. Any flavour can be put in the syrup. An excellent drink for summer.

RASPBERRY ACID.

Mrs. G. W. Pitkin.

Dissolve five ounces of tartaric acid in two quarts of water; pour it upon twelve pounds of red raspberries in a large bowl; let it stand twenty-four hours; strain it without pressing; to a pint of this liquor add one and a half pounds of white sugar; stir until dissolves. Bottle, but do not cook for several days, when it is ready for use. Two or three tablespoons in a glass of ice water will make a delicious beverage.

RASPBERRY VINEGAR.

Mrs. W. S. Walker.

To four quarts red raspberries, put enough vinegar to cover, and let them stand twenty-four hours; scald and strain it; add a pound of sugar to one pint of juice; boil it twenty minutes, and bottle; it is then ready for use and will keep years. To one glass of water add a great spoonful. It is much relished by the sick. Very nice.

RASPBERRY VINEGAR.

Mrs. Joseph B. Leake.

Fill a jar with red raspberries picked from the stalks. Pour in as much vinegar as it will hold. Let it stand ten days, then strain it through a sieve. Don't press the berries, just let the juice run through. To every pint add one pound loaf sugar. Boil it like other syrup; skim and bottle when cold.

BLACKBERRY SYRUP.

Mrs. Bausher.

To one pint of juice, put one pound of white sugar, one-half ounce of powdered cinnamon, one-fourth ounce mace, and two teaspoons cloves; boil all together for quarter of an hour, then strain the syrup, and add to each pint a glass of French brandy.

LEMON SYRUP.

Mrs. De Forrest.

Pare off the yellow rind of the lemon, slice the lemon and put a layer of lemon and a thick layer of sugar in a deep plate; cover close with a saucer, and set in a warm place. This is an excellent remedy for a cold.

SPLENDID GINGER BEER.

Mrs. H. L. Bristol.

Five gallons of water, one-half pound ginger root boiled, four pounds of sugar, one-eighth pound of cream of tartar, one bottle of essence of lemon, one ounce of tartaric acid, one quart of yeast.

GINGER WINE.

Mrs. Oliphant.

One-half pound of cinnamon bark, four ounces of pimento, two ounces of mace, three quarters of an ounce of capsicum, three quarters of a pound of ginger root, five gallons of alcohol; macerate and strain or filter, after standing fifteen days. Now make syrup, thirty pounds of white sugar, half pound of tartaric acid, one and a half pounds of cream tartar, dissolve with warm water, clarify with white of two eggs, and add soft water to make forty gallons. Colour with cochineal and let it stand six months before use.

GINGER WINE.

Mrs. Betts.

INGREDIENTS: Ten gallons of water, one pound bruised

ginger, thirty-two pounds raw sugar, ten lemons, ten Seville oranges, four pounds of raisins, one-half ounce of isinglass. Peel the fruit, and express the juice. Boil the water, ginger, and sugar half an hour; pour it boiling hot upon the peel; add the juice. When nearly cold put in a little yeast spread upon a toast. Let it stand three days, stirring it twice a day; then put it into a cask with the raisins and isinglass. Continue stirring twice a day for ten days. It must not be stopped till it has ceased to ferment. Fit for use in three months.

RED CURRANT WINE.

Mrs. Betts.

For every gallon of water take one gallon of currants off the stalks, bruise well and let them stand over night. Next morning mash them well with your hands and strain through a hair sieve. To every gallon of the liquor add four pounds of sugar. Rinse the cask well with brandy and strain the liquor again when putting in, by which you will see whether the sugar is dissolved. Lay the bung lightly on and stop it up in ten days.

BOSTON CREAM (A SUMMER DRINK).

Mrs. Kerr.

Make a syrup of four pounds of white sugar with four quarts of water; boil; when cold add four ounces of tartaric acid, one and a half ounces of essence of lemon, and the whites of six eggs beaten to a stiff froth; bottle. A wineglass of the cream to a tumbler of water, with sufficient carbonate of soda to make it effervesce.

HOT MULLED WINE.

Mrs. Bendelari.

To every pint of wine allow one large cup of water, one tablespoon of sugar, half a salt spoon of cloves, half a salt spoon of cinnamon, half a salt spoon of nutmeg. First tie your spices in a muslin bag, and put the water into a porcelain saucepan with the spices, and when it has simmered a few minutes add the wine.

CHAMPAGNE CUP.

Mrs. Bendelari.

One quart bottle of champagne, two bottles of soda water, one liqueur glass of brandy, two tablespoons of powdered sugar, a few thin strips of cucumber rind; make this just in time for use, and add a large piece of ice.

CLARET CUP.

Mrs. Bendelari.

One quart bottle of claret, one bottle of soda water, one lemon cut very thin, four tablespoons of powdered sugar, quarter of a teaspoon of grated nutmeg, one liqueur glass of brandy, one wine glass of sherry wine. Half an hour before it is to be used, put in a large piece of ice, so that it may get perfectly cold.

LEMON SYRUP.

Mrs. Christopher Patterson.

Seven pounds of loaf sugar, three quarts of water, four ounces of citric acid, one drachm of oil of lemon.

Dissolve acid in warm water; mix; don't put the acid in a brass kettle; when quite cold put in the oil of lemon and bottle.

GINGER LIQUEUR.
Mrs. Christopher Patterson.

One gallon of strong malt whiskey, four pounds of lump sugar dissolved in one pint of boiling water, five ounces of bitter almonds, five ounces of sweet almonds, five ounces of bruised ginger, the rind of six lemons; mix all in a jar; in five or six days filter and bottle.

ESSENCE OF GINGER.
Mrs. Christopher Patterson.

Infuse four ounces of well bruised ginger, and an ounce of lemon peel sliced thin in a pint and a half of strong rectified spirits (of brandy); let it be closely stopped and shaken every day.

RED CURRANT CORDIAL.
Mrs. Spence.

To two quarts of red currants, put one quart of whiskey; let it stand twenty-four hours, then bruise and strain through a flannel bag. To every two quarts of this liquor, add one pound of loaf sugar, and quarter of a pound of ginger well bruised and boiled; let the whole stand to settle, then strain or filter; bottle and cork, seal the corks tightly.

N. B.—It is an improvement to have half red raspberry juice if the flavour is liked. The above is fit for use in a month.

WHITE CURRANT CORDIAL.

Mrs. Spence.

To every quart of white currants bruised, add one quart of best whiskey, the rind of a fresh lemon pared very thin, let it stand for two days, then strain or filter. To the above add one pound of loaf sugar, quarter of an ounce of the best ginger, and juice of the lemon. Bottle and seal; it will be fit for use in a month, and the longer it is kept the better it is.

CHERRY WHISKEY.

Mrs. Spence.

Take eight quarts of fine ripe cherries; put them into a jar, then pour over them six quarts of either good whiskey or brandy; let it stand for a month, then take out the fruit, bruise it in a mortar, put it back into the liquor, and let it stand another month; strain off the liquor, and to every quart add three-quarters of a pound of loaf sugar made into a syrup; pour boiling hot into the cold liquor; let it stand to settle and cool; when quite cold bottle and cork well. Excellent, and improves by keeping.

BLACK CURRANT CORDIAL.

Mrs. Spence.

To every four quarts of black currants, picked from the stems and lightly bruised, add one gallon of the best whiskey; let it remain four months, shaking the jar occasionally; then drain off the liquor and strain; add three pounds of loaf sugar and a quarter of a pound of best cloves, slightly bruised; bottle well, and seal.

GINGER CORDIAL.

To one pound of picked currants, red or black, add one quart of whiskey, one ounce of bruised ginger; put in a stone jar and let it stand for twenty-four or thirty-six hours; strain through a flannel bag, and add half a pound of sugar; when it is all melted, bottle.

CHERRY CORDIAL.

To six pounds of cherries add three pounds of sugar and one gallon of whiskey. Shake the jar often for the first three weeks, then bottle.

LEMON SYRUP.

Pour six quarts of boiling water on five pounds of white sugar, one and a half ounces of tartaric acid, and a little whole ginger; let stand till cold; then add one small bottle of essence of lemon. Strain and bottle.

CREAM NECTAR.

Mrs. Spence.

Dissolve two pounds of crushed sugar in three quarts of water; boil down to two quarts; drop in the white of an egg while boiling; then strain, and put in tartaric acid; when cold drop in the lemon to your taste; then bottle and cork. Shake two or three times a day.

HOP BEER.

Mrs. Dickinson.

One handful of hops, boil an hour, strain, and add one pint of molasses, and enough water to make two gallons. When milk-warm, add one cup or cake of yeast; let it stand over night; skim and pour it off from he yeast carefully; add one tablespoon of wintergreen, and bottle for use.

MISCELLANEOUS.

LIME WATER.

Mrs. E. R. Lynde.

One of the most useful agents of household economy if rightly understood, is lime water. Its mode of preparation is as follows: Put a stone of fresh unslacked lime about the size of a half-peck measure into a large stone jar or unpainted pail, and pour over it slowly and carefully, (so as not to slacken too rapidly,) a teakettle full (four gallons,) of hot water, and stir thoroughly; let it settle, and then stir again two or three times in twenty-four hours. Then bottle carefully, all that can be poured off in a clear and limpid state.

USES.—It is often sold by druggists as a remedy for children's summer complaints, a teaspoon being a dose in a cup of milk, and when diarrhœa is caused by acidity of the stomach, it is an excellent remedy, and when put into milk gives no unpleasant taste, but rather improves the flavour.

When put into milk that might curdle when heated, it will prevent its so doing, and can then be used for puddings and pies. A little stirred into cream or milk, after a hot day or night, will prevent its turning when used for tea or coffee.

It is unequalled in cleansing bottles or small milk vessels, or babies' nursing bottles, as it sweetens and purifies without leaving an unpleasant odour or flavour.

A cupful, or even more, mixed in the sponge of bread or cakes made over night, will prevent it from souring.

PRESERVING AUTUMN LEAVES.
Mrs. C. H. Wheeler.

These may be easily preserved and retain their natural tints, or nearly so, by either of the following methods: As they are gathered they may be laid between the leaves of a magazine until the book is full, and left with a light weight upon them until the moisture of the leaves has been absorbed; two or three thicknesses of paper should intervene between the leaves. If the leaves are large or in clusters, take newspapers, lay them on a shelf and use in the same manner as above. Then dip the leaves into melted wax (such as is used for moulding fruits, etc.) into which you will have to put a few drops of turpentine and lay upon newspapers to harden perfectly. This will make the leaves pliable and natural, and gives sufficient gloss. Great care should be taken that the wax is of right temperature. This can be ascertained by the first leaf which is dipped in. Draw out gently over the pan both sides of the leaf and hold it up by the stem. If the wax is too hot the leaf will shrivel—if too cool it will harden in lumps on the leaf.

Another method is to iron each leaf with a middling hot iron until the moisture is all out of them. Are best without varnish.

SKELETON LEAVES.

Boil the leaves in equal parts of rain water and soft soap until you can separate the pulp from the skin;

take them out into clear water; lay the leaf to be cleaned on glass, the upper side of the leaf next to the glass; then with a tooth brush remove all pulp and skin, turn the leaf and repeat the process; when thoroughly done put the leaf to bleach in this solution: One pound sal soda, dissolved in five pints rain water; one-half pound chloride of lime, in three pints water; allow twenty-four hours for the latter to dissolve. Strain out the sediment, and pour out the clear solution of lime into the solution of sal soda. The result will be a thick butter-milk solution, otherwise the lime was not strong enough. Filter this until it is perfectly clear. For leaves, use one part of solution to one part of water; for ferns, use the solution full strength. When perfectly white, remove to clear water; let stand for several hours, changing two or three times; the last water should be a little blue; float out on paper, press in books when nearly dry. In mounting use mucilage made of five parts of gum arabic, three parts white sugar, two parts of starch; add a very little water, boil and stir until thick and white.

TO RESTORE FROZEN PLANTS.

R. H. Knapp.

As soon as discovered, pour cold water over the plant wetting every leaf thoroughly. In a few moments it will be crystallized with a thick coating of ice. In this state place it in the dark, carefully covered with a newspaper. The ice will slowly melt, leaving the plant in its original state of health.

FOR CRYSTALLIZING GRASS.

Mrs. Ludlam.

Take one and one-half pounds of rock alum, pour on three pints of boiling water; when quite cool put into a wide-mouthed vessel, hang in your grasses, a few at a time. Do not let them get too heavy, or the stems will not support them. You may again heat alum and add more grasses. By adding a little colouring it will give variety.

CAMPHOR ICE.

Mrs. A. M.

One ounce of lard, one ounce of spermaceti, one ounce of camphor, one ounce of almond oil, one-half cake of white wax; melt and turn into moulds.

CAMPHOR ICE.

Mrs. Bartlett.

One-half ounce each of camphor gum and white wax, spermaceti and sweet oil; melt slowly the hard ingredients and then add the oil.

COLD CREAM.

Mrs. Anna Marble.

Four ounces sweet almond oil, two ounces of rose water, two ounces of white wax, two ounces of cocoa butter, two of spermaceti; put a bowl in a pan of boiling water; cut the spermaceti, white wax, and cocoa butter in small pieces; put them in the bowl, also the oil and rose water. When melted, stir contents until cold.

TO BEAUTIFY TEETH.

Dissolve two ounces of borax in three pints of boiling water, and before it is cold add one teaspoon of spirits of camphor; bottle it for use. A teaspoon of this with an equal quantity of tepid water.

HAIR TONIC.
Mrs. A. M.

One-half ounce sugar of lead, one-half ounce of lac sulphur, one quart of rose water, six tablespoons castor oil.

FOR CLEANING HAIRBRUSHES.
Mrs. C. H. Wheeler.

Use spirits of ammonia and hot water; wash them well and shake the water out, drying on a coarse towel; they will look white and clean as new. Little or no soap is needed.

TO CLEAN HAIRBRUSHES.
E. A. Forsyth.

Do not use soap, but put a tablespoon of hartshorn into the water, having it only tepid, and dip up and down until clean; then dry with the brushes down, and they will be like new ones. If you do not have ammonia, use soda; a teaspoonful dissolved in the water will do very well.

JAPANESE CLEANSING CREAM.

One-fourth pound of white castile soap, three ounces of ammonia, one of ether, one of spirits of wine, one of glycerine; cut the soap fine and dissolve in one quart of rain water; then add four quarts rain water, and then all the ingredients. For cleansing silks.

SALT OF LEMON TO TAKE OUT IRON RUST.

Mrs. P.

One ounce of cream tartar, one ounce of salt of sorrel.

STARCH POLISH.

Mrs. C. Patterson.

Take one ounce of spermaceti and one ounce of white wax, melt and run it into a thin cake on a plate. A piece the size of a quarter dollar added to a quart of prepared starch gives a beautiful lustre to the clothes and prevents the iron from sticking.

COUGH MIXTURE.

Mrs. C. Patterson.

Two ounces of gum arabic, one ounce of paregoric elixir, two ounces of sugar candy, juice of one lemon; mix with six glasses of hot water. One wineglass to be taken morning, noon, and night.

TO KEEP EGGS FOR WINTER USE.

Mrs. C. Patterson.

Take a pint of unslacked lime, and a pint of salt; put them into a pail of water; the eggs must be well covered with the mixture.

RECEIPT FOR COLD.

Miss J. B. Riley.

One pound of liverwort put into four quarts of water and boiled down to one quart; add, while warm, a quarter pound of ball liquorice and a quarter pound of loaf sugar; when cool add a half pint of gin. Dose—half a large wineglass half an hour before each meal.

FOR CLOTHES THAT FADE.

One ounce sugar of lead in a pail of rain water. Soak over night.

TO WASH CALICO.

Mrs. Edward Ely.

Blue calicoes or muslins will retain their colour if one small teaspoon of sugar of lead is put into a pail of water and the articles washed in water.

BLACK CALICOES.

Wash black percales or calicoes as usual, rinse in water with a strong solution of salt. This will prevent black from running, and also colours.

TO WASH WOOLLEN BLANKETS.

Mrs. J. A. Packard.

Dissolve soap enough to make a good suds in boiling water, add a tablespoon of aqua ammonia; when scalding hot, turn over your blankets. If convenient, use a pounder, or any way to work thoroughly through the suds without rubbing on a board. Rinse well in hot water. There is usually soap enough from the first suds to make the second soft; if not, and a little soap and ammonia; and after being put through the wringer, let two persons, standing opposite, pull them into shape; dry in the sun. White flannels may be washed in the same way without skrinking.

TO WASH WOOLLEN.

E. A. Forsyth.

To every pail of water, add one tablespoon of ammonia, and the same of beef gall; wash out quickly, and rinse in warm water, adding a very little beef gall to the water. This will remove spots from carpets, making them look fresh.

TO WASH CARPETS.

E. A. Forsyth.

Spread the carpet where you can use a brush; take Irish potatoes and scrape them into a pail or tub of water and let them stand over night, using one peck to clean a large carpet; two pails of water is sufficient to let them stand in, and you can add more when ready to use; add two ounces of beef gall and use with a brush, as to scrub a floor; the particles of potato will help cleanse; when dry, brush with a broom or stiff brush.

WASHING FLUID.

Mrs. A. P. Inglehart.

Nine tablespoons unslacked lime, two pounds of sal soda, four quarts water; let this simmer half an hour, then bottle up. Take a small teacup to a boiler of water.

WASHING FLUID.

Mrs. A. W. D.

One pound sal soda, one pound potash, each dissolved in one gallon of water (separately); then mix together and bottle.

EXCELLENT FAMILY SOAP.

Mrs. F. Knapp.

INGREDIENTS.—One box of lye, five pounds of grease, one pound of resin, one and a half gallons of soft water; make in an iron pot. When the water boils, put in the lye; when this is dissolved add the grease; stir till all is melted; then add one pound of resin gradually, and boil for an hour and a half; keep stirring with a stick, and add hot water to keep up the original quantity; pour into wet tins, and let it stand for twenty-four hours; cut into bars and keep in a dry warm place for a month.

TO MAKE GOOD STARCH.

Mrs. D.

Mix the starch with cold water, add boiling water until it thickens, then add dessert spoon of sugar, and a small piece of butter. Makes a stiff and glossy finish equal to laundry.

AN EXCELLENT HARD SOAP.

Mrs. Kate Johnson.

Pour twelve quarts soft boiling water on two and one-half pounds of unslacked lime; dissolve five pounds sal soda in twelve quarts soft hot water; then mix and let them remain from twelve to twenty-four hours. Pour off all the clear fluid, being careful not to allow any of the sediment to run off; boil three and one-half pounds clean grease and three or four ounces of rosin in the above lye till the grease disappears; pour into a box and let it stand a day to stiffen and then cut in bars. It is as well to put the lime in all the water and then add the soda. After pouring off the fluid, add two or three gallons of water and let it stand with the lime and soda dregs a day or two. This makes an excellent washing fluid to boil or soak the clothes in, with one pint in a boiler of water.

CLEANING SILVER.

Mrs. O. L. Parker.

Never put a particle of soap about your silver if you would have it retain its original lustre. When it wants polish, take a piece of soft leather and whiting and rub hard. The proprietor of one of the oldest silver establishments in the city of Philadelphia says that housekeepers ruin their silver in soap suds, as it makes it look like pewter.

POLISH FOR ZINC OR TIN.

Mrs. Thos. A. Hill.

To three pints of water, add one ounce of nitric acid.

two ounces of emery, and eight ounces of pumice stone; shake well together. Any druggist will fill it for fifteen cents.

STOVE POLISH.

Mrs. O. L. Parker.

Stove lustre, when mixed with turpentine and applied in the usual manner, is blacker, more glossy, and more durable than when mixed with any other liquid. The turpentine prevents rust, and when put on an old rusty stove will make it look as well as new.

TO EXTRACT INK.

To extract ink from cotton, silk, and woollen goods, saturate the spot with spirits of turpentine and let it remain several hours; then rub it between the hands. It will crumble away without injuring either the colour or texture of the article.

TO TAKE INK OUT OF LINEN.

Dip the spotted part in pure tallow, melted; then wash out the tallow and the ink will disappear.

PATENT SOAP.

Mrs. Ludlam.

Five pounds hard soap, one quart lye, one-fourth ounce pearl-ash; place on the fire and stir well until the soap is dissolved; add one-half pint spirits of turpentine, one gill spirits hartshorn, and stir well. It is then fit for use. The finest muslin may be put to soak in this suds, and if left for a time will become beautifully white. A small portion of soap put into a little hot water, and a flannel cloth will save hard labour and a brush in cleaning paint. One who has tried it thinks it worth the price of the book.

FOR BLEACHING COTTON CLOTH.
Mrs. C. H. Wheeler.

One pound chloride of lime, dissolved and strained; put in two or three pails of water; thoroughly wet the cloth and leave it in over night; then rinse well in two waters. This will also take out mildew, and is equally good for brown cotton or white that has become yellow from any cause, and will not injure the fabric.

TO REMOVE TAR.

Rub well with clean lard, afterwards wash with soap and warm water. Apply this to either hands or clothing.

JAVELLE WATER FOR MILDEW STAINS.

One pound of chloride of lime, two of washing soda, two gallons of soft water; pour one gallon of boiling water to the ingredients to dissolve them, adding the cold water when dissolved.

COLOURING COTTON CARPET RAGS.
Mrs. S. I. Parker.

BLUE.—For five pounds of cloth, take five ounces of copperas, with two pails of water in a tin or copper boiler; set it over the fire till the copperas is dissolved and it begins to heat, then put in the cloth, stirring it frequently till it boils, one-half or three-fourths of an hour; then remove the cloth where it can drain; pour away the copperas water and take two ounces of prussiate of potash in about two pails of water in the same vessel; when it is well dissolved and hot, put in the cloth from the copperas water, stirring it thoroughly till it boils, one-half an hour, then remove the cloth; add (with care and caution, on account of the spattering which ensues) one tablespoon of oil of vitriol, and stir it well in the dye; replace the cloth, stirring it briskly till it has boiled one-half an hour. Should be well rinsed and washed in clear water to prevent the dye from making it tender after colouring.

YELLOW.—For five pounds of cloth dissolve one-half pound of sugar of lead in a tub of warm water and twelve ounces of bichromate of potash in another tub of cold water; soak, rinse, and wring the cloth in the lead water first, then in the other, and return from one to the other, till the right shade of colour is obtained.

ORANGE.—Dip the yellow coloured cloth into strong lime water; if it should not turn, boil it; rinse all well.

GREEN.—Put your blue cloth in the yellow dye in the same manner as for colouring yellow. Old calico will take a darker shade of blue or green in the same dye with the white cloth.

TO PRESERVE EGGS.

Mrs. G. Wyllie.

One pint salt, two pints fresh lime, three gallons water; mix well and put in eggs without cracking the shell; they must be kept covered with the brine.

TO PRESERVE EGGS.

Mrs. Midgley.

Take a patent pailful of spring water, pour it into a stone jar, take one pound of lime, one pint of Liverpool salt; let it stand for three days, stir it every day, then pour it off, and put in your eggs.

HOW TO MAKE UP SHIRT BOSOMS.

Take two ounces of fine gum arabic powder; put it in a pitcher and pour into it a pint or more of boiling water, according to the degree of strength you require, and then having covered it let it stand all night; in the morning pour it carefully from the dregs into a clean bottle, cork and keep it for use. A tablespoonful of gum stirred into a pint of starch made in the usual manner will give to lawn, either white or printed, a look of newness when nothing else can restore them after they have been washed.

IRONING.

To keep starch from sticking to irons rub the irons with a little piece of wax or sperm.

GREASE ERASER.

Mrs. Oliphant.

Benzine, alcohol, ether, equal parts; mix; apply with sponge (patting the spot); put a piece of blotting paper on each side and iron with a hot flat iron.

TO KEEP GLASS JARS FROM BREAKING

when pouring in boiling fruit, wrap a cold wet cloth round each jar.

TO PREVENT RED ANTS.

Put one pint of tar in an earthen vessel, pour on it two quarts of boiling hot water, and place it in your closet.

CLEANING MARBLE.

Mrs. Gray.

Dissolve a large lump of Spanish whiting in water which has previously dissolved a teaspoon of washing soda, take only sufficient water to moisten the whiting, and it will become a paste; with a flannel cloth rub the marble well, leaving it on for a while and repeating the process two or three times, if necessary. Wash off with soap and water, then dry the marble well and polish with a soft duster.

FURNITURE POLISH.

No. 1. Shellac varnish, linseed oil, and spirits of wine, equal parts. No. 2. Linseed oil, alcohol, equal parts. No. 3. Linseed oil five ounces, turpentine two ounces, oil of vitriol one-half ounce.

CLEANING WHITE PAINT.

Mrs. C. Belford.

Spirits of ammonia, used in sufficient quantity to soften the water and ordinary hard soap, will make the paint look white and clean with half the effort of any other method I have ever tried. Care should be taken not to have too much ammonia, or the paint will be injured.

HARD SOAP.

Mrs. Mary A. Odell.

Six pounds of clean grease, six pounds of sal soda, three pounds of stone lime; slake the lime and put it into four gallons of soft water; add the sal soda, and when dissolved let it settle. Pour off the water into an iron kettle, and add the grease melted, and boil. If the soap does not come after boiling a few minutes, add more soft water till it is of the consistency of honey. Wet a tub and pour the hot soap into it. When cold, cut into pieces and lay it away to dry. Always make soap in an iron kettle.

THE SICK ROOM.

Egg Gruel.—Boil eggs from one to three hours until hard enough to grate; then boil new milk and thicken with the egg, and add a little salt. Excellent in case of nausea.—Mrs. Bartlett.

Gruel for Infants.—To make a gruel for infants suffering from marasmus, take one pint of goat's milk and the yolks of two eggs boiled sufficiently hard to reduce to an impalpable powder; add a pint of boiling water, a little salt or sugar, and administer by a nursing bottle.—Dr. Small.

Beef Tea.—To one pound of lean beef add one and one-half tumblers of cold water; cut the beef in small pieces, cover and let it boil slowly for ten minutes, and add a little salt after it is boiled. Excellent.

Beef Jelly for Invalids.—Three small onions, three small or one and one-half large carrots, a few whole cloves and black pepper, one small teaspoon of sugar, one slice of ham, two calf's feet, one and a half pounds of beef. Put in the onions and other ingredients in succession. Place the ham on top, then the calf's feet, and lastly the beef; no water; put on the side of the range, and let it stand until reduced to a soft mass, then add a quart of water and let it boil one hour; strain and let stand until cold, when take off the fat. Use by dissolving a little in hot water.—Mrs. J. A. Ellis.

PANADA.—Two thick slices of stale bread half an inch in thickness; cut off the crust, toast them a nice brown, cut them into squares of two inches in size, lay them in a bowl, sprinkle a little salt over them and pour on a pint of boiling water.

FEVER AND AGUE.—Four ounces galangal root in a quart of gin, steeped in a warm place; take often.—MRS. R. A. SIBLEY.

FOR A CAKED BREAST.—A HIGHLAND REMEDY.—Bake large potatoes, put two or more in a woollen stocking; crush them soft and apply to the breast as hot as can be borne; repeat constantly, till relieved.—MRS. G. B. WYLLIE.

TO CURE A STING OF BEE OR WASP.—Mix common earth with water to about the consistency of mud. Apply at once.—MRS. STORY.

AN INDIAN REMEDY FOR A CAKED BREAST OR SWOLLEN GLANDS.—Gather mullein leaves, saturate in hot vinegar, and apply to the skin very hot; cover with flannel and keep repeating till cured.—MRS. G. B. WYLLIE.

MEDICINAL RECEIPTS.

GRANDMOTHER'S SALVE FOR EVERYTHING.—Two pounds of rosin and half a teacup of mutton tallow after it is hard, half as much beeswax, and half an ounce of camphor gum; put all together into an old kettle, and let it dissolve and just come to a boil, stirring with a stick; then take half a pail of warm water, just the chill off, pour it in and stir carefully until you can get your hands around it. Two persons must each take half and pull like candy until quite white and brittle; put a little grease on your hands to prevent sticking, and keep them wet all the time. Wet the table, roll out the salve, and cut it with a knife. Keep it in a cool place.—MRS. GARDNER.

CHOLERA REMEDY.—Mix in a small bottle equal parts of tincture of opium (laudanum), rhubarb, capsicum (red pepper, double strength), camphor, and spirits of nitre, essence of peppermint double strength. Shake well, and cork tight. Dose: From five to thirty drops every fifteen minutes. Dose for children, from two to ten drops.—MRS. GARDNER.

FIG PASTE FOR CONSTIPATION.—One-half pound of good figs chopped fine, one-half pint of molasses, two ounces powdered senna leaves, one drachm fine powdered coriander seed, one drachm of fine powdered cardamom seed. Put the molasses on stove and let it come to a boil, then stir in all the rest and bring to a boil again. A teaspoonful once in a while is a dose. It will keep, when covered, for a year.—MRS. GARDNER.

CURE FOR BOILS.—ISAIAH, xxxviii. 21.—*Go thou and do likewise.*

FOR CANKER SORE MOUTH.—Burn a corn cob and apply the ashes two or three times a day.

CURE FOR CORNS.—The strongest acetic acid, applied night and morning, will cure hard and soft corns in a week.

RING WORM.—Put a penny into a tablespoon of vinegar; let it remain until it becomes green, and wash the ring worm with this two or three times a day.

CURE FOR CHILBLAINS.—Place red hot coals in a vessel, and throw upon them a handful of corn meal; hold the feet in the dense smoke, renewing the coals and meal, till the pain is relieved. This has been known to make very marked cures when all other remedies have failed.

CURE FOR RHEUMATISM AND BILIOUS HEADACHE.—Finest Turkey rhubarb, half an ounce, carbonate magnesia, one ounce; mix intimately; keep well corked in glass bottle. Dose: One teaspoonful, in milk and sugar, the first thing in the morning; repeat till cured. Tried with success.—F. A. K.

TOOTHACHE.—At a meeting of the London Medical Society Dr. Blake, a distinguished physician, said that he was able to cure the most desperate case of toothache, unless the disease was connected with rheumatism, by the application of the following remedy: Alum reduced to an impalpable powder, two drachms; nitrous spirit of ether, seven drachms; mix and apply to the tooth. Tried with success.

GREASE FROM CLOTH.—Grease can be removed from cloth by a paste of fuller's earth and turpentine. This should be rubbed on the fabric until the turpentine has evaporated and a white powder produced. The latter can be brushed off, and the grease will have disappeared.

TO MEND CHINA.—Take a very thick solution of gum arabic in water, and stir into it plaster of Paris until the mixture becomes of a proper consistency. Apply it with a brush to the fractured edges of the china, and stick them together. In three days the articles cannot be broken in the same place. The whiteness of the cement renders it doubly valuable.

HOW TO CURE A BONE FELON.—Of all painful things can there be any so excruciatingly painful as a bone felon? We know of none that the flesh is heir to, and, as this malady is quite frequent and the subject of much earnest consideration, we give the latest recipe for its cure, which is given by that high authority, the London *Lancet*:—" As soon as the pulsation which indicates the disease is felt, put directly over the spot a fly blister, about the size of your thumb nail, and let it remain for six hours, at the expiration of which time, directly under the surface of the blister, may be seen the felon, which can be instantly taken out with the point of a needle or a lancet."

How to get rid of Flies.—A clergyman, writing from Ireland, says :—" For three years I have lived in town, and during that time my sitting room has been free from flies, three or four only walking about my breakfast table, while all my neighbours' rooms were crowded. I often congratulated myself on my escape, but never knew the reason of it until two days ago. I then had occasion to move my goods to another house, while I remained on for two days longer. Among other things moved were two boxes of geraniums and calceolarias, which stood in my window, the latter always being open to its full extent top and bottom. The boxes were not gone half an hour before my room was as full of flies as those around me. This, to me, is a new discovery, and perhaps it may serve to encourage others in that which is always a source of pleasure, and which now proves also to be a source of comfort, viz., window gardening."

Smallpox Remedy.—The following remedy a friend tried in Ohio in a case of confluent smallpox, when the doctor had little hope of saving the patient, and it saved the woman's life. The remedy is sure in scarlet fever. "I herewith append a recipe' which has been used to my own knowledge in a hundred cases. It will prevent or cure the small pox, even though the pittings are filling. When Jenner discovered cow pox in England, the world of science hurled an avalanche of fame upon his head, and when the most scientific school of medicine in the world (that of Paris), published this panacea for the small pox, it passed unheeded. It is unfailing as fate, and conquers in every instance. It is harmless when taken by a well person. It will also cure scarlet fever. Take sulphate of zinc, one grain; fox glove (*digitalis*) one grain; half a teaspoon of water. When thoroughly mixed, add four ounces water. Take a spoonful every hour, and either disease will disappear in twelve hours. For a child, smaller doses, according to age."

For Hydrophobia.—Franklin Dyer, a highly respectable farmer of Galena, Kent county, Md., gives the following as a sure cure for the bite of a mad dog. He has tested it with most gratifying results: Elecampane is a plant well known and found in many gardens. Immediately after being bitten, take one and a half ounces of the root of the plant, the green root is preferable. The dried, to be found in drug stores, will answer; bruise it, put it in a pint of fresh milk, boil down to half a pint, strain, and when cold drink it, fasting at least six hours afterwards. The next morning repeat the dose, fasting, using two ounces of the root. On the third morning, take another dose prepared as the last, and this will be sufficient. After each dose, nothing to be eaten for at least six hours. I had a son who was bitten by a mad dog eighteen years ago, and four other children in the neighbourhood were also bitten. They took the above, and are now alive and well. I have known many who were cured. It is supposed that the root contains a principle, which, being taken up by the blood in its circulation, counteracts or neutralizes the deadly effect of the virus of hydrophobia. I feel so much confidence in this simple remedy that I am willing you should give my name in connection with this statement.

For Felon.—Take common rock salt, as used for salting down pork or beef, dry in an oven, then pound it fine and mix with spirits of turpentine in equal parts; put it in a rag and wrap it around the parts affected; as it gets dry put on more, and in twenty-four hours you are cured. The felon will be dead. No harm to try it, as I have with success.

Cure for Neuralgia.—A friend who suffered horrible pains from neuralgia, hearing of a noted physician in Germany who invariably cured the disease, went to him, and was permanently cured after a short sojourn. The doctor gave him the remedy, which was nothing but a poultice and tea made from our common field thistle. The leaves are macerated and used as a poultice on the parts affected, while a small quantity of the same is boiled down to the proportion of a quart to a pint, and a small wine glass of the decoction drank before each meal. Our friend says he has never known it to fail of giving relief, while in almost every case it has effected a cure. God gave herbs for the healing of the nations.

Tincture of Iodine on Corns.—Dr. Bajis states that corns may be rapidly cured by the application of the Tincture of Iodine; the corn disappearing in the course of a few days, if touched with the Tincture several times a day. If the corn be situated between the toes, it should be covered with a piece of linen steeped in a mixture of the Tincture and Glycerine.—Mrs. C. Patterson.

FLANNELS FOR FOMENTATION.—Fold the flannel the size to fit over a pot of boiling water, and cover with a lid; in a few minutes it will be hotter than if wrung out of boiling water and yet dry at the corners; roll it up covered, and convey quickly to the patient.—J. K. GILMOUR.

FOR HOARSENESS.—Squeeze the juice of half a lemon in a pint bowl, add loaf sugar (two tablespoons), one full teaspoon of glycerine, and one full tablespoon of whiskey; pour over this boiling hot water to nearly fill the bowl, and drink hot just before going to bed.

FOR SORE THROAT.—Cut slices of salt pork or fat bacon; simmer a few moments in hot vinegar, and apply to throat as hot as possible. When this is taken off, as the throat is relieved, put around a bandage of soft flannel. A gargle of equal parts of borax and alum, dissolved in water, is also excellent. To be used frequently.

HEALING LOTION.—One ounce glycerine, one ounce rose-water, ten drops carbolic acid. This preparation prevents and cures chapping of the skin, and at the same time bleaches it. It is also excellent for sore lips and gums. I consider it an indispensable adjunct to the toilet table.—Mrs. A. YOCUM.

TO STOP BLEEDING.—A handful of flour bound on the cut.—MRS. A. M.

TO PREVENT CONTAGION FROM ERUPTIVE DISEASES.— Keep constantly, in plates or saucers, sliced raw onions in the sick room, if possible. As fast as they become discoloured, replace by fresh ones. During any epidemic of skin diseases that are eruptive, onions, except those taken fresh from the earth, are unsafe, as they are peculiarly sensitive to disease.

To Restore from Stroke of Lightning.—Shower with cold water for two hours; if the patient does not show signs of life, put salt in the water, and continue to shower an hour longer.

For Toothache.—Of powdered alum and fine salt, equal quantities; apply to the tooth and it will give speedy relief.—Mrs. Bartlett.

For Headache.—Pour a few drops of ether on one-half ounce of gum camphor and pulverize; add to this an equal quantity of carbonate ammonia pulverized; add twenty drops peppermint; mix and put in an open-mouthed bottle and cork.—Mrs. A. M. Gibbs.

Salve for Chilblains.—Fry out nicely a little mutton tallow; into this while melted, and after it is nicely strained, put an equal quantity of coal oil; stir well together while it is cooling.

To Remove Discolouration from Bruises.—Apply a cloth wrung out in very hot water, and renew frequently until the pain ceases. Or, apply raw beefsteak.

Cure for Wasp Sting.—Apply a poultice of saleratus water and flour, and bind on the sting. Apply slices of raw onion for a bee sting.

Cure for Summer Complaint.—Two ounces tincture rhubarb, one of paregoric, one-half of essence of peppermint, one-half of essence of annis, one-half of prepared chalk. Dose for adult, one teaspoon in a little water; take as often as needed.—Mrs. L. Bradley.

THE BEST DEODORIZER.—Use bromo-chloralum in the proportion of one tablespoon to eight of soft water; dip cloths in this solution and hang in the rooms; it will purify sick rooms of any foul smells. The surface of anything may be purified by washing well and then rubbing over with a weakened solution of bromo-chloralum. A weak solution is excellent to rinse the mouth with often, when from any cause the breath is offensive. It is also an excellent wash for sores and wounds that have an offensive odour.

TO DESTROY BED BUGS, MOTHS, AND OTHER VERMIN.—Dissolve alum in hot water, making a very strong solution; apply to furniture or crevices in the walls with paint brush. This is sure destruction to those noxious vermin, and invaluable because easily obtained, is perfectly safe to use, and leaves no unpleasant traces behind. When you suspect moths have lodged in the borders of carpets, wet the edges of the carpets with a strong solution; whenever it reaches them, it is certain death.

HOW TO SELECT MEATS.—An English journal gives the following hints on this subject:—"Good and wholesome meat should be neither of a pale rosy or pink colour, nor of a deep purple. The first denotes the diseased condition, the last proves the animal has died a natural death. Good meat has more of a marble look, in consequence of the branching of the veins which surround the adipose cells. The fat, especially of the inner organs, is alway firm and suety, and never moist, while in general the fat from diseased cattle is flabby and watery, and more often resembles jelly or boiled parchment. Wholesome meat will always show itself firm and elastic to the touch, and exhibit no dampness, while diseased meat will appear soft and moist, in fact often more wet, so that the liquid substances run out of the blood when pressed hard. Good meat has very little smell, while unsound meat has a disagreeable, cadaverous smell, and diffuses a certain medicinal odour. This can be distinctly proved by cutting the meat through with a knife and smelling the blade, or pouring warm water over it. Lastly, bad meat has the peculiarity that it shrinks considerably in the boiling; wholesome meat rather swells, and does not lose an ounce in weight.

BILLS OF FARE.

In the accompanying Bills of Fare, the arrangement of the various courses will be suggested by the form in which they are given:

MENU.

BREAKFAST—No. 1.

Fine Hominy. Buttered Toast.
Beefsteak.
French Rolls. Potatoes a la Creme.
Buckwheat Cakes.
Tea. Coffee. Chocolate.

BREAKFAST—No. 2.

Broiled Spring Chickens.
Home Rolls. Irish Potatoes.
Scrambled Eggs. Fried Oysters.
Rye and Indian Loaf.
Coffee. Tea. Chocolate.

BREAKFAST—No. 3.

White Fish. Potatoes.
Muffins.
Fried Ham. Egg Omelette.
Coffee. Tea. Chocolate.

LUNCHES.

LUNCH PARTY—No. 1.

Beef Tea, served in small porcelain cups.
Cold Chicken and Oyster and other forms of Croquettes.
Chicken Salad. Minced Ham Sandwiches.
Escalloped Oysters.
Tutti Frutti. Chocolate Cream.
Cake Basket of Mixed Cake.
Mulled Chocolate.
Mixed Pickles. Biscuits, etc.
Ice Cream and Charlottes can either be added or substituted. For twenty guests, allow one gallon.

LUNCH PARTY—No. 2.

Oyster Pie. Boiled Partridge. Cold Ham.
Sweet Pickles. Sandwiches.
Pound and Fruit Cake. Pyramids of Wine Jelly.
Blanc Mange. Snow Jelly.
Pineapple Flummery.
Kisses. Macaroons. Ice Cream.

DINNERS.

DINNER—No. 1.

FIRST COURSE.

Oyster Soup, with Celery.

SECOND COURSE.

Roast Turkey.
Croquettes of Rice. Sweet and Irish Potatoes.

THIRD COURSE.

Quail on Toast.
Vegetables. Pickles. Escalloped Tomatoes.
Macaroni. Jelly.

DESSERT.

Almond Pudding.
Mince Pie. Lemon Pie.
Cheese. Fruits. Nuts.
Coffee.

DINNER—No. 2.

FIRST COURSE.

Raw Oysters.
White and Brown Soup.

SECOND COURSE.

Boiled White Fish, with Sauce and Sliced Lemon.

THIRD COURSE.

Roast Beef.

FOURTH COURSE.

Roast Turkey. Ducks.
Vegetables in season. Croquettes of Rice or Hominy.
Cranberry Sauce. Currant Jelly.

DESSERT.

Cream Custard. Lemon Pie.
Fruits. Nuts.
Coffee.

TEA.

TEA—No. 1.

Tea. Coffee. Chocolate.
Biscuits.
Oyster Sandwiches. Chicken Salad.
Cold Tongue.
Cake and Preserves.
Ice Cream and Cake later in the evening.

TEA—No. 2.

Tea, Coffee, or Chocolate.
Escalloped or Fried Oysters. Muffins.
Sliced Turkey and Ham.
Cold Biscuits.
Sardines and Sliced Lemons.
Thin slices of Bread, rolled. Sliced Pressed Meats.
Cake in variety.

SUPPERS.

SUPPER—No. 1.

Cold Roast Turkey. Chicken Salad.
Quail on Toast.
Ham Croquettes. Fricasseed Oysters.
Charlotte Russe. Vanilla Cream.
Chocolate Cake. Cocoanut Cake.
Mixed Cakes.
Fruit.
Coffee and Chocolate.

SUPPER—No. 2.

Cold Roast Partridges or Ducks.
Oyster Patties. Cold Boiled Ham. Dressed Celery.
Oysters or Minced Ham Sandwiches.
Raw Oysters. Chicken Croquettes or Fricasseed Oysters.
Wine Jelly. Ice Cream. Biscuit Glace. Cakes.
Fruits. Chocolate. Coffee.
Pickles and Biscuits.

ALLOWANCE OF SUPPLIES FOR AN ENTERTAINMENT.

In inviting guests, it is safe to calculate that out of one hundred and fifty, but two-thirds of the number will be present. If five hundred are invited, not more than three hundred can be counted upon as accepting.

Allow one quart of oysters to every three persons present. Five chickens (or, what is better, a ten-pound turkey, boiled and minced), and fifteen heads of celery, are enough for chicken salad for fifty guests; one gallon of ice cream to every twenty guests; one hundred and thirty sandwiches for one hundred guests; and six to ten quarts of wine jelly for each hundred. For a company of twenty, allow three chickens for salad; one hundred pickled oysters; two moulds of Charlotte Russe; one gallon of cream; and four dozen biscuits.

COLD LUNCHES FOR WASHING DAYS, OR OTHER DAYS OF EXTRA LABOUR.

LUNCH No. 1.—Cold corn beef, nicely sliced; baked potatoes; bread, butter, and pickles. Dessert—mince pie and cheese.

LUNCH No. 2.—Chicken pie; baked potatoes; rolled bread or biscuit. Dessert—cake and custard.

LUNCH No. 3.—First course: Raw oysters, with lemon and crackers. Second course: Cold veal, with jelly and Saratoga potatoes; bread and butter. Dessert—cherry pie with cheese.

LUNCH No. 4.—Casserole of fish, with mushroom catsup; bread and butter. Dessert—pie with cheese.

ECONOMICAL DINNERS.

SUNDAY.—Roast beef, potatoes, and greens. Dessert—pudding or pie, cheese.

MONDAY.—Hashed beef, potatoes, and bread pudding.

TUESDAY.—Broiled beef, vegetables, apple pudding.

WEDNESDAY.—Boiled pork, beans, potatoes, greens, and pie or rice pudding.

THURSDAY.—Roast or broiled fowl, cabbage, potatoes, lemon pie, cheese.

FRIDAY.—Fish, potato croquettes, escalloped tomatoes, pudding.

SATURDAY.—*A la mode* beef, potatoes, vegetables, suet pudding and mince pie, cheese.

www.ingramcontent.com/pod-product-compliance
Lightning Source LLC
Chambersburg PA
CBHW030358230426
43664CB00007BB/650